CAMBRIDGE
UNIVERSITY PRESS

 UNIVERSITY of CAMBRIDGE
ESOL Examinations

MW01102450

Cambridge English

IELTS
TRAINER

剑桥雅思
官方模考题精讲精练

Official Cambridge preparation materials for IELTS

（英）**Louise Hashemi**
（英）**Barbara Thomas** 编著

 西安交通大学出版社
XI'AN JIAOTONG UNIVERSITY PRESS

图书在版编目(CIP)数据

剑桥雅思官方模考题精讲精练 /(英)哈希米
(Hashemi,L.),(英)托马斯(Thomas,B.)编著. —西
安:西安交通大学出版社,2012(2016.11 重印)
　ISBN 978-7-5605-4408-3

　Ⅰ.①剑⋯　Ⅱ.①哈⋯ ②托⋯　Ⅲ.①IELTS—题解
Ⅳ.①H319.6

中国版本图书馆 CIP 数据核字(2012)第 123705 号

陕版出图字:25-2012-132 号

This is a reprint edition of the following title published by Cambridge University Press:

IELTS Trainer Six Practice Tests with Answers and Audio CDs(3)(ISBN:9780521128209)

ⓒ Cambridge University Press 2011

This reprint edition for the People's Republic of China (excluding Hong Kong, Macau and Taiwan) is published by arrangement with the Press Syndicate of the University of Cambridge, Cambridge, United Kingdom.

ⓒ Cambridge University Press and Xi'an Jiaotong University Press 2012

This reprint edition is authorized for sale in the People's Republic of China (excluding Hong Kong, Macau and Taiwan) only. Unauthorized export of this reprint edition is a violation of the Copyright Act. No part of this publication may be reproduced or distributed by any means, or stored in a database or retrieval system, without the prior written permission of Cambridge University Press and Xi'an Jiaotong University Press.

此版本仅限在中华人民共和国境内(不包括香港、澳门特别行政区及台湾省)销售。未经授权出口此版本属违法行为。未经剑桥大学出版社和西安交通大学出版社书面同意,本书任何部分不得以任何方式被翻印或传播,不得载入数据或检索系统。

书　　名	剑桥雅思官方模考题精讲精练
编 著 者	(英)Louise Hashemi　(英)Barbara Thomas
责任编辑	孙冠群
封面设计	大愚设计+黄　蕊
出版发行	西安交通大学出版社
地　　址	西安市兴庆南路 10 号(邮编:710049)
电　　话	(010)62605588　62605019(发行部)　(029)82668315(总编室)
读者信箱	dywh@xdf.cn
印　　刷	北京鑫海达印刷有限公司
字　　数	375 千
开　　本	880mm×1230mm　1/16
印　　张	14.75
版　　次	2016 年 11 月第 1 版第 8 次印刷
书　　号	ISBN 978-7-5605-4408-3/H・1385
定　　价	49.00 元

版权所有　侵权必究

如有缺页、倒页、脱页等印装质量问题,请拨打服务热线:010-62605166。

Contents

Introduction

雅思简介

国际英语语言测试系统（International English Language Testing System），简称"雅思"（IELTS），是一项用来测试需要到英语国家学习或者工作的人的英语能力的考试，并已得到全球的广泛认可。

雅思考试分两种：学术类（适用于本科或研究生阶段留学）和一般培训类（适用于非学位水平的职业或培训项目、中学入学或移民）。这两种类型的考试均由听力、阅读、写作和口语四个单项测试组成。其中，学术类和一般培训类的听力、口语单项题目相同，阅读和写作单项的题目不同。

本书的适用对象

本书适用于所有雅思学术类考生。本书可在课堂上用做教材，也可用做自学参考书。本书的目标读者是那些希望在雅思考试中取得6分及以上成绩的考生。

本书简介

本书包含6套雅思考试模拟测试题，每套测试题都包含听力、阅读、写作和口语单项测试。Test 1和Test 2中附有进一步的练习和学习指导。6套模拟测试题的难度都与真题难度相当。

在Test 1中，每部分的测试都包含**Training**（练习）和**Exam practice**（模拟测试）两大块：

● **Training**部分提供了考试信息和练习题，帮助考生备考。在听力、写作和口语测试部分，Test 1主要讲解和练习了语法、词汇以及与这几部分相关的功能语言，而这些练习以修正雅思考生在考试中出现的常见错误为基础，这些错误都收录在剑桥学习者语料库（Cambridge Learner Corpus，以下简称"CLC"）中（参见下文）。写作部分包含雅思考生作文和官方范文的节选。

● **Exam practice**部分除了测试题之外，还包含答题策略提示和相关题目解题指导，一步一步地指导考生完成测试题。雅思听力和阅读部分涵盖各式各样的题目，而同一题型未必每次都出现在试题的同一板块。这些模拟测试题便体现了这一多样性；在Test 1和Test 2的测试中，考生会遇到雅思考试的所有主要题型。

Test 2除了回顾Test 1中的主要题型，还包含了Test 1没有涉及的题型训练。Test 2中的**Training**部分要比Test 1中的短。Test 2也包含**Exam practice**，并就如何解题给出一些提示和建议。

Tests 3-6均为完整的模拟测试题，不包含答题指导或练习。这4套模拟测试题包含Test 1和Test 2中出现的各种题型，并涵盖了各种不同的话题和文章类型。这4套模拟测试题可以让考生有机会练习在Test 1和Test 2中掌握的答题策略和技巧。

每套模拟测试题都附有答案详解（参见下文）。

如何使用本书

Test 1 Training

- 对于测试题的每个Section（如Listening Section 1，第10页），首先读一下**What is...?**部分，这部分主要描述了该Section包含的题型。有的Section还包含**What does it test?**，主要描写了诸如试题各部分主要考查哪种技能（如识别关键信息，理解说话者的观点）等内容。

- 通读**Task information**，这部分详细描述了接下来要出现的题型。

- 浏览标有**Tip!**的信息，这部分给出了有关考试策略和语言知识的大致建议。

- 在做**Exam practice**部分的练习之前，先完成各Section的**Useful language**部分的练习。这些练习可以帮助考生拓展必要的技能，并提供与Test 1中的试题直接相关的练习。练习均附答案和详解。很多练习还包含了对雅思考生常犯的语言错误的展示和纠正，这些错误都收录在CLC中。

- 查看标有**Advice**的方框，里面是针对具体问题给出的实用指导。

- 在听力部分，需使用MP3播放器播放光盘中相应的音频文件。

- 在Test 1的写作部分中，很多练习都是以CLC的雅思范文以及雅思考生作文使用的语言为基础的，参考答案同样如此，且这些答案都体现了最优秀的考生应达到的标准。练习题附有答案和详解。这些练习最后构成与模拟测试部分类似的测试练习，但不完全一样。

- 在口语部分，一些练习可以形成一组适用于Part 1问题的个性化的、实用的回答；其他练习主要训练在Part 2的对话和Part 3的讨论中必备的语言技巧。这些练习可以用来和搭档一起做限时练习，也可以用来独自练习。

Test 1 Exam practice

- 在做模拟测试题之前，先读听力、阅读和写作各Section中的**Action plan**部分。对于雅思考试中诸多不同的题型，**Action plan**部分会告诉考生如何用最佳方法解答每一种题型，取得高分，并避免浪费时间。

- 仔细按照**Action plan**中的步骤完成题目，并充分利用**Tip!**和**Advice**中提供的帮助信息。

- 所有题目均附解析，详细地解释了选项正确或错误的原因。听力部分提供了完整的听力原文，并用下画线标出了包含正确答案的内容。

Test 2 Training

- 回答**Review**中的问题以提醒自己注意测试的每个部分。如果需要的话，可以使用与Test 1的相互参照来核对自己的答案。

- 完成写作和口语部分的练习。该口语部分将Test 1中介绍的答题策略和技巧扩展到口语测试中可能会问及的话题中。写作部分修正了Test 1中涉及的答题策略，并且进一步提供了更有针对性的写作练习。很多练习都是以CLC提供的雅思考生作文为基础的。

Test 2 Exam practice

- 回答每一个**Action plan reminder**中的问题。这些问题与Test 1中介绍的答题策略相关。如果需要的话，你可以使用相互参照查看Test 1中相应的内容。

- 通读**Action plans**，了解没有在Test 1中出现的新题型。充分利用**Tip!**和**Advice**中提供的有用信息来完成测试，并通过本书的答案详解部分核对答案。

Tests 3–6 Exam practice

- 可能的话，尽量在考试环境下做这几套模拟测试题，并且运用在指导性的Test 1和Test 2中学到的答题技巧和语言知识。

- 口语部分最好和搭档一起进行，这样可以方便互相提问题。如果条件不允许，则要按题目说明独立完成口语的三个部分。可以准备一块手表，严格遵守时间规定。录下自己的回答并听听自己的录音，这样可以帮助自己发现哪些地方还需多加练习。

考生可以以任意顺序完成Tests 3–6，但是每套题一定要在规定时间内完成。

剑桥学习者语料库 (Cambridge Learner Corpus)

剑桥学习者语料库（CLC）大量收集了参加过剑桥ESOL英语测试的全球各地考生所写的考卷，目前已经收录了85,000多份，而且数量一直在增加。它是剑桥国际语料库（Cambridge International Corpus，以下简称"CIC"）的一个组成部分，由剑桥大学出版社和剑桥ESOL考试中心共同维护建设。CLC目前收集的考卷来自：

- 85,000名考生
- 100种不同的第一语言
- 180个不同的国家

在本书写作部分的练习题和考生作文节选中，有如下标记的便是来自CLC的内容：

本书的其他内容

- 本书第173–231页的答案详解部分给出了正确答案和必要的解析（尤其是在Test 1和Test 2中）。在有些地方，例如多项选择题部分，也分析了其他选项错误的原因。
- 本书提供了听力部分完整的听力原文，并用下画线标出了包含正确答案的内容。
- 本书的最后提供了阅读和听力部分的答题纸。在实际参加考试前，考生应对这些有所了解，以便知道如何正确标记和书写答案。
- 光盘内包含了6套雅思模拟测试题的听力音频文件。书中涉及听力录音的部分均以特殊图标标示：

🎧 01 🎧 02 🎧 03

国际英语语言测试系统（雅思）

雅思的级别

雅思考试没有通过与否之说。考生会得到一个在1–9分之间的等级分。获得9分的考生英语使用流利、精确，词汇量大，极少犯错，将有能力在专业和学术环境下运用英语。获得7分的考生能够有效地理解英语和用英语进行沟通，能够使用一些复杂的英语，尽管可能会有错误，但并不影响交流。成绩在5分或者5分以下意味着考生只掌握有限的英语，而且语法、发音等方面的错误会导致误解。

不同的组织和机构会公布各自对录用者的雅思成绩的要求。

评分

听力单项测试包含40道题，每答对1题得1分。

阅读单项测试包含40道题，每答对1题得1分。学术类和培训类的阅读测试部分按同样的标准进行评分。但是由于学术类阅读测试的文章总体上比培训类的难度大一些，所以分数相同的情况下，培训类阅读要求考生答对更多的题目。

写作单项测试（学术类和培训类）从以下几个方面进行评分：任务完成情况（Task 1）、任务回答情况（Task 2）、连贯与衔接、词汇量、语法多样性和准确性。考官为以上每项标准分别评等级分，且这几项标准所占权重相同。

口语单项测试中，考官按以下四项标准分别评等级分：语言的流利度和连贯性、词汇量、语法多样性和发音，这几项标准所占权重相同。

考生的每一项技能测试（听力、阅读、写作和口语）都会采用1–9分的等级评分制来测评，4个单项独立记分且同等重要。4个单项所得分数经过平均后四舍五入的成绩即为最终成绩。每个考生都会收到成绩报告单，记录考生的总分和4个单项的分别得分。按照下面列出的1–9分的评分标准，雅思考试的总分和4个单项分均允许整分或者半分。

如果考生在考试环境下完成本书模拟测试题，那么考生的阅读和听力两部分都要达到将近20分才能使总成绩达到5.5分左右。要想达到7分的话，阅读和听力两部分都要达到将近30分才行。

雅思成绩等级

9 卓越使用者——精通英语用法：语体得当，用词准确，口语流利，沟通无障碍。

8 优秀使用者——精通英语用法，偶尔语言组织不准确或不恰当；遇到不熟悉的情况可能会出现理解错误；能够进行复杂、具体的论证。

7 良好使用者——熟练掌握英语用法，只是偶尔在某些情况下出现用法不准确、不恰当和理解错误；大体而言可以很好地处理复杂的语句，并能够理解详细的论证。

6 合格使用者——大体上能有效掌握英语用法，但是有时会出现用法不准确、不恰当或理解错误；能够运用并理解相当复杂的句子，尤其是在比较熟悉的领域。

5 普通使用者——部分掌握英语用法，在大多数情况下能理解大意，不过很可能会出现很多错误；在自身熟悉的领域应该可以进行基本的沟通。

4 有限使用者——只限在熟悉领域内的基本运用能力；在理解和表达方面经常遇到困难；无法使用复杂句式。

3 极其有限使用者——只有在非常熟悉的领域内才能进行比较基本的沟通；交流经常中断。

2 间歇性使用者——无法进行真正的交流，只有在熟悉领域和紧急需要时，能以单词或短句传达最基本的信息；在英语口语和书面语理解方面都非常困难。

1 非使用者——除了能够使用个别单词，基本上无法用英语进行交流。

0 没有参加考试——没有可供评估的信息。

更多有关评分和考试成绩的信息，请查阅剑桥ESOL官网（地址参见本书第9页）。

雅思考试内容

雅思考试包含4个单项测试，每个单项各含2、3或4个部分。每部分的考查事项详见下文表格。

听力 大约30分钟，最后有10分钟的时间把答案誊写到答题纸上。

- 学术类和培训类的题目一致。

- 前两个Section的话题主要基于社交或生活场景，后两个Section则都是与教育或培训相关的场景。

- 4个Section的难度依次递增。

- 每个Section的录音只听一遍。

- 每道题的答题说明都在试卷上。

- 每个Section开始前都有一段短暂的停顿，考生可以利用这段时间查看题目。如果一个Section中有一个以上的任务，那么在下一个任务的录音内容开始前也会有短暂的停顿。

- 每个Section开始之前都能听到一段对接下来的录音内容的简短介绍，但这段内容不会印在试卷上。

- 听力测试结束后，考生会有10分钟的时间把答案誊写到答题纸上。

- 誊写答案时，正确的拼写非常重要。

Section	题量	听力录音内容	题型 （每个Section包含以下一项或多项任务）	题目信息
1	10	两个谈话者之间的一段对话或采访，就日常生活话题给出并交换看法	完成笔记	第10、67页
			完成表格	第61页
2	10	一段独白（有时由另一个说话者发起），提供与日常生活话题相关的信息，例如一次广播节目或者某个导游的一次谈话	完成图表	第21、62页
			补全句子	第68页
			完成流程图	第17页
3	10	2个、3个或者4个谈话者之间的有关教育或者培训的情景对话	标记地图	第64页
			标注图解	第17页
			配对题	第14、66页
4	10	在某个学术场景下的一段独白，例如一次讲座或演示	多项选择题	第14、63、65页

学术类阅读 1小时

● 本书阅读测试仅适用于学术类考试。参加一般培训类考试的考生可参考剑桥ESOL考试中心的网站。两种类型的阅读测试都采用相同的形式，但所选文章在话题、文体、语言难度和风格方面有所不同。

● 三篇文章的长度加起来大约2,750个词。

Passage	题量	文章类型	题型 （每部分包含以下一项或多项任务）	题目信息
1	13 （2项或3项任务）	文章可能选自图书、期刊、杂志、报纸或网站。这些文章均适合本科生或研究生阅读，并不针对学科专业研究，适宜兴趣阅读。	多项选择题	第34、76、80页
			配对题	第28、34、73、82页
			判断True/False/Not Given	第23、71页
2	13 （3项任务）		判断Yes/No/Not Given	第34、81页
			信息定位	第28页
			完成笔记、图表或流程图	第23、72页
3	14 （3项任务）		完成概要或句子	第28、77页
			标注图解	第23页

学术类写作　1小时

本书写作测试仅适用于学术类考试。参加一般培训类考试的考生可参考剑桥ESOL考试中心的网站。

Task	建议时间和分数比例	题型和字数	题目信息
1	20分钟 占写作总分的三分之一	总结图表或表格中给出的信息 不少于150字	第40、87页
2	40分钟 占写作总分的三分之二	写一篇作文，讨论某种观点或想法 不少于200字	第48、90页

口语　11-14分钟

学术类和一般培训类都适用。

考生要直接面对考官，进行一对一的面试，并且面试过程会被录音。

Part	时间	题型	题目信息
1	4-5分钟	自我介绍并讨论一些日常话题	第55、91页
2	1分钟的准备时间 2分钟的谈话	准备并讨论考官给出的话题，接着再回答一两个与话题相关的问题	第57、92页
3	4-5分钟	就Part 2中的话题和考官进行讨论，并且主动创造机会讨论更抽象的问题和看法	第59、94页

更多信息

本书所提供的有关雅思考试的信息仅为对雅思考试的概述。想要了解有关雅思考试的详细信息，如题型、测试重点和备考信息，请参考《雅思手册》（*IELTS Handbook*），本书可通过剑桥ESOL考试中心获取（地址如下）或通过其官方网站下载：
www. Cambridge ESOL. org。

University of Cambridge ESOL Examinations
1 Hills Road
Cambridge CB1 2EU
United Kingdom

What is Listening Section 1?

- a conversation between two people, either face to face or on the phone
- the subject is a topic of general interest (e.g. booking a holiday or course of study)
- one or two tasks (e.g. note completion)
- an example and 10 questions

What does it test?

- understanding specific information (e.g. dates, everyday objects, places, etc.)
- spelling

Useful language: spelling

If you are asked to write the name of a street, person, company, etc., it will be spelt for you. You need to be very familiar with the names of the letters of the alphabet as you only hear them once.

🎧 02 **1** **Listen and repeat the names of these letters.**

A E I S

🎧 03 **2** **Now listen to these letters and put them in the correct column according to how we pronounce their names.**

C F G H J K L N O R T U V W X Y

Four of the letters don't fit in any of the columns. Which are they?

A	E	I	S
	C		

🎧 04 **3** **Listen to some words being spelt out and write down what you hear. Read the word you have written. Can you say it? If not, maybe you missed a vowel!**

1 Address: 23 .... Road
2 Name of company: .... Limited
3 Name: Anna ....
4 Meeting place: .... School
5 Name of village: ....
6 Website address: www. .... .com

> **Tip!** When a letter is repeated, we say 'double', e.g. EE is 'double E'.

Task information: *Note completion*

This task requires you to fill the gaps in the notes someone makes during a conversation. The notes are in the same order as the information you hear. There are other similar completion tasks that you will see: tables (e.g. Test 1 Section 4), sentences (e.g. Test 3 Section 4) and forms (e.g. Test 2 Section 1).

You have to:

- listen to a conversation – you hear it once only.
- write one/two/three words or a number or date in each gap in the notes.
- write the exact words you hear.
- spell everything correctly.
- transfer your answers to the answer sheet after all four listening sections.

Useful language: numbers

🎧 **05** **Listen to these sentences and write the number you hear in the gaps.**

1 .... King Street
2 Family ticket costs $ ....
3 Mobile phone number: ....
4 Theatre opened in ....
5 Secretary is in Room ....
6 Cost of flight: £ ....

Tip! The numbers you write in the exam will be a year, a price, a phone number or part of an address, etc.

Advice

3 When we say a phone number, we can pronounce 0 as 'oh', or say 'zero'.

6 When we talk about money we say, for example 'four pound(s)/dollar(s)/euro(s) fifty' (£4.50 / $4.50 / €4.50).

Useful language: dates

🎧 **06** **Listen to these sentences and write the dates you hear in the gaps.**

1 The course begins on ....
2 Date of birth: ....
3 Date of appointment: ....
4 The wedding will take place on ....
5 Date of arrival in New York: ....
6 Date of interview: ....

Advice

2 We say dates like 1985 or 2014 as 'nineteen eighty-five' and 'twenty fourteen'. For years between 2000 and 2010, we can say, for example, 'two thousand and one'.

Tip! You can write a date in different ways to get a mark (e.g. 3rd March, March 3 or 3 March). This fits the 'one word and/or a number' in the instruction.

Useful language: measurements

🎧 **07** **Listen to these sentences and write the measurement you hear in the gaps.**

1 Mount Everest is .... high.
2 Distance from Wellington to Auckland: ....
3 John's height: ....
4 Add .... flour to sugar.
5 Weight: ....
6 Width of desk: ....

Tip! You can write the whole measurement or an abbreviation (e.g. 25 metres/meters or 25m, 19 kilometres/kilometers or 19km).

Useful language: deciding what to write in the gaps

Look at the sample exam task below and complete this table.

Tip! Predicting what type of word will go into each gap helps you to be ready to hear it during the recording.

Which gaps need ...		What tells you this?
a date?	1	
a distance?		
only numbers?		
a price?		
a website address?		
nouns:		
• a meal or kind of food?		
• a place?		
• a facility?		
• clothes or a piece of equipment?		
• an event?		

Pony-trekking holiday

Example	Answer
Holiday lasts	..........8.......... days.

Holiday starts on **1** ....

Children must be over **2** .... years.

Group rides **3** .... each day on average.

Hats provided but not **4** ....

Holiday costs **5** £.................... per person

All food included except **6** ....

Camp site has a **7** ....

Find more information at www. **8** .... .com

At least one day is spent riding in the **9** ....

A **10** .... will take place one evening.

Action plan for *Note completion*

1 Look at the instructions to find out how many words you can write.

2 Look at the heading and read through the notes. There is time to do this before you listen.

3 Look at the gaps and think about what kinds of word or number are needed (e.g. a date, a distance, an address, a noun).

4 Listen to the introduction, which tells you what the recording is about.

5 Listen carefully to the conversation and focus on each question in turn. As soon as you've written the answer to one question, listen for the answer to the next.

Tip! Write an answer in every gap even if you aren't sure about it. A guess might get a mark but an empty space can't!

08 *Questions 1–10*

Complete the notes below.

*Write no more than **TWO WORDS AND/OR A NUMBER** for each answer.*

Tip! Remember you only hear the recording once.

Tip! If one of your answers is more than two words and a number, it is wrong!

Cycling holiday in Austria

Example	Answer
Most suitable holiday lasts	..........10.......... days.

Holiday begins on **1** ....

No more than **2** .... people in cycling group.

Each day, group cycles **3** .... on average.

Some of the hotels have a **4** ....

Holiday costs **5** £ .... per person without flights.

All food included except **6** ....

Essential to bring a **7** ....

Discount possible on equipment at www. **8** .... .com

Possible that the **9** .... may change.

Guided tour of a **10** .... is arranged.

Advice

The words you hear are usually different from the words in the notes, except for the word(s) you have to write.

1 Make sure you write the whole date.

2 What question does the woman ask which tells you the answer is coming? Which words in the man's answer mean 'no more than'?

3 Which word tells you the answer is coming? Which words do you hear that mean 'on average'?

6 If the word you hear is plural, don't forget to write the 's'.

7 Which words do you hear which tell you that you will soon hear the answer?

8 Write only the missing word(s). There's no need to write www. and .com on the answer sheet.

10 You must spell everything correctly but both American and British English spelling are acceptable here. Check your spelling when you transfer your answers.

What is Listening Section 2?

- a talk / speech / announcement / recorded message / radio excerpt given by one person, sometimes with an introduction by another person
- the subject is a topic of general interest (e.g. what's on, a place of interest)
- usually two tasks (e.g. multiple choice, matching, completing a flow-chart)
- ten questions – there is a brief pause in the recording before the start of the next task

What does it test?

- understanding specific factual information
- selecting relevant information from what you hear

Task information: *Multiple choice (three options)*

Multiple-choice questions usually focus on the details. They follow the order of the recording.

You have to:

- listen to the recording – you hear it ONCE only.
- choose from options A, B or C to answer a question or complete a statement so that it means the same as the recording.
- transfer your answers to the answer sheet after all four listening sections.

There is another kind of multiple-choice task – see Test 2 Listening Section 2.

Task information: *Matching information*

Matching information requires you to listen to detailed information and relate it to a number of places, people, etc.

You have to:

- listen to part of the recording – you hear it ONCE only.
- match one piece of information from the box to each question.
- transfer your answers to the answer sheet after all four listening sections.

There are other kinds of matching task (e.g. Test 2 Listening Section 3, Test 4 Listening Section 3).

Useful language: paraphrasing

In many IELTS tasks, you have to choose a correct answer from a number of options. The options express ideas using different words from the recording.

Match these phrases (1–10) to ones with similar meanings (a–j).

1	a wide variety	a	a convenient location
2	recently	b	a special occasion
3	easy to get to	c	not long ago
4	no more than	d	looks out over
5	a peaceful spot	e	a huge range
6	birthday	f	has changed
7	has a view of	g	the maximum number
8	is different	h	kitchen equipment
9	upmarket	i	a quiet place
10	saucepans	j	luxury

Action plan for *Multiple choice (three options)*

1 Read the questions. They give you an idea of what the recording will be about and what information you should listen for.

2 Listen to the introduction. It tells you what the recording is about.

3 Follow the recording by listening for the answer to each question.

Tip! Listen out for key words, so that you know which question to answer.

4 As soon as you've chosen the answer to a question, listen for the answer to the next one.

5 Check your answers and then transfer them to the answer sheet at the end of the Listening test.

🎧09 *Questions 11–14*

Choose the correct letter, A, B or C.

Advice

11   The market is now situated

    A   under a car park.
    B   beside the cathedral.
    C   near the river.

11 The prepositions on the recording are different from the ones here. Check that the answer you choose means the same as what you hear.

12   On only one day a week the market sells

    A   antique furniture.
    B   local produce.
    C   hand-made items.

12 Think about the kinds of word you might hear before you listen (e.g. what is 'local produce'?).

13   The area is well known for

    A   ice cream.
    B   a cake.
    C   a fish dish.

13 Although the questions follow the order of the recording, each set of options (A, B, C) may not.

14   What change has taken place in the harbour area?

    A   Fish can now be bought from the fishermen.
    B   The restaurants have moved to a different part.
    C   There are fewer restaurants than there used to be.

*14 Read the question carefully. You need to listen for what has **changed**.*

Action plan for *Matching information*

1 Read the options in the box. Think about words you might hear that have a similar meaning.

> **Tip!** At the end of the first task there is a pause. Use this time to read the questions for the next task.

2 Listen to the instructions for the task (if this is the first task).

3 Look at the names of places, people or things that you need to match to the options.

4 Look at the options in the box while you listen to the recording. Choose one answer to each question.

> **Tip!** If you can't choose between two answers for one question, write them both down for now. One might be the answer to a later question, then you will know you can't choose it twice.

5 Check your answers and then transfer them to the answer sheet at the end of the Listening test. Make sure you transfer the answers for both tasks!

⌒09 Questions 15–20

Which advantage is mentioned for each of the following restaurants?

*Choose **SIX** answers from the box and write the correct letter, **A–H**, next to questions 15–20.*

> **Tip!** You can only choose each option (Advantages A–H) once, so two of the options aren't needed.

> **Tip!** The options are in alphabetical order, not in the order you hear them.

> **Advice**
>
> **B** *For some restaurants you will hear information about parking but it might not be 'easy'.*
>
> **D** *You will hear information about service but it might not be 'excellent'. The answer is only correct if the meaning matches exactly what you hear.*

> **Tip!** The restaurants (15–20) are in the order you hear them so listen for each one in turn.

```
                  Advantages

A    the decoration
B    easy parking
C    entertainment
D    excellent service
E    good value
F    good views
G    quiet location
H    wide menu
```

15	Merrivales	....
16	The Lobster Pot	....
17	Elliots	....
18	The Cabin	....
19	The Olive Tree	....
20	The Old School Restaurant	....

What is Listening Section 3?

- a discussion between two to four speakers (e.g. between one or more students and/or a university teacher)
- the subject is some aspect of academic life (e.g. a past or future project)
- up to three tasks (e.g. flow-chart, multiple choice, labelling a diagram)
- 10 questions – there is a brief pause in the discussion between the parts that relate to each of the tasks

What does it test?

- identifying key facts and ideas and how they relate to each other
- identifying speakers' attitudes and opinions

Task information: *Flow-chart completion*

Flow-chart completion requires you to follow the development of a discussion. The steps in the flow-chart are in the same order as what you hear.
You have to:

- listen to part of the discussion – you hear it **once** only.
- choose one option (**A**, **B**, **C**, etc.) from the box to complete each space in the flow-chart according to what you hear.
- transfer your answers to the answer sheet after all four listening sections.

There is another kind of *flow-chart completion* task – see Test 5 Listening Section 4.

Task information: *Diagram labelling*

Diagram labelling requires you to transfer the information you hear to a simple picture or plan. You need to follow language expressing where things are.
You have to:

- listen to part of the discussion – you hear it **once** only.
- choose the correct words from a list to label the diagram.
- write **A**, **B**, **C**, etc. in the spaces on the diagram. There are always more words in the box than you need.
- transfer your answers to the answer sheet after all four listening sections.

There are other kinds of *diagram-labelling* task (e.g. Test 2 Listening Section 2, Test 5 Listening Section 3).

Action plan for *Flow-chart completion*

1 Read the instructions and check how many gaps there are in the flow-chart.

2 Look at the heading of the flow-chart to find out the topic of the discussion.

3 Look at the flow-chart and try to predict what the discussion will be about.

4 Read the list of options in the box.

Tip! Look at each line of the flow-chart in turn. Think about which of the words in the box might fit each space.

5 Listen carefully to the conversation, using the flow-chart to help you follow it.

Tip! The words you hear before the missing word may be synonyms of the words in the flow-chart.

6 Transfer your answers to the answer sheet at the end of the Listening test. Make sure you transfer the answers for both tasks!

Complete the flow-chart below.

Choose **SIX** answers from the box and write the correct letter, **A–I**, next to questions 21–26.

A	actors
B	furniture
C	background noise
D	costumes
E	local council
F	equipment
G	shooting schedule
H	understudies
I	shopowners

FILM PROJECT

visit locations and discuss **21** ....

contact the **22** .... about roadworks

plan the **23** ....

hold auditions and recheck availability
of the **24** ....

choose the **25** .... from the volunteers

rehearse

collect **26** .... and organise food and
transport

 Tip! Look at the list in the box and the flow-chart before you begin.

Advice

A–I These items may be mentioned in any order.

Three of them will not be needed.

Tip! Focus on each question in turn. As soon as you have answered one question, look at the next line.

Advice

21 The answer must be something they plan to talk about when they go somewhere.

22 Probably a person or organisation.

24 The answer comes after they have talked about auditions. Listen out for words which mean 'recheck' and 'availability'.

25 This answer is likely to be A, H or I because they are people.

26 The answer will come after they have talked about rehearsals.

Tip! As soon as the first part ends, look at the next task.

Action plan for *Diagram labelling*

1 Look at the instructions and check how many parts of the diagram you have to label.

2 Look at the heading of the diagram to find out the topic of the discussion.

3 Look at the diagram and read the labels.

Tip! You hear the information you need in the same order as the numbering of the diagram.

4 Read the list in the box. Think about what you might hear.

Tip! There are always more items in the box than you need.

5 Transfer your answers to the answer sheet at the end of the test. Make sure you transfer the answers for both tasks!

🎧10 *Questions 27–30*

Choose four answers from the box and write the correct letter,
A–G, *next to questions 27–30.*

Tip! The words in the list may be mentioned in any order.

A	lights
B	fixed camera
C	mirror
D	torches
E	wooden screen
F	bike
G	large box

Tip! Three of these items will not be needed. They may refer to things which are not in the diagram, or things which you do not have to label.

Old water-mill

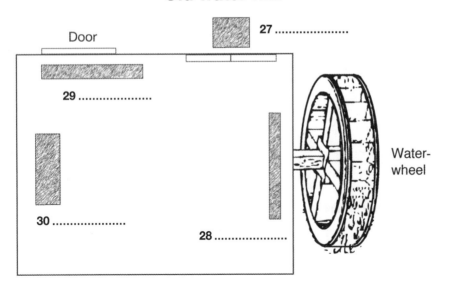

Advice

27 Where is the first object you have to label – inside or outside the mill?

28 This is near a labelled object. What is the object?

What is Listening Section 4?

- a lecture, talk or presentation, usually in front of an audience
- the subject is a topic of academic interest (e.g. a scientific or historical subject)
- up to three tasks (e.g. completing notes, a table or flow-chart)
- 10 questions

What does it test?

- understanding and distinguishing between ideas: reasons, causes, effects, consequences, etc.
- following the way the ideas are organised (e.g. main ideas, specific information, attitude) and the speaker's opinion
- accurate spelling

Task information: *Table completion*

Table completion requires you to follow a talk, step by step, and complete a table which gives a record of the information and ideas that you hear.

You have to:

- listen to a lecture or talk – you hear it once only.
- write one, two or three words in each gap in the table.
- write the exact words you hear. Remember to write only the missing word(s).
- spell your answers correctly on the answer sheet.
- transfer your answers to the answer sheet after all four listening sections.

Useful language: following the speaker

When completing a table (or notes, flow-chart, etc.), it is important to listen for verbal signals that show when the speaker is moving from one aspect of the topic to another. This helps you to be in the right place for each answer.

Here are four kinds of verbal signal you can listen for:

A Introducing a new aspect of the topic
B Developing the topic further
C Introducing an example
D Referring back

Read these expressions and mark each one A, B, C or D to show what kind of verbal signal it could be. For some expressions, you can use more than one letter.

1 The reason for this was ...
2 Now I want to explain a little about ...
3 Among these well-established trades, one was ...
4 Next there's the problem of ...
5 Another experiment demonstrates ...
6 I've been asked to talk to you about ...
7 It's important to recognise ...
8 Now I'd like to talk about ...
9 Anyway, for all these reasons ...
10 And another thing was ...
11 So I want to start by ...
12 Before I talk to you in detail about ...
13 I'm going to describe for you ...
14 The first one concerns ...
15 Another way of doing this was ...
16 Another interesting result ...
17 So, we've looked briefly at ...
18 Lastly, but this is really important ...
19 Another variation is ...
20 I'll now tell you how ...

Action plan for *Table completion*

1 Look at the instructions and check how many words you must write in each gap.

2 Look at the heading of the table which tells you what the recording is about.

3 Read the column headings.

4 Look at each row of the table in turn and think about the kind of word(s) you need to complete it.

Tip! The question numbers run horizontally across each row.

5 Listen and complete each gap.

6 Move on to the next row each time the speaker talks about something new.

Tip! Keep up with the speaker. If you miss an answer, forget it and move on to the next. Fill any gaps at the end with a guess.

7 Transfer your answers to the answer sheet at the end of the test.

 Questions 31–40

Tip! The answers are words which are not in the table.

Complete the table below.

Tip! You will hear the exact word you need to write, but its context may be worded differently from the table.

Write **NO MORE THAN TWO WORDS** *for each answer.*

Tip! Focus on each row in turn as you listen.

EXOTIC PESTS			
Origin	**Name**	**New habitat**	**Notes**
Australia	red-backed spider	New Zealand and Japan	even on island in middle of **31** ....
England	rabbit	Australia	800 years ago: imported into England to be used for **32** ....
America	fire ants	**33** .... in Brisbane	imported by chance
Australia	**34**	Scotland	deliberately introduced in order to improve **35** .... (not effective)
New Zealand	flatworm	**36** .... Europe	accidental introduction inside imported **37** ....
Japan	**38**	Australian coastal waters	some advantages
Australia	budgerigar	urban areas of south-east **39**	smaller flocks because of arrival of **40** .... in recent years

Advice

31 *You know the answer is coming when you hear about New Zealand and Japan.*

32 *Listen for information about 800 years ago.*

33 *You know the answer is coming when you hear this place or these animals.*

38 *The extra information between answers is sometimes quite long, sometimes quite short.*

What is Reading Passage 1?

- a text of up to 900 words, usually factual or descriptive
- two or three tasks, with a total of 13 questions (e.g. True/False/Not given, short-answer questions, diagram labelling)
- usually slightly easier than Passages 2 and 3

What does it test?

- understanding texts which could be included in an academic course
- the ability to follow an argument and opinions
- a range of reading skills including reading for main ideas and detail as well as understanding the structure of a text at sentence and paragraph level

Task information: *True/False/Not given*

True/False/Not given requires you to compare the information given in a series of statements with information given in the text and decide if they are the same.

You have to:

- read statements which are in the same order as the information in the text.
- scan the text to find the information you need.
- decide if the idea given in each statement agrees with the text (True), or contradicts the text (False), or if there is no information about it in the text (Not given).

Task information: *Diagram labelling*

Diagram labelling requires you to understand a detailed description, and relate it to information in a diagram. This task is often found where the text is concerned with a process or a description of something.

You have to:

- scan the text to find specific information.
- find one, two or three words or a number in the text which complete each sentence or notes and copy them into the gaps. If you spell the word(s) wrongly, you will lose marks.

Task information: *Flow-chart completion*

Flow-chart completion requires you to understand a description of a process or sequence of events.

You have to:

- scan the text to find specific information, using the words in the flow-chart to help you locate the parts you need. This may be one or more parts of the text or the whole text. The information is not always in the same order as the flow-chart.
- find one, two or three words or a number in the text which answer each question and copy them into the gaps.

There is another kind of completion task - see Test 2 Reading Passage 2.

NOW FOLLOW THE ACTION PLANS ON PAGES 25–27

*You should spend about 20 minutes on **Questions 1–13**, which are based on Reading Passage 1 below.*

Walking with dinosaurs

Peter L. Falkingham and his colleagues at Manchester University are developing techniques which look set to revolutionise our understanding of how dinosaurs and other extinct animals behaved.

The media image of palaeontologists who study prehistoric life is often of field workers camped in the desert in the hot sun, carefully picking away at the rock surrounding a large dinosaur bone. But Peter Falkingham has done little of that for a while now. Instead, he devotes himself to his computer. Not because he has become inundated with paperwork, but because he is a new kind of palaeontologist: a computational palaeontologist.

What few people may consider is that uncovering a skeleton, or discovering a new species, is where the research begins, not where it ends. What we really want to understand is how the extinct animals and plants behaved in their natural habitats. Drs Bill Sellers and Phil Manning from the University of Manchester use a 'genetic algorithm' – a kind of computer code that can change itself and 'evolve' – to explore how extinct animals like dinosaurs, and our own early ancestors, walked and stalked.

The fossilised bones of a complete dinosaur skeleton can tell scientists a lot about the animal, but they do not make up the complete picture and the computer can try to fill the gap. The computer model is given a digitised skeleton, and the locations of known muscles. The model then randomly activates the muscles. This, perhaps unsurprisingly, results almost without fail in the animal falling on its face. So the computer alters the activation pattern and tries again ... usually to similar effect. The modelled 'dinosaurs' quickly 'evolve'. If there is any improvement, the computer discards the old pattern and adopts the new one as the base for alteration. Eventually, the muscle activation pattern evolves a stable way of moving, the best possible solution is reached, and the dinosaur can walk, run, chase or graze. Assuming natural selection evolves the best possible solution too, the modelled animal should be moving in a manner similar to its now-extinct counterpart. And indeed, using the same method for living animals (humans, emu and ostriches) similar top speeds were achieved on the computer as in reality. By comparing their cyberspace results with real measurements of living species, the Manchester team of palaeontologists can be confident in the results computed showing how extinct prehistoric animals such as dinosaurs moved.

The Manchester University team have used the computer simulations to produce a model of a giant meat-eating dinosaur. It is called an acrocanthosaurus which literally means 'high spined lizard' because of the spines which run along its backbone. It is not really known why they are there but scientists have speculated they could have supported a hump that stored fat and water reserves. There are also those who believe that the spines acted as a support for a sail. Of these, one half think it was used as a display and could be flushed with blood and the other half think it was used as a temperature-regulating device. It may have been a mixture of the two. The skull seems out of proportion with its thick, heavy body because it is so narrow and the jaws are delicate and fine. The feet are also worthy of note as they look surprisingly small in contrast to the animal as a whole. It has a deep broad tail and powerful leg muscles to aid locomotion. It walked on its back legs and its front legs were much shorter with powerful claws.

Falkingham himself is investigating fossilised tracks, or footprints, using computer simulations to help analyse how extinct animals moved. Modern-day trackers who study the habitats of wild animals can tell you what animal made a track, whether that animal was walking or running, sometimes even the sex of the animal. But a fossil track poses a more considerable challenge to interpret in the same way. A crucial consideration is knowing what the environment including the mud, or sediment, upon which the animal walked was like millions of years ago when the track was made. Experiments can answer these questions but the number of variables is staggering. To physically recreate each scenario with a box of mud is extremely time-consuming and difficult to repeat accurately. This is where computer simulation comes in.

Falkingham uses computational techniques to model a volume of mud and control the moisture content, consistency, and other conditions to simulate the mud of prehistoric times. A footprint is then made in the digital mud by a virtual foot. This footprint can be chopped up and viewed from any angle and stress values can be extracted and calculated from inside it. By running hundreds of these simulations simultaneously on supercomputers, Falkingham can start to understand what types of footprint would be expected if an animal moved in a certain way over a given kind of ground. Looking at the variation in the virtual tracks, researchers can make sense of fossil tracks with greater confidence.

The application of computational techniques in palaeontology is becoming more prevalent every year. As computer power continues to increase, the range of problems that can be tackled and questions that can be answered will only expand.

Action plan for *True/False/Not given*

1 Look at the title and information below it and decide who or what the text is about.

2 Read the text very quickly to get an idea of what it is about. Don't worry about words you don't understand.

3 Look at the questions and underline the important words.

4 Find the paragraph which mentions the information in the first question. Read that paragraph carefully and decide if the answer is True, False or Not given.

5 Now do the same for the other questions.

 Tip! The information you need for each question is not evenly spaced through the text. Some may be close together and some further apart. There may be some paragraphs which do not relate to any of the questions.

Questions 1–6

Do the following statements agree with the information given in Reading Passage 1?

In boxes 1–6 on your answer sheet, write

TRUE	*if the statement agrees with the information*
FALSE	*if the statement contradicts the information*
NOT GIVEN	*if there is no information on this*

 Tip! You will always be able to find the answer by reading the text. You never need to use your own general knowledge.

Tip! Two questions following each other may have the same answer. There is always at least one True, one False and one Not given answer.

1 In his study of prehistoric life, Peter Falkingham rarely spends time on outdoor research these days.

2 Several attempts are usually needed before the computer model of a dinosaur used by Sellers and Manning manages to stay upright.

3 When the Sellers and Manning computer model was used for people, it showed them moving faster than they are physically able to.

4 Some palaeontologists have expressed reservations about the conclusions reached by the Manchester team concerning the movement of dinosaurs.

5 An experienced tracker can analyse fossil footprints as easily as those made by live animals.

6 Research carried out into the composition of prehistoric mud has been found to be inaccurate.

Advice

1 The answer is in the first paragraph. Sometimes the first question is about information in a later paragraph and the first few paragraphs don't have a True/False/Not given question.

2 Which paragraph do you need to read? Which words tell you? You need to read several sentences to find the answer.

4 Which sentence talks about the conclusions made by the Manchester team about the movement of dinosaurs? What does it say about the opinions of other palaeontologists?

Action plan for *Diagram labelling*

If a diagram is the first task for a text, read the text through very quickly before you follow this plan so that you have a general idea of the text's structure and argument.

1 Look at the instructions and see how many words you must write.

2 Look at the heading to the diagram. This will help you find the information you need in the text.

3 Read the questions, underline the important words and decide what kind of word(s) you need for the answer (e.g. noun, verb, adjective).

4 Find the part of the text which you need and read it carefully.

Tip! The answers are usually in one or two paragraphs but they may be in a different order in the text from the questions.

5 For each question, underline the word(s) in the text which fit(s) the gap and copy it/them.

Tip! You will always be able to find the exact word(s) you need in the text.

6 Read the labels again to make sure they make sense.

Questions 7–9

Label the diagram below.

Choose **NO MORE THAN ONE WORD** *from the passage for each answer.*

Write your answers in boxes 7–9 on your answer sheet.

Tip! Sometimes you only need to write one word, sometimes two or three. Read the instructions carefully.

Tip! Which paragraph(s) talk(s) about a model of an acrocanthosaurus?

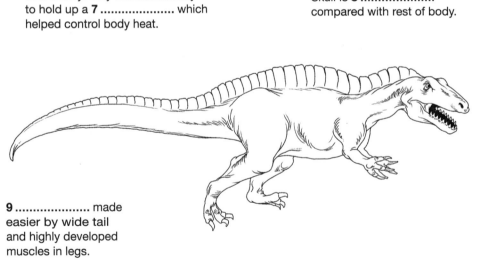

A model of an acrocanthosaurus

Dinosaur's name comes from spines. One theory: they were necessary to hold up a **7** .... which helped control body heat.

Skull is **8** .... compared with rest of body.

9 .... made easier by wide tail and highly developed muscles in legs.

Advice

7 *There are several theories about the spines. Which one talks about 'body heat'? Which words are used?*

8 *What kind of word do you need to look for?*

9 *Find the sentences which talk about the tail and legs. Which word means the same as 'made easier'?*

Action plan for *Flow-chart completion*

If a flow-chart is the first task for a text, read the text through very quickly before you follow this plan so that you have a general idea of the text's structure and argument.

1 Look at the instructions and see how many words you must write.

2 Read the heading to the flow-chart. This will help you find the part(s) of the text you need.

3 Read the flow-chart. Underline the important words in each question and decide what kind of word(s) you need (e.g. noun, verb, adjective).

4 Find the part(s) of the text you need and read it carefully.

5 For each question, underline the word(s) in the text which fit(s) the gap and copy it/them.

Tip! You never need to change the word you copy (e.g. from a noun into a verb, or from singular to plural).

6 Read the sentences again to make sure they make sense.

Questions 10–13

Complete the flow-chart below.

*Write **NO MORE THAN TWO WORDS** for each answer.*

Tip! Check the instructions and make sure you write the correct number of words.

Tip! Some parts of the flow-chart don't have a gap in them. They help you to find the right part of the text.

Peter Falkingham's computer model

Mud is simulated with attention to its texture and thickness and how much **10** .... it contains.

A virtual foot produces a footprint in the mud.

The footprint is dissected and examined from all angles.

Levels of **11** .... are measured within the footprint.

Multiple simulations relate footprints to different types of **12** ....

More accurate interpretation of **13** .... is possible.

Advice

10 *Copy the word carefully. Don't make a spelling mistake.*

13 *You need two words for this answer.*

What is Reading Passage 2?

- a text of up to 900 words
- two or three different tasks, with a total of 13 or 14 questions

Task information: *Locating information*

Locating information requires you to scan a text to find specific information in a paragraph.

You have to:

- read a text divided into labelled paragraphs.
- read statements which focus on details in a paragraph.
- find which paragraph contains the information in each question. The answer may be in one sentence or phrase in a paragraph, or you may need to read more than one sentence.

Task information: *Matching names*

Matching names requires you to relate information, ideas or opinions in the text to a number of people, places, dates, etc.

You have to:

- read a list of statements and match them to a list of options by finding the information in the text. You may have to match people, cities, projects, businesses, schools, theories, plants or dates with events, techniques, discoveries, facilities, etc.
- for each question, write the letter of the statement which matches it. DON'T put the letter of the paragraph where you find the answer.

There are other kinds of matching task – see Test 2 Reading Passage 2.

Task information: *Summary completion*

Summary completion requires you to understand the main points of part of the text.

You have to:

- read the summary and identify the part(s) of the text to which it refers. The information may not be in the same order as in the text.
- complete the gaps in the summary by choosing a word or words from the text.

There is another kind of summary task (e.g. Test 4 Reading Passage 3).

NOW FOLLOW THE ACTION PLANS ON PAGES 31–33

*You should spend about 20 minutes on **Questions 14–26**, which are based on Reading Passage 2 below.*

The robots are coming – or are they?

What is the current state of play in Artificial Intelligence?

A Can robots advance so far that they become the ultimate threat to our existence? Some scientists say no, and dismiss the very idea of Artificial Intelligence. The human brain, they argue, is the most complicated system ever created, and any machine designed to reproduce human thought is bound to fail. Physicist Roger Penrose of Oxford University and others believe that machines are physically incapable of human thought. Colin McGinn of Rutgers University backs this up when he says that Artificial Intelligence 'is like sheep trying to do complicated psychoanalysis. They just don't have the conceptual equipment they need in their limited brains'.

B Artificial Intelligence, or AI, is different from most technologies in that scientists still understand very little about how intelligence works. Physicists have a good understanding of Newtonian mechanics and the quantum theory of atoms and molecules, whereas the basic laws of intelligence remain a mystery. But a sizeable number of mathematicians and computer scientists, who are specialists in the area, are optimistic about the possibilities. To them it is only a matter of time before a thinking machine walks out of the laboratory. Over the years, various problems have impeded all efforts to create robots. To attack these difficulties, researchers tried to use the 'top-down approach', using a computer in an attempt to program all the essential rules onto a single disc. By inserting this into a machine, it would then become self-aware and attain human-like intelligence.

C In the 1950s and 1960s great progress was made, but the shortcomings of these prototype robots soon became clear. They were huge and took hours to navigate across a room. Meanwhile, a fruit fly, with a brain containing only a fraction of the computing power, can effortlessly navigate in three dimensions. Our brains, like the fruit fly's, unconsciously recognise what we see by performing countless calculations. This unconscious awareness of patterns is exactly what computers are missing. The second problem is robots' lack of common sense. Humans know that water is wet and that mothers are older than their daughters. But there is no mathematics that can express these truths. Children learn the intuitive laws of biology and physics by interacting with the real world. Robots know only what has been programmed into them.

D Because of the limitations of the top-down approach to Artificial Intelligence, attempts have been made to use a 'bottom-up' approach instead – that is, to try to imitate evolution and the way a baby learns. Rodney Brooks was the director of MIT's Artificial Intelligence laboratory, famous for its lumbering 'top-down' walking robots. He changed the course of research when he explored the unorthodox idea of tiny 'insectoid' robots that learned to walk by bumping into things instead of computing mathematically the precise position of their feet. Today many of the descendants of Brooks' insectoid robots are on Mars gathering data for NASA (The National Aeronautics and Space Administration), running across the dusty landscape of the planet. For all their successes in mimicking the behaviour of insects, however, robots using neural networks have performed miserably when their programmers have tried to duplicate in them the behaviour of higher organisms such as mammals. MIT's Marvin Minsky summarises the problems of AI: 'The history of AI is sort of funny because the first real accomplishments were beautiful things, like a machine that could do well in a maths course. But then we started to try to make machines that could answer questions about simple children's stories. There's no machine today that can do that.'

E There are people who believe that eventually there will be a combination between the top-down and bottom-up, which may provide the key to Artificial Intelligence. As adults, we blend the two approaches. It has been suggested that our emotions represent the quality that most distinguishes us as human, that it is impossible for machines ever to have emotions. Computer expert Hans Moravec thinks that in the future robots will be programmed with emotions such as fear to protect themselves so that they can signal to humans when their batteries are running low, for example. Emotions are vital in decision-making. People who have suffered a certain kind of brain injury lose the ability to experience emotions and become unable to make decisions. Without emotions to guide them, they debate endlessly over their options. Moravec points out that as robots become more intelligent and are able to make choices, they could likewise become paralysed with indecision. To aid them, robots of the future might need to have emotions hardwired into their brains.

F There is no universal consensus as to whether machines can be conscious, or even, in human terms, what consciousness means. Minsky suggests the thinking process in our brain is not localised but spread out, with different centres competing with one another at any given time. Consciousness may then be viewed as a sequence of thoughts and images issuing from these different, smaller 'minds', each one competing for our attention. Robots might eventually attain a 'silicon consciousness'. Robots, in fact, might one day embody an architecture for thinking and processing information that is different from ours – but also indistinguishable. If that happens, the question of whether they really 'understand' becomes largely irrelevant. A robot that has perfect mastery of syntax, for all practical purposes, understands what is being said.

Action plan for *Locating information*

1 Look at the title and subtitle and decide who or what the text is about.

2 Read the questions quickly and see what else you can predict about the text.

3 Read the text very quickly to get a general idea of what it is about.

4 Read each question carefully and find the part of the text which contains the same information as the question.

Tip! Some paragraphs may contain the answers to more than one question and some paragraphs may not contain any answers.

5 Check that the paragraph you choose as the answer has exactly the same information as the question.

段落信息题
I a reference
‖ mention
an account = explanation

an example & examples.

Questions 14–20

Reading Passage 2 has six paragraphs, *A–F*.

Which paragraph contains the following information?

Write the correct letter, A–F, in boxes 14–20 on your answer sheet.
NB You may use any letter more than once.

14 an insect that proves the superiority of natural intelligence over Artificial Intelligence

15 robots being able to benefit from their mistakes

16 many researchers not being put off believing that Artificial Intelligence will eventually be developed

17 an innovative approach that is having limited success

18 the possibility of creating Artificial Intelligence being doubted by some academics

19 no generally accepted agreement of what our brains do

20 robots not being able to extend their intelligence in the same way as humans

Advice

14 Scan the text quickly to find any paragraphs which mention insects. Read those paragraphs carefully. Which matches the information in the question? You need to find a reference to a particular insect rather than insects in general.

15 Scan the text quickly to find which paragraph talks about robots learning from their mistakes. Most of the paragraphs talk about the things robots aren't good at but only one paragraph mentions them learning from mistakes.

16 All the paragraphs mention researchers but which paragraph mentions some who are positive about the future of Artificial Intelligence? Which words in the text mean 'not being put off'?

17 Check the tense in this question. Find a paragraph in the text which mentions an innovative approach. Is it having limited success now?

18 The important word here is 'doubted'.

19 Find a phrase which means 'generally accepted agreement'. An idea in the text will probably be expressed in the question with different words.

Action plan for *Matching names*

If *Matching names* is the first task for a text, read the text through very quickly before you follow this plan so that you have a general idea of the text's structure and argument.

1 Look at the list of names. Find them in the text and underline them.

Tip! Sometimes the names are in more than one place.

2 For each name, read all the things that person says.

3 For each name, choose the statement which matches one of the things they say. Each name can be matched with only one statement.

Tip! There are two statements which don't match any of the names.

Questions 21–23

Look at the following people (Questions 21–23) and the list of statements below.

Match each person with the correct statement, **A–E**.

Write the correct letter, **A–E**, in boxes 21–23 on your answer sheet.

D **21**   Colin McGinn

B **22** C Marvin Minsky

A **23**   Hans Moravec

A	Artificial Intelligence may require something equivalent to feelings in order to succeed.
B	Different kinds of people use different parts of the brain.
C	Tests involving fiction have defeated Artificial Intelligence so far.
D	People have intellectual capacities which do not exist in computers.
E	People have no reason to be frightened of robots.

Tip! Write the letter of the correct statement, *not* the paragraph where you find the answer.

Advice

In which paragraphs can you find the opinions of these people? Other people are also quoted in the text but their opinions are not important here.

21 Read what Colin McGinn says and match it to one of the statements. Why is A wrong?

22 Marvin Minsky is quoted in two different paragraphs. Read what he says in both places and match one of the statements to what he says.

23 Read what Hans Moravec says and match it to one of the statements.

Action plan for *Summary completion*

If *Summary completion* is the first task for a text, read the text through very quickly before you follow this plan so that you have a general idea of the text's structure and argument.

1 Read the instructions and check how many words you have to write.

2 Locate the part(s) of the text you need by reading the summary and underlining important words. The title of the summary may help you.

Tip! The information you need may be in one paragraph or it may be spread over a longer part of the text.

3 Look at each numbered gap and decide what kind of word(s) you need (e.g. noun, verb, adjective).

4 Read the relevant part(s) of the text and underline the word(s) which you think fit(s) in each gap.

5 Write the words in the gaps and then read the summary again. It should make sense and summarise exactly what the text says.

Tip! Write each word exactly as it appears in the text. Check if it is singular or plural.

Questions 24–26

Complete the summary below.

Choose **ONE WORD ONLY** from the passage for each answer.

Write your answers in boxes 24–26 on your answer sheet.

When will we have a thinking machine?

Despite some advances, the early robots had certain weaknesses. They were given the information they needed on a 24 .disc.... . This was known as the 'top-down' approach and enabled them to do certain tasks but they were unable to recognise 25 patterns Nor did they have any intuition 直觉 or ability to make decisions based on experience. Rodney Brooks tried a different approach. Robots similar to those invented by Brooks are to be found on 26 .M...... where they are collecting information.

Advice

Underline the important words in the summary before you start. Which part of the text will you read? Which words in the text mean 'early robots'?

Which word in the summary means 'shortcomings'? Find the part of the text which explains the 'top-down' approach and read it.

24 Find the sentence about how robots were given information. Which word will you write?

25 Find the part of the text about what robots cannot recognise. Which word will you write?

26 Find the part of the text about Rodney Brooks.

What is Reading Passage 3?

- a text of up to 950 words
- two or three different tasks, with a total of 13 or 14 questions (e.g. Yes/No/Not given, multiple choice and summary completion)
- usually slightly more challenging than Passages 1 and 2

Task information: *Yes/No/Not given*

Yes/No/Not given requires you to identify and understand opinions, ideas and attitudes.

You have to:

- read statements which focus on the writer's ideas as expressed in the text. The statements are in the same order as the ideas in the text.
- scan the text to find where the writer discusses the relevant topic.
- decide if the idea given in each statement agrees with opinions/ideas of the writer (Yes), or contradicts them (No), or if there is no information about that idea in the text (Not given).

Task information: *Multiple choice*

Multiple choice requires both general and detailed understanding of the text.

You have to:

- read questions or incomplete statements which focus on the ideas and information in the text. The questions are in the same order as the ideas in the text. They may refer to a small part of the text, or a long section of it. Occasionally, the last question may refer to the text as a whole.
- choose the correct option **A**, **B**, **C** or **D** to answer the question or complete the statement so that it means the same as the text. There is *never* more than one correct option.

Task information: *Matching sentence endings*

Matching sentence endings requires you to understand a number of significant ideas expressed in the text.

You have to:

- read the first halves of some sentences. These are in the same order as the information in the text so the information relating to the first half-sentence will be found in the text before the information relating to the second half-sentence, and so on.
- choose the ending for each half-sentence from a number of options **A**, **B**, **C**, etc. so that the complete sentence correctly expresses an idea or opinion in the text.

NOW FOLLOW THE ACTION PLANS ON PAGES 37–39

You should spend about 20 minutes on **Questions 27–40**, which are based on Reading Passage 3 below.

Endangered languages

'Never mind whales, save the languages',
says Peter Monaghan, graduate of the Australian National University

Worried about the loss of rainforests and the ozone layer? Well, neither of those is doing any worse than a large majority of the 6,000 to 7,000 languages that remain in use on Earth. One half of the survivors will almost certainly be gone by 2050, while 40% more will probably be well on their way out. In their place, almost all humans will speak one of a handful of megalanguages – Mandarin, English, Spanish.

Linguists know what causes languages to disappear, but less often remarked is what happens on the way to disappearance: languages' vocabularies, grammars and expressive potential all diminish as one language is replaced by another. 'Say a community goes over from speaking a traditional Aboriginal language to speaking a creole*,' says Australian Nick Evans, a leading authority on Aboriginal languages, 'you leave behind a language where there's very fine vocabulary for the landscape. All that is gone in a creole. You've just got a few words like 'gum tree' or whatever. As speakers become less able to express the wealth of knowledge that has filled ancestors' lives with meaning over millennia, it's no wonder that communities tend to become demoralised.'

If the losses are so huge, why are relatively few linguists combating the situation? Australian linguists, at least, have achieved a great deal in terms of preserving traditional languages. Australian governments began in the 1970s to support an initiative that has resulted in good documentation of most of the 130 remaining Aboriginal languages. In England, another Australian, Peter Austin, has directed one of the world's most active efforts to limit language loss, at the University of London. Austin heads a programme that has trained many documentary linguists in England as well as in language-loss hotspots such as West Africa and South America.

At linguistics meetings in the US, where the endangered-language issue has of late been something of a flavour of the month, there is growing evidence that not all approaches to the preservation of languages will be particularly helpful. Some linguists are boasting, for example, of more and more sophisticated means of capturing languages: digital recording and storage, and internet and mobile phone technologies. But these are encouraging the 'quick dash' style of recording trip: fly in, switch on digital recorder, fly home, download to hard drive, and store gathered material for future research. That's not quite what some endangered-language specialists have been seeking for more than 30 years. Most loud and untiring has been Michael Krauss, of the University of Alaska. He has often complained that linguists are playing with non-essentials while most of their raw data is disappearing.

Who is to blame? That prominent linguist Noam Chomsky, say Krauss and many others. Or, more precisely, they blame those linguists who have been obsessed with his approaches. Linguists who go out into communities to study, document and describe languages, argue that theoretical linguists, who draw conclusions about how languages work, have had so much influence that linguistics has largely ignored the continuing disappearance of languages.

Chomsky, from his post at the Massachusetts Institute of Technology, has been the great man of theoretical linguistics for far longer than he has been known as a political commentator. His landmark work of 1957 argues that all languages exhibit certain universal grammatical features, encoded in the human mind. American linguists, in particular, have focused largely on theoretical concerns ever since, even while doubts have mounted about Chomsky's universals.

* a language developed from a mixture of two different languages

Austin and Co. are in no doubt that because languages are unique, even if they do tend to have common underlying features, creating dictionaries and grammars requires prolonged and dedicated work. This requires that documentary linguists observe not only languages' structural subtleties, but also related social, historical and political factors. Such work calls for persistent funding of field scientists who may sometimes have to venture into harsh and even hazardous places. Once there, they may face difficulties such as community suspicion. As Nick Evans says, a community who speak an endangered language may have reasons to doubt or even oppose efforts to preserve it. They may have seen support and funding for such work come and go. They may have given up using the language with their children, believing they will benefit from speaking a more widely understood one.

Plenty of students continue to be drawn to the intellectual thrill of linguistics field work. That's all the more reason to clear away barriers, contend Evans, Austin and others. The highest barrier, they agree, is that the linguistics profession's emphasis on theory gradually wears down the enthusiasm of linguists who work in communities. Chomsky disagrees. He has recently begun to speak in support of language preservation. But his linguistic, as opposed to humanitarian, argument is, let's say, unsentimental: the loss of a language, he states, 'is much more of a tragedy for linguists whose interests are mostly theoretical, like me, than for linguists who focus on describing specific languages, since it means the permanent loss of the most relevant data for general theoretical work'. At the moment, few institutions award doctorates for such work, and that's the way it should be, he reasons. In linguistics, as in every other discipline, he believes that good descriptive work requires thorough theoretical understanding and should also contribute to building new theory. But that's precisely what documentation does, objects Evans. The process of immersion in a language, to extract, analyse and sum it up, deserves a PhD because it is 'the most demanding intellectual task a linguist can engage in'.

Action plan for *Yes/No/Not given*

1 Look at the title and subtitle and think about who or what the text is about.

2 Read the text very quickly. Don't worry about words you don't understand.

3 Look at the statements. Underline the important words.

4 Find the part of the text which discusses the ideas in the first statement. Read it carefully.

5 Decide whether the first statement agrees with what the writer says in the text. Choose *Yes, No* or *Not given*.

Tip! Be sure to read enough to check you have understood the writer's views properly.

6 Do the same for the other statements.

Questions 27–32

Do the following statements agree with the views of the writer in Reading Passage 3?

In boxes 27–32 on your answer sheet, write

YES	*if the statement agrees with the views of the writer*
NO	*if the statement contradicts the views of the writer*
NOT GIVEN	*if it is impossible to say what the writer thinks about this*

27 By 2050 only a small number of languages will be flourishing.

28 Australian academics' efforts to record existing Aboriginal languages have been too limited.

29 The use of technology in language research is proving unsatisfactory in some respects.

30 Chomsky's political views have overshadowed his academic work.

31 Documentary linguistics studies require long-term financial support.

32 Chomsky's attitude to disappearing languages is too emotional.

 Tip! Remember, it is the **writer's** views you need to check, not other people's.

Advice

27 Are the ideas in the question referred to in the first or second paragraph?

28 Which words in the statement suggest an attitude towards the work of Australian linguists? Is it critical or positive?

29 What does 'the use of technology' mean? Find this in the text. Read around the sentence where it is mentioned. Why is it mentioned?

30 Think carefully about the implications of 'overshadowed'. What does the writer say about Chomsky's political views?

Action plan for *Multiple choice*

If the *multiple-choice* questions are the first task for a text, read the text through quickly before you follow this plan so that you have a general idea of the text's structure and argument.

1 Read each question or incomplete statement and the options A–D.

2 Find the part of the text that you need and think about what the answer might be. Make sure you read far enough to cover everything relevant to the question.

3 Reread all four options carefully and choose the one you believe to be correct.

Tip! Be careful – the incorrect options may use similar words to those in the text, but they will be clearly wrong.

Questions 33–36

Choose the correct letter, A, B, C or D.

33 The writer mentions rainforests and the ozone layer

    A   because he believes anxiety about environmental issues is unfounded.

    B   to demonstrate that academics in different disciplines share the same problems.

    C   because they exemplify what is wrong with the attitudes of some academics.

    D   to make the point that the public should be equally concerned about languages.

34 What does Nick Evans say about speakers of a creole?

    A   They lose the ability to express ideas which are part of their culture.

    B   Older and younger members of the community have difficulty communicating.

    C   They express their ideas more clearly and concisely than most people.

    D   Accessing practical information causes problems for them.

35 What is similar about West Africa and South America, from the linguist's point of view?

    A   The English language is widely used by academics and teachers.

    B   The documentary linguists who work there were trained by Australians.

    C   Local languages are disappearing rapidly in both places.

    D   There are now only a few undocumented languages there.

36 Michael Krauss has frequently pointed out that

    A   linguists are failing to record languages before they die out.

    B   linguists have made poor use of improvements in technology.

    C   linguistics has declined in popularity as an academic subject.

    D   linguistics departments are underfunded in most universities.

Tip! Multiple-choice questions follow the order of the text.

Advice

33 Look at the first paragraph and find where the writer mentions rainforests and the ozone layer. Choose the answer which supports what we know about the writer's views.

34 Find the part of the text where Nick Evans talks about the speakers of a creole. What does he say about them? Remember to read the footnote here.

35 Find the part of the text which mentions these places. 'Hotspot' is used here as a metaphor. What do you think it implies? Which words describe these hotspots?

36 Be careful – Krauss is mentioned more than once. What do you think 'playing with non-essentials' refers to?

Action plan for *Matching sentence endings*

If *Matching sentence endings* is the first task for a text, read the text through very quickly before you follow this plan so that you have a general idea of the text's structure and argument.

1 Read the first incomplete sentence.

2 Find the part or parts of the text that you need. Make sure you read far enough to cover everything relevant to the question.

3 Read the options carefully and choose the one you believe to be correct.

Tip! There are two or three options which do not match any of the first halves of sentences, but they may seem very close in meaning until you read them carefully.

4 Read each of the other incomplete sentences and repeat Steps 2 and 3 above.

Tip! There may be more than one part of the text which mentions the subject of the sentence. It's important to find the right one.

Questions 37–40

Complete each sentence with the correct ending, **A–G**, below.

Write the correct letter, **A–G**, in boxes 37–40 on your answer sheet.

37 Linguists like Peter Austin believe that every language is unique

38 Nick Evans suggests a community may resist attempts to save its language

39 Many young researchers are interested in doing practical research

40 Chomsky supports work in descriptive linguistics

A	even though it is in danger of disappearing.
B	provided that it has a strong basis in theory.
C	although it may share certain universal characteristics.
D	because there is a practical advantage to it.
E	so long as the drawbacks are clearly understood.
F	in spite of the prevalence of theoretical linguistics.
G	until they realise what is involved.

Tip! The first halves contain clues to help you locate the correct parts of the text.

Tip! These questions work in a similar way to multiple-choice questions such as Question 33, but there are more options to choose from. There is still only one correct answer for each question, however!

Advice

37 Austin is mentioned in several paragraphs but only one concerns his beliefs about language. What does 'Austin and Co.' mean?

38 Be careful – you need Evans's opinion here.

39 What is the opposite of 'practical' in this context?

Tip! Read the sentence endings carefully. The linking words (*even though, provided that*, etc.) can be very important to the meaning.

What is Writing Task 1?

- a writing task based on data which is presented as a graph or bar chart, or a diagram of a process, machine or device

What does it test?

- expressing the information concisely and accurately
- use of an appropriate academic style (formal or neutral)
- accurate grammar, spelling and punctuation
- clear organisation of your ideas

Task information

This task requires you to recognise and select important and relevant points from the data.

You have to:

- summarise the data you are given in at least 150 words.
- plan, write and check your work in 20 minutes.
- write about the most important parts of the data.
- make comparisons and contrasts as appropriate.
- draw attention to relevant features of the data and interpret them.

STRATEGIES

Before you write

A   Reading the question

Read the task below and think about the questions in boxes 1–5. This is the kind of task you will see in Writing Task 1.

*1 Read the **question** carefully. What does the first part of the question tell you?*
*What **three** things does the rest of the question remind you to do?*

You should spend about 20 minutes on this task.

The bar chart below gives information about the percentage of the population living in urban areas in the whole world and in different parts of the world.

Summarise the information by selecting and reporting the main features, and make comparisons where relevant.

Write at least 150 words.

*2 Look at the **bar chart**. Give yourself time to understand it. The **title** gives you information about its purpose. What does the title of this bar chart tell you?*

*3 Look at the **key** of the bar chart. What do the three bars represent? (The **key** of a chart, graph or map explains its symbols, shading or colours.)*

*4 Look at the **numbers** on the bar chart. What do they represent?*

*5 Look at the **labels** along the x-axis (at the bottom). What information does the bar chart contain?*

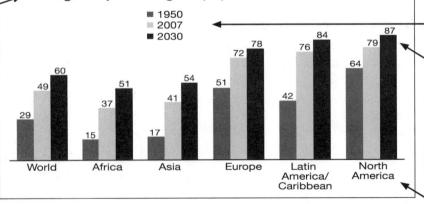

Changes in percentage of population in urban areas

■ 1950
▨ 2007
■ 2030

	1950	2007	2030
World	29	49	60
Africa	15	37	51
Asia	17	41	54
Europe	51	72	78
Latin America/ Caribbean	42	76	84
North America	64	79	87

B Understanding the data

Read these sentences about the bar chart on the previous page. Which of them report the data correctly? Mark them ✔ (correct) or ✘ (incorrect).

Can you explain why the incorrect statements are wrong? Can you correct them?

1 *In North America, we can see that 64% of people already lived in cities by 1950, increasing to 79% by 2007.*

2 This bar chart gives information about the percentage of the population living in urban areas in six regions of the world in three different years, 1950, 2007 and 2030.

3 According to the chart, there is a much greater change in Africa than in North America.

4 *According to the chart, more North Americans already live in cities than in the rest of the world.*

5 In Africa only 15% of the population lived in urban areas in the middle of the last century, but this had risen to 37% by 2007.

6 According to this chart, there will be twice as many Latin Americans and Caribbeans living in cities in 2030 as there were eighty years earlier.

7 *In 2030 the percentage of the world's population living in urban areas is predicted to be just over twice what it was in 1950.*

C Selecting from the data

Look again at the task on page 40. Select which parts of the data in the bar chart are most relevant to the task. Use a highlighter pen or make notes.

Now check your answers to Exercise B and study the corrected sentences. Which sentences could you use for the following parts of your summary?

1 an opening statement of what the whole bar chart is about (find one sentence)

2 the main piece of information which you understand from the data (find one sentence)

3 a comparison or contrast, supported by data from the chart (find at least three sentences)

> **Tip!** The longest part of your summary will be comparing and contrasting. The opening sentence and main information will be **at most** two sentences each.

D Writing a summary

1 When you have analysed the data you have to interpret, and planned what you are going to write, you are ready to write your summary. Use the words in the box to fill the spaces in the sample answer below.

| compares | doubled | greatest | in spite of |
| marked | shows | smaller | whereas |

The bar chart **1** .... the percentage of the world's population living in urban areas in 1950 and **2** .... this with the percentage in 2007 and the projected percentage for 2030.

The proportion of the world's population living in cities will have **3** .... between 1950 and 2030. However, the change is less **4** .... in some regions than others. In North America, for example, we can see that 64% of people already lived in cities by 1950, increasing to 79% by 2007, **5** .... in Africa only 15% of the population lived in urban areas in 1950, but this rose to 37% by 2007. This represents the **6** .... change from rural to urban living, even though the percentage of Africans in cities is still **7** .... than the world average. It is also noticeable that, according to the bar chart, the proportion of the population of Latin America and the Caribbean in cities will be higher than Europe by 2030, **8** .... being lower in 1950.

2 Which is the longest part of this answer – the opening, the main idea or the comparisons and contrasts?

After you write

E Checking your answer

Read the answer at the top of page 43 as if you were checking your own work in the test. Decide whether the candidate has answered the question satisfactorily.

1 There is one spelling error. Can you find it?

2 Now correct her errors.

    a Correct 1 and 2. Find the other places where the candidate repeats these errors.

    b Fill the marked space 3 with a suitable word.

    c Correct the grammar in the other highlighted words and phrases.

    d Suggest another word to use instead of repeating 'part(s)' every time.

IELTS candidate's summary

In the chart we can see the percentage of the population who live in urban 1 area in the years 1950, 2007 and 2030. The first three columns show us the 2 result in the whole world and the other columns show the result in different parts of the world. What is very obvious from the chart is that the number of people living in urban area and also 3 .... moving to urban area is growing quite fast in all parts of the world and there 4 isn't any part that the percentage has come down. It 5 is also seen that in North America and 6 the Latin America this percentage is higher than other parts. 7 By comparing the proportion of people in cities in the rest of the world, Europe, Asia and Africa respectively have the highest percentages. The increase in the number of people in urban area is such that it is estimated that in the year 2030, approximatly 60% of the people in the world will be living in urban area.

Some of these errors are habits influenced by the writer's first language. Can you identify your own habitual errors?

Tip! Make a note of your habitual errors and check for them when you write.

Useful language: contrasting facts and ideas

We contrast facts and ideas between sentences using expressions such as *However, By contrast, On the other hand*, etc. We contrast facts and ideas within a sentence using words such as *whereas* and *while*.

1 💿 **What mistake has this IELTS candidate made?**

The profits of company C declined over these fifteen years. On the other hand the overall profits of company B also declined.

2 💿 **What mistake has this IELTS candidate made?**

The money spent by governments on research has decreased in developing countries. Whereas in industrialised countries it has doubled.

3 **Without looking back at the sample answer on page 42, fill the spaces with *whereas*, or *however*, then check your answers.**

The proportion of the world's population living in cities will have doubled between 1950 and 2030. **a** .... , the change is less marked in some regions than others. In North America, for example, we can see that 64% of people already lived in cities by 1950, increasing to 79% by 2007, **b** .... in Africa only 15% of the population lived in urban areas in 1950.

4 ◉ **Choose the correct word or phrase in italics in these IELTS candidates' sentences.**

1 USA has the highest percentage of this group *while/however* Vietnam has the lowest.

2 In 1990, industrialised countries were spending twice as much on research compared to 1980. *Whereas/On the other hand*, expenditure in developing countries decreased during this period.

3 New Zealand has the highest percentage of women working in parliament. *By contrast/While*, Italy has the lowest percentage of all the countries shown.

4 Going out to restaurants accounted for 15% of free time activities, *whereas/on the other hand* only about 12% of the time was used for meeting friends and socialising.

5 People aged 14–24 went to the cinema most often at this time. *However/Whereas* the percentage of people over fifty was lowest.

5 **Contrast the facts and ideas in five of these pairs of sentences, using a different word or expression from the box for each one.**

One pair of sentences does not offer contrasting ideas. Suggest a way of combining the two sentences to emphasise this.

by contrast	however	on the other hand
whereas	while	

1 For the workforce, working conditions have always been more important than wages. Profitability has been the main concern of the management.

2 In the United States, people tend to eat early in the evening. In Spain, few people eat before nine o'clock.

3 The students at the state university showed an improved performance in the tests. Attending a private college enabled students to increase their test scores.

4 Home computers were a rarity in the 1980s. The majority of families have at least one computer now.

5 Car ownership has risen sharply in rural areas. The provision of public transport has declined.

6 A sense of humour is rated as essential by 90% of women who are looking for a partner. Only 70% of women say they want to meet someone wealthy.

6 **Now use the words in the box in Exercise 5 and write some sentences about a topic you are interested in.**

Useful language: expressing percentages, proportions and quantities

Try to vary the way you refer to quantities in your writing. Look at these expressions for 90% and write down ways you could refer to 10%.

90%	10%
ninety percent (of)	....
a high percentage (of)	....
nine-tenths (of)	....
nine out of ten	....
the vast majority of	....
most (of)	....
nearly all (of)	....

Useful language: talking about numbers as they get bigger and smaller

1 Match these verbs with their opposites.

1	to rise	**a**	to decrease
2	to increase	**b**	to shrink
3	to go up	**c**	to halve
4	to grow	**d**	to contract
5	to double	**e**	to fall
6	to expand	**f**	to go down

2 Which verbs from Exercise 1 can you use with these groups of words?

1 things that can be counted (e.g. number of homeowners/students, etc.)

2 things that can be described in terms of size (e.g. a company)

3 things that have monetary value (e.g. cost of living, price of houses)

3 Complete the sentences with appropriate verbs from Exercise 1 in the correct tense.

1 Audiences at the theatre ...... if another cinema opens. (–)

2 The cost of living ...... in the last forty years. (+)

3 Losing our best customer ...... our income. (÷ 2)

4 Computer use ...... sharply in the past few years. (+)

5 The company's profits ...... in 2009. (x 2)

6 Interest rates ...... if the government follows this policy. (–)

Useful language: writing about information in a chart or graph

⊙ **Look at the pairs of sentences written by IELTS candidates. Choose the correct one in each pair (a or b) and underline the correct phrase.**

1 **a** It can be seen that 96% of the prison population are males.
   b It is seen that 96% of the prison population are males.

2 **a** There is clear that almost 30% of men work over 45 hours a week.
   b It is clear that almost 30% of men work over 45 hours a week.

3 **a** It is easy to be seen that the number of people increased.
   b It is easy to see that the number of people increased.

4 **a** The pie chart represents the main types of employment.
   b The pie chart shows the main types of employment.

5 **a** The graphs indicate information about total government spending.
   b The graphs provide information about total government spending.

6 **a** From the charts we can find out travelling abroad is becoming more popular.
   b From the charts we can see travelling abroad is becoming more popular.

Test 1 Exam practice / Writing Task 1

In the IELTS exam, it is important not to spend more than 20 minutes on Task 1, otherwise you may not have enough time for Writing Task 2, which is longer and is worth twice as many marks.

Tip! When practising you will probably need more than 20 minutes at first. Keep a note of how long you take and try reducing the time for each practice test until you can do Task 1 in 20 minutes.

Action plan for *Bar chart* and other graphs

Before you write

This Action plan refers to a bar chart. Follow the same Action plan for other graphs and diagrams. The bar chart is similar to the one on page 40 but NOT the same.

1 Look at the task on page 47 and read the question carefully. Think about what the first part of the question tells you.

2 Look at the bar chart and decide what the title, key, labels and numbers mean.

3 Make notes or highlight the data you want to include in your summary:

opening statement	
main information	
comparison or contrast	

4 Write your summary. Try to include the language you practised in the exercises on pages 43–45. Use the ideas in the the task and title but avoid copying them word for word.

After you write

5 Read through what you have written.

Check for

- **meaning** – does it give correct information, according to the chart?
  - have you supported your ideas with data from the chart?

- **grammatical slips** – do your verbs agree with their subjects?
  - have you used the correct prepositions?
  - have you used articles correctly?, etc.

- **spelling** – have you copied words correctly?
  - have you avoided habitual mistakes?

- **length** – have you written at least 150 words?

6 Correct any mistakes neatly, but do not rewrite the whole essay.

Writing Task 1

Advice

Do NOT copy this sentence into your answer, you will lose marks.

Remember to select and compare, but do NOT challenge the data or introduce new information.

You don't gain extra marks for writing more than 150 words, but you will lose marks if you write less.

You should spend about 20 minutes on this task.

The bar chart below gives information about the percentage of the population living in urban areas in different parts of the world.

Summarise the information by selecting and reporting the main features, and make comparisons where relevant.

Write at least 150 words.

Changes in percentage of population in urban areas

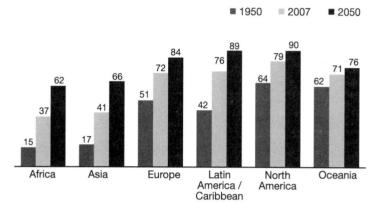

What is Writing Task 2?

- a formal discussion essay

What does it test?

- expressing and evaluating ideas
- use of an appropriate style
- grammar, spelling and punctuation
- paragraphing

Task information

This task requires you to present arguments in a clear and well-organised way.

You have to:

- write at least 250 words in 40 minutes.
- discuss the idea expressed in the task.
- give your opinion and support it with relevant examples.
- conclude with a brief statement of your final opinion.

STRATEGIES

Before you write

A   Reading the question

Read the task below and think about the questions in the boxes. This is the kind of task you will see in Writing Task 2.

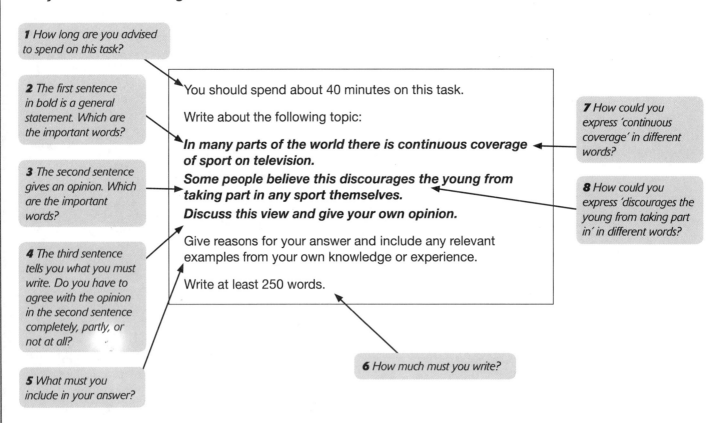

1 How long are you advised to spend on this task?

2 The first sentence in bold is a general statement. Which are the important words?

3 The second sentence gives an opinion. Which are the important words?

4 The third sentence tells you what you must write. Do you have to agree with the opinion in the second sentence completely, partly, or not at all?

5 What must you include in your answer?

You should spend about 40 minutes on this task.

Write about the following topic:

In many parts of the world there is continuous coverage of sport on television.
Some people believe this discourages the young from taking part in any sport themselves.
Discuss this view and give your own opinion.

Give reasons for your answer and include any relevant examples from your own knowledge or experience.

Write at least 250 words.

7 How could you express 'continuous coverage' in different words?

8 How could you express 'discourages the young from taking part in' in different words?

6 How much must you write?

B Planning your answer

Before you start writing your answer, it is essential to plan what you want to say and to organise it. This is one way of presenting your answer:

Stage 1	An **introduction** restating the view expressed in the question and giving a brief reaction to it
Stage 2	A **discussion** of why some people hold this view, with examples or comments supporting it and against it
Stage 3	Your own **opinion**, supported by **examples**
Stage 4	Your final **conclusion**

Match these notes for Writing Task 2 on page 48 to Stages 1–4 above.

a *some watch instead of taking part but not the young*
...**Stage 4**...

b *most countries, many TV channels, including sport – people obviously like it but watching sport not necessarily alternative to participating*
....

c *teachers/parents see teenagers watching TV sport, worry because not active but teens need to relax – exam pressure*
....

d *my neighbourhood, teenagers – lots of sport – admire sports stars on TV – want to emulate them but older people watch instead of playing – office workers, no exercise*
....

C Developing a clearly structured argument

Using the correct words and phrases to tie your ideas together gives your writing coherence and makes your ideas easy to follow.

1 Read this model answer and fill gaps 1–5 with expressions a–e, and gaps 6–10 with expressions f–j.

Nowadays, in most countries, there are numerous television channels to choose from and these include non-stop broadcasting of sport. **1**.....................many people must be interested in watching sport throughout the day and night. However, **2**.....................watching sport makes people less keen on participating in it. Teachers and parents may be concerned when they see teenagers spending time watching sport on television and fear that they are not active enough. While there may be some justification for this, **3**.....................young people are often under pressure, for example to do well in exams. They need to relax and give their minds and bodies a break.

4..................... the young do not tend to watch sport rather than participating in it. The teenagers in my neighbourhood regularly play football after school and at weekends they play in matches or go to the tennis courts or the swimming pool. **5**..................... they all support various famous clubs and admire sports stars. These stars are their role models and watching them on television encourages participation in sporting activities **6**..................... the young try to emulate the people they admire.

7..................... I have observed that some older people spend their evenings and weekends in front of the television, following sports such as international golf or motor racing. **8**..................... many of these are middle-aged men (it tends to be men) who spend their days sitting at a desk in an office and who get very little exercise **9**..................... they need it more than most.

10..................... although I accept that there are some people who may be discouraged from participating in sport because they can watch it on television instead, in my view this does not generally apply to the young.

a it does not necessarily follow that

b Therefore it would appear that

c it is also true that

d As well as this,

e In my experience,

f By contrast,

g In conclusion,

h Moreover,

i in spite of the fact that

j because

2 Which of the stages 1–4 in Exercise B on page 49 takes up more than one paragraph in this answer? Why?

Useful language: style

1 Compare the language of A and B below. Which style is more suitable for an essay?

> **A**
>
> I think, from what I've seen, kids are getting more and more lazy.
>
> And this is because of the way grown-ups behave – they let their kids do nothing for much too long.

> **B**
>
> In my opinion, it is noticeable that children are becoming increasingly lazy.
>
> Moreover, this is a result of adult behaviour as children are permitted to remain inactive for longer than they should.

2 Here are some language features of A. Can you find examples of them?

1 short verb forms
2 informal vocabulary
3 using a dash (–) instead of a linking word
4 simple vocabulary
5 repetition for emphasis
6 a conjunction / linking word at the beginning of a sentence

3 Now look at B. Can you find examples of these language features?

1 noun instead of verb
2 passive verb
3 impersonal structure
4 formal vocabulary
5 modal verb
6 an adverb at the beginning of a sentence

4 ⊙ Choose the most appropriate phrases in *italics* for use in an essay from these IELTS candidates' sentences.

1 If *you don't like / people dislike* sport, *you probably won't / they are unlikely to* do it.
2 *I think / As I see it*, 24-hour sports programmes *make no difference / don't matter*.
3 I liked watching football matches on *television / TV*, but I *rarely played / didn't play much*.

Useful language: impersonal structures

1 ⊙ Find and correct the errors in these IELTS candidates' sentences.

1 This is true that in some countries people do not like tourism.
2 That is obviously necessary to prepare yourself for such activities.
3 There is no doubt true that the media play a role in our lives.
4 This is a fact that increasing numbers of young people are leaving home.

2 Explain the meaning of these impersonal phrases.

1 It is unfortunate that
2 It is undeniable that
3 It is understandable that
4 It is generally accepted that
5 It is regrettable that
6 It is frequently asserted that
7 It is often assumed that
8 It is no doubt true that

3 Now make sentences with the phrases in Exercise 2 above, using the ideas in this box, or your own.

> students / affordable accommodation
> children / cartoons
> music / universal language
> careless driving / accidents

Example

It is undeniable that students often have difficulty finding affordable accommodation.

Useful language: *the* and no article

⊙ When you check your essay, make sure that your use of articles is correct. Read these sentences from IELTS candidates' essays and write *the* or – in each gap.

1 We should not overemphasise .... importance of .... wealth.

2 Films, books and .... Internet can provide almost all of .... necessary information.

3 In conclusion, it is not .... money that can solve children's problems, but .... love and .... good teaching.

4 A high level of .... education and .... development of .... technology affects agricultural societies.

5 In conclusion, I find that .... advantages of .... international tourism outweigh .... disadvantages.

6 If .... governments had more effective policies for these children who grow up in .... poverty, ... children would have more chance to contribute to .... society.

Useful language: giving reasons

⊙ Look at the pairs of extracts from IELTS candidates' essays. Choose the correct one in each pair and underline the correct phrase.

1 a This is not true for a number of reasons.

  b This is not true because of a number of reasons.

2 a Some people have a wide knowledge of the world as a result from travelling.

  b Some people have a wide knowledge of the world as a result of travelling.

3 a In society today, by the advance of science and technology, people know more than they used to.

  b In society today, because of the advance of science and technology, people know more than they used to.

4 a They gave free educational materials to the children. So that the children were more likely to attend classes.

  b They gave free educational materials to the children so that the children were more likely to attend classes.

5 a I assume the reason of this is that media companies are producing better films nowadays.

  b I assume the reason for this is that media companies are producing better films nowadays.

6 a In those countries women's rights are more developed and, as a consequence, women are more fairly treated there.

  b In those countries women's rights are more developed, as a consequence, women are more fairly treated there.

Useful language: paragraphing

Read this essay by a strong IELTS candidate. It is a good answer. However, it does not have paragraphs, which will lose marks. Mark each place where you think she should start a new paragraph and write 'new para' in the margin. Explain your decisions.

IELTS candidate's essay

These days, it is noticeable that young people are becoming less interested in team games, sports and other forms of exercise. It is my belief that this is mainly because of our everyday work, which is increasingly sedentary. Besides, I think every person would admit that sitting and relaxing is much easier than moving and running and sweating. The question is, how much of this laziness is because of the sports programmes on television? From one point of view it could be true that these programmes make young people lazy. However, this may be because some people who like sport, and also like watching sports, are attracted to the television programmes and spend so much time watching sport that there is no spare time for them to participate themselves. By contrast, watching sport may encourage some other young people to take up sport, as these individuals might like that sport and consequently want to try it to see how it feels. Watching such programmes on television can make us feel that we want to be active, want to play basketball, or go swimming and so on. Thus, I would suggest that there are positive aspects of watching sports programmes. In my opinion, the fundamental issue is the reason why we like sport. Does an individual like sport merely as a spectator or as a participant? If the reason is simply the pleasure of watching other people playing volleyball or football or even dancing, that person will never want to be among those who take part. However, if a person enjoys being active and joining in, then sports programmes will never prevent this.

> **Tip!** Do not attempt to learn model or sample answers and rewrite them in the exam. Your composition will not fit the task exactly, even if it is about a similar subject. The examiners can recognise a prepared answer and you will lose a lot of marks.

Action plan

Before you write

1 Look at the task below and read the question carefully. The question that you have to answer is printed in **bold italics**, but remember to read all the rest of the question too.

2 Underline the important parts of the task.

Tip! You are marked on the quality of your English, not how good your ideas are.

3 Consider alternative language to express the ideas in the task.

Tip! You will lose marks if you copy the wording of the instructions. Use your own words.

4 Make notes on the task before you begin to write your essay. Your notes should cover the four essential points described in Exercise B on page 49: introduction; discussion of the view expressed; your own opinion; conclusion.

5 Now write your composition.

After you write

6 Read through your answer. Correct any mistakes neatly, but do not rewrite the whole essay.

7 Check for

- **overall structure** – have you included the four essential points?

- **paragraphing** – do you start a new paragraph for each new idea?

- **coherence** – have you linked your ideas together clearly?

- **style** – have you used appropriately formal language?

- **grammar, spelling and punctuation** – are your verb forms correct? Are your adverbs spelt correctly? Have you used capitals, apostrophes and full stops correctly?

- **your habitual errors** – what are these? (see Writing Task 1 page 43)

Tip! If you have forgotten to use paragraphs, mark them in the correct places and write 'new para' in the margin.

You should spend about 40 minutes on this task.
Write about the following topic:

In many parts of the world there is continuous coverage of sport on television. Some people believe this discourages the young from taking part in any sport themselves.
Discuss this view and give your own opinion.

Give reasons for your answer and include any relevant examples from your own knowledge or experience.

Write at least 250 words.

Tip! Allow at least five minutes for planning before you write and another five minutes for checking at the end.

Tip! If you don't have an opinion, invent one!

Speaking Part 1

What is Speaking Part 1?

- a short introductory conversation lasting 4–5 minutes

What does it test?

- your ability to talk about personal experiences and interests

Tip! Don't forget to take your passport or ID card to the exam room!

Task information

You are required to answer questions about everyday topics.

You have to:

- talk about some aspects of your life such as your family and friends, home, studies/work, leisure activities, etc.
- answer each question appropriately – usually in one or two sentences.

Useful language: topics

The topics in Part 1 are usually things that you can talk about easily.

1 You may be asked about where you live. Think about your home town, city or village. What is it like? Underline any of the expressions below that you could use to talk about it. Make a note of other expressions you need.

City/Town etc.	(big) city (medium-sized) town (tiny) village port
Position	to the north/east etc. of … in the mountains on the coast not far from …
Description	the capital in a rural/industrial/commercial region has a population of … famous for …
Part of the city/town	in the centre (of) on the outskirts (of) in a suburb on a housing estate on a busy street in a built-up area
Building/Street etc.	convenient crowded quiet modern typical traditional friendly isolated
Countryside/Landscape	mountainous flat agricultural popular with tourists

2 Make similar tables for yourself with useful words and expressions for other topics, e.g. family and friends, leisure activities, food.

Tip! In Part 1 you will be asked questions on topics which are very familiar. It's important not to memorise answers – just try and talk about the topic naturally.

3 Look at the questions about your home town on page 60 and practise saying the answers.

Tip! Answer the questions you are asked. Your answers needn't be more than one or two sentences. Don't give a long speech in this Part.

Useful language: adding information to your answers

1 Look at these questions and answers about learning English (1–5).
For each possible answer in italics, underline the correct alternative.

   1 How long have you been learning English?

     Since six years. / <u>*For six years.*</u>

   2 Do most children learn English in your country?

     Yes, they do. / Yes, they are.

   3 What can you remember about your early lessons?

     They were fun. / They were funny.

   4 Have you studied any other languages?

     I have studied Spanish until I was 14. / I studied Spanish until I was 14.

   5 What advice would you give to someone who wants to start learning English?

     Go to a class. / Go to the class.

2 The answers in Exercise 1 are too short. Choose one piece of extra
information to add to each answer.

   a You learn much faster with a teacher and it's hard to be motivated on
your own.

   b We start learning when we are seven and most people continue until
they leave school. I think it's a good idea to start young.

   c Apart from English, we could choose between Spanish and Portuguese.
I chose Spanish but I've given it up now.

   d I started when I was ten years old.

   e Our teacher used to play a lot of games with us. But we had to work
hard too.

Tip! Never answer questions with one word, or just *Yes* or *No*. Give an extra piece of
information or a reason.

3 Look at the questions above about learning English and practise
answering them about yourself.

Speaking Part 2

What is Speaking Part 2?

- a short talk

What does it test?

- your ability to talk for about two minutes
- your ability to organise your ideas and speak fluently

Task information

You are required to prepare and talk about a topic given to you during the test by the examiner.

You have to:

- read a card with a task on it.
- make notes on each of the separate parts of the task. You have a minute or two to do this.
- talk about the topic in the task, answering the questions on the card.
- stop talking when the examiner tells you to.
- answer some follow-up questions.

Useful language: adjectives for describing people

Here are some characteristics you might admire in different people. Which other adjectives from the box could describe each of these people a–e? Write them in the gaps.

amusing	cheerful	considerate	courageous	determined	encouraging
entertaining	~~imaginative~~	inventive	optimistic	reliable	sympathetic	witty

a   a creative person   imaginative   ....
b   a funny person   ....
c   a kind person   ....
d   a positive person   ....
e   a strong person   ....

Tip! Use a wide range of adjectives when you are describing someone or something.

Useful language: making notes

1   Look at the task on page 60. Underline the important words. Read the notes one candidate made for this task.

Tip! Use the preparation time to think about what you will say even if you don't write very much.

> Who? my brother, five years older
> Kind of person? fun, energetic, patient
> Relationship? cycling + fishing together during holidays, no time when busy
> (I got upset)
> Influence? balance work/play, gave me confidence

Think about what the candidate might say using the notes.

2   Look at the task on page 60 again and write some notes for yourself.

3 Here are some useful phrases you might want to use in your talk. Can you add any more?

> What I really admired about X was …
> X was a … kind of person
> I respected X because …
> The best times were …
> X made me feel …
> We used to …
> X inspired / encouraged / supported / stood up for me
> X was always there for me

 Tip! Answer all the questions. You needn't answer them in the order on the card and you needn't spend an equal amount of time on each one. You may have more to say about some questions than others.

Useful language: giving a talk

1 Make sure you introduce the topic. Here are some suggestions of ways to begin.

> The person / What I want to talk about is …
> I'd like to tell you about X …
> I've chosen to talk about …

2 Look at the notes you made in Making notes, Exercise 2. Record yourself talking for two minutes. Use a clock to time yourself.

3 Listen to what you said and think about how to improve it. Think about these questions.
- Did you introduce the topic?
- Did you use the correct tenses?
- Did you use a range of vocabulary?
- Did you connect your sentences?
- Did you cover all the points on the card (not necessarily in that order)?
- Did you speak clearly?

4 Look at the two follow-up questions on page 60 and think of your answers. You only need to give short answers to these.

5 Practise talking about the topics below for two minutes. Don't forget to make some notes and time yourself for each one.
- your favourite music and why you like it
- a special day, what you did, why it was important
- a place you have visited, why you went there, what you did and if you enjoyed it

 Tip! You must talk about the topic on the card. Remember, what you say doesn't have to be completely true or exciting and you don't need any special knowledge.

Speaking Part 3

What is Speaking Part 3?

- a discussion of general and abstract ideas lasting 4–5 minutes

What does it test?

- your ability to analyse and discuss ideas in depth

Task information

You are required to answer questions which relate to the topic in Part 2.

You have to:

- offer your opinions and give reasons for them.

Useful language: giving opinions

(O) There are errors in the phrases below used by IELTS candidates.
Correct the mistakes so that you have a list of expressions for giving your opinion.
(Sometimes there is more than one mistake in a phrase.)

        In
1 ~~From~~ my opinion, ...
2 As far as I am concern, ...
3 There are several reasons about my opinion.

4 I strongly disagree the idea that ...
5 I am completely agree to this opinion.
6 From the point of my view, ...

Here are some more expressions used by IELTS candidates. Three of these are not good English. Tick (✓) the ones you could use to give your opinion.

7 It seems to me that ...
8 According to my point of view, ...
9 It is my view that ...
10 In my own opinion, I think ...

11 Personally, I think that ...
12 What I think is that ...
13 According to me, ...

Useful language: easily confused words and expressions

1   (O) Here are some examples of language used by IELTS candidates.
Underline the correct word in italics in each sentence.

1 Parents should be more *restricted* / *strict* with their children.
2 Children who are *grown up* / *brought up* by working parents are more independent.
3 Children who live in *extended* / *joint* families tend to have better social skills.
4 A lot of children do not respect *elder* / *elderly* people because they have so little contact with them.
5 Children from *sole* / *single* parent families are often close to their grandparents.
6 Schools should punish children for bad *behaviour* / *behaving*.
7 Children whose parents *let* / *allow* them to do what they want learn to make their own rules.
8 Children who are spoilt do not learn how to behave in *the society* / *society*.

2 Read the statements in Exercise 1 again and decide if you agree or disagree with each one. Look at the task on page 60 and think about what you would say. Practise saying your answers.

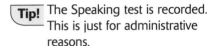

Test 1 Exam practice / Speaking

Speaking Part 1

The examiner will ask you some questions about yourself.

Let's talk about your home town.

Where do you come from?
What is it like there?
Do you like living there?
Have you always lived there?
What is the countryside like near your home town?

The examiner will then ask you some questions about one or two other topics, for example:

Now let's talk about learning English.

How long have you been learning English?
Do most children learn English in your country?
What can you remember about your early lessons?
Have you studied any other languages? Which language do you find easier?
What advice would you give to someone who wants to start learning English?

Tip! The Speaking test is recorded. This is just for administrative reasons.

Tip! Listen to the tense in the question so you use the right one in your answer.

Speaking Part 2

The examiner will give you a topic on a card like the one on the right and ask you to talk about it for one to two minutes. Before you talk you'll have one minute to think about what you're going to say. The examiner will give you some paper and a pencil so you can make notes if you want to.

The examiner may ask one or two more questions when you have finished, for example:

Did the person you've described influence other people too?
Are you similar to this person?

> **Describe someone who influenced you when you were a child.**
> **You should say:**
> who the person was
> what kind of person he/she was
> what your relationship was like
> **and explain how he/she influenced you.**

Tip! The examiner will tell you when to start speaking.

Speaking Part 3

The examiner will ask some more general questions which follow on from the topic in Part 2.

Do children nowadays have too many toys, electronic games and so on?
Do parents give their children toys instead of paying attention to them?
Is it the responsibility of parents or schools to teach children how to behave well?
Do children learn better if they have fun at school, or if the teachers are strict?
Do you think attitudes towards bringing up children differ in different parts of the world?
What about respect for older people, does that vary in different countries?

Tip! The examiner may ask you some questions during your talk.

Tip! Don't worry if you haven't finished when the examiner tells you to stop.

Tip! You are given a mark across all three parts, not a different mark for each part separately.

Review

1 How many speakers will you hear?

2 How many times will you hear the recording?

3 How many questions do you have to answer?

4 Does each task in this section have the same number of questions?

5 Is there an example answer?

6 What information do you have to listen for in Section 1?

7 Do you have to write the exact words you hear?

8 Is spelling important in Section 1?

9 When do you transfer your answers to the answer sheet?

Action plan reminder

Form completion

1 How do you know how many words to write?

2 Do you have time to look at the task before you hear the recording?

3 What can you learn from the words around the gaps?

4 How can you lose marks in this task?

◀ **Page 13** *Test 1 Listening Section 1 Action plan*

🎧 12 **Questions 1–6**

Complete the form below.

Write **NO MORE THAN TWO WORDS** for each answer.

PRIME RECRUITMENT
Employee record

Example	*Answer*
Surname	..........Riley........

Email	1 .... @worldnet.com
Nationality	2 ....
Reference (professional)	Name: John Keen Job: manager of 3 ....
Reference (personal)	Name: Eileen Dorsini Job: 4 ....
Special qualifications	current 5 .... certificate certificate of competence in 6 ....

Tip! You don't have to write the same number of words in each space.

Tip! There is always an example in Listening Section 1 but not in the rest of the Listening test. As soon as you hear the answer to the example, listen for the answer to Question 1.

Advice

2 Be careful to write a nationality, not the name of a country.

3 What kind of word(s) do you need here?

4 Is this the same kind of word as for Question 3?

Action plan reminder

Table completion

1 How do you know how many words to write?

2 What should you check before the recording begins?

3 How will you know when an answer is coming?

 Page 22 *Test 1 Listening Section 4 Action plan*

 Questions 7–10

Complete the table below.

Write **NO MORE THAN ONE WORD** *for each answer.*

Tip! You need a different number of words in this part!

PRIME RECRUITMENT CHILDCARE VACANCIES			
Location	**Name**	**Children**	**Special requirements**
London	Benton	girl and boy	be keen on 7 ....
near Oxford	Granger	8 .... boys	be animal-lover
9	Campbell	four girls	be willing to 10 .... when camping

Advice

7 *What kind of word is needed here?*

8 *This word probably indicates how many boys.*

9 *Be ready for a place name.*

10 *What kind of word do you need here?*

Review

1 How many speakers will you hear?

2 How many times will you hear the recording?

3 How many tasks are there usually?

4 How many questions do you have to answer?

5 Does each task have the same number of questions?

6 Is there an example?

7 What does Section 2 test?

Action plan for *Multiple choice (five options)*

1 Read the question(s) and the list of items A–E. This will give you an idea of what you will hear and what information you should listen for.

Tip! You will probably hear all the things A–E mentioned, but only TWO of them will be the correct answer for the questions.

2 Listen for the answers to each question.

3 There will be a pause during the recording at the end of the first task. During the pause read the questions in the second task.

◄ **Page 15** *Test 1 Listening Section 2 Action plan*

🎧13 *Questions 11 and 12*

*Choose **TWO** letters, **A–E**.*

Which **TWO** sources of funding helped build the facility?

A   the central government

B   local government

C   a multinational company

D   a national company

E   city residents

Tip! You'll hear the information for Questions 11 and 12 before the information for Questions 13 and 14.

Advice

11 & 12 What is a 'source of funding'?

🎧13 *Questions 13 and 14*

*Choose **TWO** letters, **A–E**.*

Which **TWO** pre-existing features of the site are now part of the new facilities?

A   football stadium

B   playing fields

C   passenger hall

D   control tower

E   aircraft hangars

Advice

13 & 14 What does 'pre-existing' mean? In what kind of place would you find things like C–E?

Action plan for *Map labelling*

1 Look at the map and read the instructions.

Tip! This task is similar to, but not exactly the same as, a diagram labelling task.

2 Try to understand what the map shows and how to describe the location of each of the places marked.

Tip! The letters on the map are *not* in the same order as the places you hear mentioned, but the places in the questions are in the right order.

3 Read the instructions, so you know what to write (e.g. a word or a letter).

4 Use the places already marked on the map to help you follow the recording.

5 Write the names of the places on the map as you listen.

6 Write the letters next to the question numbers at the end.

Tip! The speaker will say exactly where you are on the map at the beginning.

🎧 **13** *Questions 15–20*

Label the map below.

*Write the correct letter, **A–H**, next to questions 15–20.*

Tip! There are some letters on the map which you don't need to use.

15	hotel	....
16	transport hub	....
17	cinema	....
18	fitness centre	....
19	shops	....
20	restaurant	....

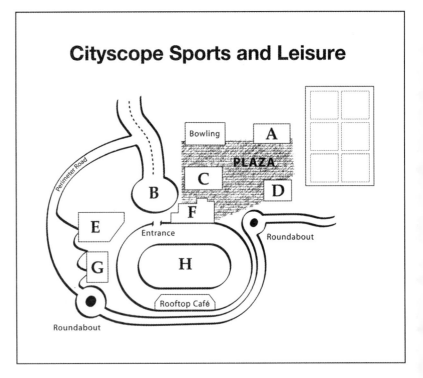

Cityscope Sports and Leisure

Review

1 Is the topic about academic situations or is it more general?

2 How many speakers are there?

3 How many times do you hear the recording?

4 How many questions do you have to answer?

5 Does each task have the same number of questions?

6 When are you given time to read the questions?

Action plan reminder

Multiple choice

1 Are the questions (21, 22, etc.) in the same order as the recording?

2 Are the options (A, B, C, etc.) in the same order as the recording?

3 How do you know the answer to the next question is coming?

4 What should you do before you listen?

Page 15 Test 1 Listening Section 2 Action plan

 Questions 21–25

Choose the correct letter, A, B or C.

21 What is Chloe concerned about?

    A her knowledge of maths
    B her ability to write essays
    C her lack of business experience

22 Which of the following does Ivan feel he has improved?

    A his computer skills
    B his presentation skills
    C his time management

23 What does Chloe especially like about the course?

    A She won't have to do a final examination.
    B She can spend time working in a business.
    C She can study a foreign language.

24 Ivan is pleased that the university is going to have

    A more lecture rooms.
    B a larger library.
    C more courses.

25 What does Ivan advise Chloe to do?

    A contact his tutor
    B read about some other universities
    C visit the university

Tip! Read the questions to give you an idea of what the conversation is about.

Advice

Which speaker is thinking of doing the course? What kind of course is it?

21 What does Ivan say which tells you that you need to listen for the answer?

22 Ivan mentions all of the options but he only feels one has improved.

23 What words does Chloe use to say she especially likes something?

Action plan for *Matching A, B and C*

1 Read the options (A, B, C) you have to choose from.

2 Listen carefully to hear the words in the numbered questions, and decide which option from A, B and C is closest in meaning to what the speaker says.

3 Choose an answer to each of the questions. The questions are in the order you hear them.

Tip! There may sometimes be more than three options (A, B, C) to choose from.

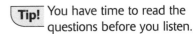 **Questions 26–30**

What does Chloe decide about the following subjects?

*Write the correct letter, **A**, **B** or **C**, next to questions 26–30.*

Tip! You have time to read the questions before you listen.

A	She will study it.
B	She won't study it.
C	She might study it.

Subjects

26 Public relations ....

27 Marketing ....

28 Taxation ....

29 Human resources ....

30 Information systems ....

Advice

Only put A or B as your answer if Chloe is definite in what she says.

26 *Listen for Chloe's final opinion.*

27 *Chloe sometimes disagrees with Ivan about whether a course is useful or not.*

29 *What expression does Chloe use which matches A, B or C?*

30 *When a speaker makes a statement followed by 'but ...', listen carefully to what comes after 'but' as that will probably give you the answer.*

Review

1 How many speakers are there?
2 What kind of topic might you hear?
3 How many times do you hear the recording?
4 How many questions do you have to answer?
5 Does each task always have the same number of questions?
6 When are you given time to read the questions?

Action plan reminder

Note completion

1 Do you write the same number of words in each gap?
2 Are the gaps in the same order as the information you hear?

Tip! Use the information and the headings in the notes to find your place in the recording.

3 What should you think about when you look at the gaps?
4 Are the words you need all on the recording?
5 Do you have to spell the words correctly?

◀ **Page 13** *Test 1 Listening Section 1 Action plan*

 Questions 31–35

Complete the notes below.

*Write **NO MORE THAN TWO WORDS** for each answer.*

History of weather forecasting

Early methods

- Almanacs connected the weather with the positions of different
  31 .... at particular times.

Invention of weather instruments

- A hygrometer showed levels of **32** .... (Nicholas Cusa 1450)
- Temperature variations first measured by a thermometer containing
  33 .... (Galileo Galilei 1593)
- A barometer indicated air pressure (Evangelista Torricelli 1643)

Transmitting weather information

- The use of the **34** .... allowed information to be passed around the world.
- Daily **35** .... were produced by the French from 1863.

Advice

The lecture begins with an introduction. Which word tells you to listen for the first answer?

32 Check the words you write make sense. (The names and the dates will help you hear the answer.)

33 Be careful! The answer may not be what you expect from general knowledge.

Action plan reminder

Sentence completion

1 Do you write the same number of words in each gap?

2 Are the questions in the same order as the information you hear?

3 Are the words you need all on the recording?

◀ **Page 13** *Test 1 Listening Section 1 Action plan*

 Questions 36–40

Complete the sentences below.

Write **NO MORE THAN TWO WORDS** *for each answer.*

Producing a weather forecast

36 Weather observation stations are found mostly at .... around the country.

37 Satellite images use the colour orange to show ....

38 The satellites give so much detail that meteorologists can distinguish a particular ....

39 Information about the upper atmosphere is sent from instruments attached to a ....

40 Radar is particularly useful for following the movement of ....

Tip! The second task will be on a different aspect of the first topic. The title will help you.

Advice

36 *The word 'mostly' is important.*

37 *Listen for 'orange' which tells you the answer is coming.*

39 *Listen for a word which means 'instruments'.*

Review

1 How many questions do you have to answer?

2 Does each task have the same number of questions?

3 How long should you spend on this passage?

NOW FOLLOW THE ACTION PLAN REMINDER ON PAGE 71

*You should spend about 20 minutes on **Questions 1–13**, which are based on Reading Passage 1 below.*

Our Vanishing Night
Most city skies have become virtually empty of stars
by Verlyn Klinkenborg

Tip! Read the title and subtitle which tell you what the topic is.

Tip! Quickly skim the passage to get a general idea of what it is about and the topic of each paragraph. Don't worry about words you don't understand and don't spend too long trying to work out what they mean. If you read on, they may be explained anyway.

If humans were truly at home under the light of the moon and stars, it would make no difference to us whether we were out and about at night or during the day, the midnight world as visible to us as it is to the vast number of nocturnal species on this planet. Instead, we are diurnal creatures, meaning our eyes are adapted to living in the sun's light. This is a basic evolutionary fact, even though most of us don't think of ourselves as diurnal beings any more than as primates or mammals or Earthlings. Yet it's the only way to explain what we've done to the night: we've engineered it to meet our needs by filling it with light.

This kind of engineering is no different from damming a river. Its benefits come with consequences – called light pollution – whose effects scientists are only now beginning to study. Light pollution is largely the result of bad lighting design, which allows artificial light to shine outward and upward into the sky, where it is not wanted, instead of focusing it downward, where it is. Wherever human light spills into the natural world, some aspect of life – migration, reproduction, feeding – is affected.

For most of human history, the phrase 'light pollution' would have made no sense. Imagine walking toward London on a moonlit night around 1800, when it was one of Earth's most populous cities. Nearly a million people lived there, making do, as they always had, with candles and lanterns. There would be no gaslights in the streets or squares for another seven years.

Now most of humanity lives under reflected, refracted light from overlit cities and suburbs, from light-flooded roads and factories. Nearly all of night-time Europe is a bright patch of light, as is most of the United States and much of Japan. In the South Atlantic the glow from a single fishing fleet – squid fishermen luring their prey with metal halide lamps – can be seen from space, burning brighter on occasions than Buenos Aires.

In most cities the sky looks as though it has been emptied of stars and taking their place is a constant orange glow. We've become so used to this that the glory of an unlit night – dark enough for the planet Venus to throw shadows on Earth – is wholly beyond our experience, beyond memory almost. And yet above the city's pale ceiling lies the rest of the universe, utterly undiminished by the light we waste.

We've lit up the night as if it were an unoccupied country, when nothing could be further from the truth. Among mammals alone, the number of nocturnal species is astonishing. Light is a powerful biological force, and on many species it acts as a magnet. The effect is so powerful that scientists speak of songbirds and seabirds being 'captured' by searchlights on land or by the light from gas flares on marine oil platforms, circling and circling in the thousands until they drop. Migrating at night, birds are apt to collide with brightly lit buildings; immature birds suffer in much higher numbers than adults.

Insects, of course, cluster around streetlights, and feeding on those insects is a crucial means of survival for many bat species. In some Swiss valleys the European lesser horseshoe bat began to vanish after streetlights were installed, perhaps because those valleys were suddenly filled with light-feeding pipistrelle bats. Other nocturnal mammals, like desert rodents and badgers, are more cautious about searching for food under the permanent full moon of light pollution because they've become easier targets for the predators who are hunting them.

Some birds – blackbirds and nightingales, among others – sing at unnatural hours in the presence of artificial light. Scientists have determined that long artificial days – and artificially short nights – induce early breeding in a wide range of birds. And because a longer day allows for longer feeding, it can also affect migration schedules. The problem, of course, is that migration, like most other aspects of bird behavior, is a precisely timed biological behavior. Leaving prematurely may mean reaching a destination too soon for nesting conditions to be right.

Nesting sea turtles, which seek out dark beaches, find fewer and fewer of them to bury their eggs on. When the baby sea turtles emerge from the eggs, they gravitate toward the brighter, more reflective sea horizon but find themselves confused by artificial lighting behind the beach. In Florida alone, hatchling losses number in the hundreds of thousands every year. Frogs and toads living on the side of major highways suffer nocturnal light levels that are as much as a million times brighter than normal, disturbing nearly every aspect of their behavior, including their night-time breeding choruses.

It was once thought that light pollution only affected astronomers, who need to see the night sky in all its glorious clarity. And, in fact, some of the earliest civic efforts to control light pollution were made half a century ago to protect the view from Lowell Observatory in Flagstaff, Arizona. In 2001 Flagstaff was declared the first International Dark Sky City. By now the effort to control light pollution has spread around the globe. More and more cities and even entire countries have committed themselves to reducing unwanted glare.

Action plan reminder

True/False/Not given

1 Will the questions focus on author opinion or factual information?

2 Are the questions in the same order as the information you need in the text?

3 Will there always be at least one True, one False and one Not given answer?

4 Is there an answer in every paragraph?

5 Look at the text. What will you do first?

6 Look at the questions. What will you do before you look for the answers?

◀ **Page 25** *Test 1 Reading Passage 1 Action plan*

Questions 1–7

Do the following statements agree with the information given in Reading Passage 1?

In boxes 1–7 on your answer sheet, write

TRUE	*if the statement agrees with the information*
FALSE	*if the statement contradicts the information*
NOT GIVEN	*if there is no information on this*

Tip! Use the words in the statements to find the part of the text you need to read carefully for each question. Remember – the text may use different words from the questions.

Tip! If you find the right part of the text but you can't find the answer, the answer is 'Not given'.

Advice

1 The first paragraph is about human beings in general. Underline the sentence about how most of us think of ourselves.

2 The text mentions 'bad lighting design'. Does this refer to how strong the lights are or which way they point?

3 Find the paragraph about London in 1800. Read the whole paragraph and then answer the question.

4 Find the part of the text about fishermen. What does it say about their awareness of light pollution?

5 Find the paragraph which mentions Venus. What does it say about when we can see the shadows?

6 Find the part of the text which mentions Swiss valleys. Read about both kinds of bats to get the right answer.

7 Look at the paragraph about astronomers. Find the words which mean 'the first attempts to limit light pollution' and read the rest of the sentence. The first sentence and 'in fact' also help you to answer the question.

1 Few people recognise nowadays that human beings are designed to function best in daylight.

2 Most light pollution is caused by the direction of artificial lights rather than their intensity.

3 By 1800 the city of London had such a large population, it was already causing light pollution.

4 The fishermen of the South Atlantic are unaware of the light pollution they are causing.

5 Shadows from the planet Venus are more difficult to see at certain times of year.

6 In some Swiss valleys, the total number of bats declined rapidly after the introduction of streetlights.

7 The first attempts to limit light pollution were carried out to help those studying the stars.

Action plan reminder

Table completion

1 What important information do the instructions give you?

2 What should you think about when you look at the gaps?

3 Are the words you need all in the text?

4 Can you change words or use different words with the same meaning for your answer?

5 Do you have to spell the words correctly?

 Page 27 *Test 1 Reading Passage 1 Action plan*

Questions 8–13

Complete the table below.

Choose **NO MORE THAN THREE WORDS** *from the passage for each answer.*

Write your answers in boxes 8–13 on your answer sheet.

CREATURE	EFFECTS OF LIGHT
Songbirds and seabirds	The worst-affected birds are those which are **8** .... They bump into **9** .... which stand out at night.
Desert rodents and badgers	They are more at risk from **10** ....
Migrating birds	Early migration may mean the **11** .... are not suitable on arrival.
Sea turtles	They suffer from the decreasing number of **12** ....
Frogs and toads	If they are near **13** .... , their routines will be upset.

Tip! When you have completed the table, read it through. Do your answers make sense? For example, in 8, 11 and 12 you need an adjective as well as a noun.

Tip! Look at the headings of the columns. For each kind of creature you are going to look at the ways they are affected by light.

Tip! For each question find the part of the text which is about those creatures. They are in the same order as the text.

Tip! Some of the words you need will be singular and some will be plural. Copy them carefully.

Advice

Do all the gaps need nouns or noun phrases?

8 *Which words mean 'worst-affected'?*

9 *Which paragraph is about songbirds and seabirds? Which word means 'bump into'? Why are 'searchlights' and 'oil platforms' wrong?*

10 *There is one sentence about desert rodents and badgers. Which words say they are 'at risk'?*

11 *Which paragraph is about migration? Which words mean 'on arrival'? What does the text say is not suitable?*

12 *There are three sentences about sea turtles. What is there a lack of? Which words tell you? Does this make the turtles suffer? Why is 'artificial lighting' wrong?*

13 *Which paragraph is about frogs and toads? Which words in the text mean 'their routines will be upset'? What are they near when this happens?*

Review

1 How many questions do you have to answer?

2 Does each task have the same number of questions?

3 How long should you spend on this passage?

Action plan for *Matching paragraph headings*

Tip! If there is a *Matching paragraph headings* task, it is always before the text to encourage you to read the headings before you read the text.

1 Check how many headings there are and how many paragraphs there are in the text.

2 Read the first paragraph of the text quickly. Underline the main ideas and choose the best heading.

3 Do the same for the other paragraphs. You can only use each heading once.

Tip! If you are not sure about one paragraph, do the rest of the task and go back when you haven't got so many headings to choose from.

You should spend about 20 minutes on **Questions 14–26**, which are based on Reading Passage 2 on pages 74–75.

Questions 14–20

Reading Passage 2 has seven paragraphs, **A–G**.

Choose the correct heading for **A–G** from the list of headings below.

Tip! The headings are about the main ideas in each paragraph, not about one or two details.

Write the correct number, **i–x**, in boxes 14–20 on your answer sheet.

List of Headings

i   A comparison between similar buildings

ii   The negative reaction of local residents

iii An unusual job for a psychologist

iv   A type of building benefiting from prescribed guidelines

v   The need for government action

vi   A failure to use available information in practical ways

vii Academics with an unhelpful attitude

viii A refusal by architects to accept criticism

ix   A unique co-operative scheme

x   The expanding scope of environmental psychology

14   Paragraph **A**
15   Paragraph **B**
16   Paragraph **C**
17   Paragraph **D**
18   Paragraph **E**
19   Paragraph **F**
20   Paragraph **G**

Advice

14 Whose response surprised Chris Spencer?

15 Does Paragraph B focus on a particular situation or a general one?

Is there a psychologist in the building?

— CHRISTIAN JARRETT reports on psychology's place in new architectural development. —

A The space around us affects us profoundly – emotionally, behaviourally, cognitively. In Britain that space is changing at a pace not seen for a generation. Surely psychology has something to say about all this change. But is anyone listening? 'There is a huge amount of psychology research that is relevant, but at the moment we're talking to ourselves,' says Chris Spencer, professor of environmental psychology at the University of Sheffield. Spencer recalls a recent talk he gave in which he called on fellow researchers to make a greater effort to communicate their findings to architects and planners. 'I was amazed at the response of many of the senior researchers, who would say: "I'm doing my research for pure science, the industry can take it or leave it". But there are models of how to apply environmental psychology to real problems, if you know where to look. Professor Frances Kuo is an example.

B Kuo's website provides pictures and plain English summaries of research conducted by her Human Environment Research Laboratory. Among these is a study using police records that found inner-city Chicago apartment buildings surrounded by more vegetation suffered 52 per cent fewer crimes than apartment blocks with little or no greenery. Frances Kuo and her co-researcher William Sullivan believe that greenery reduces crime – so long as visibility is preserved – because it reduces aggression, brings local residents together outdoors, and the conspicuous presence of people deters criminals.

C 'Environmental psychologists are increasingly in demand,' says David Uzzell, professor of environmental psychology. 'We're asked to contribute to the planning, design and management of many different environments, ranging from neighbourhoods, offices, schools, health, transport, traffic and leisure environments for the purpose of improving quality of life and creating a better people–environment fit.' Uzzell points to the rebuilding of one south London school as a striking example of how building design can affect human behaviour positively. Before its redesign, it was ranked as the worst school in the area – now it is recognised as one of the country's twenty most improved schools.

D Uzzell has been involved in a pioneering project between MSc students in England and Scotland. Architecture students in Scotland acted as designers while environmental psychology students in England acted as consultants, as together they worked on a community project in a run-down area of Glasgow. 'The psychology students encouraged the architecture students to think about who their client group was, to consider issues of crowding and social cohesion, and they introduced them to psychological methodologies, for example observation and interviewing local residents about their needs.' The collaborative project currently stands as a one-off experiment. 'Hopefully these trainee architects will now go away with some understanding of the psychological issues involved in design and will take into account people's needs,' says Uzzell.

E Hilary Barker, a recent graduate in psychology, now works for a design consultancy. She's part of a four-person research team that contributes to the overall work of the company in helping clients use their office space more productively. Her team all have backgrounds in psychology or social science, but the rest of the firm consists mainly of architects and interior designers. 'What I do is pretty rare to be honest,' Barker says. 'I feel very privileged to be able to use my degree in such a way.' Barker explains that the team carries out observational studies on behalf of companies, to identify exactly how occupants are using their building. The companies are often surprised by the findings, for example that staff use meeting rooms for quiet, individual work.

F One area where the findings from environment–behaviour research have certainly influenced building is in hospital design. 'The government has a checklist of criteria that must be met in the design of new hospitals, and these are derived largely from the work of the behavioural scientist Professor Roger Ulrich,' Chris Spencer says. Ulrich's work has shown, for example, how the view from a patient's window can affect their recovery. Even a hospital's layout can impact on people's health, according to Dr John Zeisel. 'If people get lost in hospitals, they get stressed, which lowers their immune system and means their medication works less well. You might think that way-finding round the hospital is the responsibility of the person who puts all the signs up, but the truth is that the basic layout of a building is what helps people find their way around,' he says.

G Zeisel also points to the need for a better balance between private and shared rooms in hospitals. 'Falls are reduced and fewer medication errors occur' in private rooms, he says. There's also research showing how important it is that patients have access to the outdoors and that gardens in hospitals are a major contributor to well-being. However, more generally, Zeisel shares Chris Spencer's concerns that the lessons from environmental psychology research are not getting through. 'There is certainly a gap between what we in social science know and the world of designers and architects,' says Zeisel. He believes that most industries, from sports to film-making, have now recognised the importance of an evidence-based approach, and that the building trade needs to formulate itself more in that vein, and to recognise that there is relevant research out there. 'It would be outrageous, silly, to go ahead with huge building projects without learning the lessons from the new towns established between 30 and 40 years ago,' he warns.

Action plan for *Selecting two answers from multiple choice (five-option)*

1 Read the question carefully and make sure you understand what you have to look for. Underline the important words.

2 Scan the text quickly. Find a reference in the text to each option and check to see if it answers the question. You only have to find two so don't keep checking if you are satisfied you have found the answers.

Tip! Some of the options may be close together and there may be some parts of the text you don't need to look at.

3 When you have found the answers, write the letters.

Questions 21 and 22

*Choose **TWO** letters, A–E.*

Write the correct letters in boxes 21 and 22 on your answer sheet.

Which **TWO** of the following benefits are said to arise from the use of environmental psychology when planning buildings?

- A   better relationships between staff
- B   improved educational performance
- C   reduction of environmental pollution
- D   fewer mistakes made by medical staff
- E   easier detection of crime

Tip! The options A–E are in the order that they appear in the text.

Advice

A What does research find out about office staff?

B In the parts of the text which refer to schools and universities, is improved educational performance mentioned?

C Does the text refer to levels of pollution in the environment?

D Which paragraphs talk about hospitals?

E What positive point is made about crime in the text?

Questions 23 and 24

*Choose **TWO** letters, A–E.*

Write the correct letters in boxes 23 and 24 on your answer sheet.

Which **TWO** of the following research methods are mentioned in the passage?

- A   the use of existing data relating to a geographical area
- B   measuring the space given to a variety of activities
- C   watching what people do in different parts of a building
- D   analysing decisions made during the planning of a building
- E   observing patients' reactions to each other

Advice

*Each option **A–E** describes a research method and its context. When you choose your answers, make sure the whole statement is correct.*

Action plan for *Sentence completion*

1 Look at the instructions and check how many words you must write.

2 Underline key words in each sentence. Decide what kinds of word you need for each gap (e.g. noun, adjective, etc.).

3 The sentences follow the order of the information in the text. Find the part of the text you need for each one.

4 Mark the words you need in the text.

5 Copy them exactly and make sure you spell correctly.

Questions 25–26

Complete the sentences below.

*Choose **NO MORE THAN TWO WORDS** from the passage for each answer.*

Write your answers in boxes 25 and 26 on your answer sheet.

25   The students from England suggested that the Scottish students should identify their ....

26   John Zeisel believes that if the .... of a building is clear, patient outcomes will improve.

Advice

25 *You need two words here.*

26 *Think about the meaning of 'patient outcomes' before looking for the answer.*

Review

1 How many tasks are there usually in this part?

2 Does each task have the same number of questions?

3 How long should you spend on this passage?

NOW FOLLOW THE ACTION PLAN REMINDER ON PAGE 80

*You should spend about 20 minutes on **Questions 27–40**, which are based on Reading Passage 3 below.*

Have teenagers always existed?

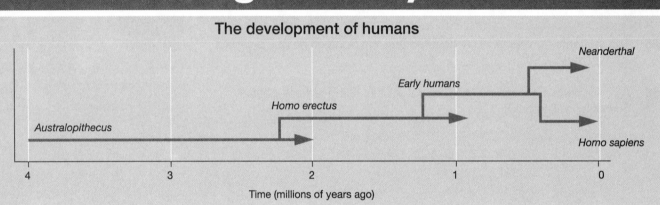

The development of humans

Time (millions of years ago)

Our ancestor, *Homo erectus*, may not have had culture or even language, but did they have teenagers? That question has been contested in the past few years, with some anthropologists claiming evidence of an adolescent phase in human fossil. This is not merely an academic debate. Humans today are the only animals on Earth to have a teenage phase, yet we have very little idea why. Establishing exactly when adolescence first evolved and finding out what sorts of changes in our bodies and lifestyles it was associated with could help us understand its purpose. Why do we, uniquely, have a growth spurt so late in life?

Until recently, the dominant explanation was that physical growth is delayed by our need to grow large brains and to learn all the behaviour patterns associated with humanity – speaking, social interaction and so on. While such behaviour is still developing, humans cannot easily fend for themselves, so it is best to stay small and look youthful. That way your parents and other members of the social group are motivated to continue looking after you. What's more, studies of mammals show a strong relationship between brain size and the rate of development, with larger-brained animals taking longer to reach adulthood. Humans are at the far end of this spectrum. If this theory is correct, and the development of large brains accounts for the teenage growth spurt, the origin of adolescence should have been with the evolution of our own species (*Homo sapiens*) and Neanderthals, starting almost 200,000 years ago. The trouble is, some of the fossil evidence seems to tell a different story.

The human fossil record is extremely sparse, and the number of fossilised children minuscule. Nevertheless, in the past few years anthropologists have begun to look at what can be learned of the lives of our ancestors from these youngsters. One of the most studied is the famous Turkana boy, an almost complete skeleton of *Homo erectus* from 1.6 million years ago found in Kenya in 1984. Accurately assessing how old someone is from their skeleton is a tricky business. Even with a modern human, you can only make a rough estimate based on the developmental stage of teeth and bones and the skeleton's general size.

You need as many developmental markers as possible to get an estimate of age. The Turkana boy's teeth made him 10 or 11 years old. The features of his skeleton put him at 13, but he was as tall as a modern 15-year-old. Susan Anton of New York University points to research by Margaret Clegg who studied a collection of 18th- and 19th-century skeletons whose ages at death were known. When she tried to age the skeletons without checking the records, she found similar discrepancies to those of the Turkana boy. One 10-year-old boy, for example, had a dental age of 9, the skeleton of a 6-year-old but was tall enough to be 11. 'The Turkana kid still has a rounded skull, and needs more growth to reach the adult shape,' Anton adds. She thinks that *Homo erectus* had already developed modern human patterns of growth, with a late, if not quite so extreme, adolescent spurt. She believes Turkana boy was just about to enter it.

If Anton is right, that theory contradicts the orthodox idea linking late growth with development of a large brain. Anthropologist Steven Leigh from the University of Illinois goes further. He believes the idea of adolescence as catch-up growth does not explain why the growth rate increases so dramatically. He says that many apes have growth spurts in particular body regions that are associated with reaching maturity, and this makes sense because by timing the short but crucial spells of maturation to coincide with the seasons when food is plentiful, they minimise the risk of being without adequate food supplies while growing. What makes humans unique is that the whole skeleton is involved. For Leigh, this is the key.

According to his theory, adolescence evolved as an integral part of efficient upright locomotion, as well as to accommodate more complex brains. Fossil evidence suggests that our ancestors first walked on two legs six million years ago. If proficient walking was important for survival, perhaps the teenage growth spurt has very ancient origins. While many anthropologists will consider Leigh's theory a step too far, he is not the only one with new ideas about the evolution of teenagers.

Another approach, which has produced a surprising result, relies on the minute analysis of tooth growth. Every nine days or so the growing teeth of both apes and humans acquire ridges on their enamel surface. These are like rings in a tree trunk: the number of them tells you how long the crown of a tooth took to form. Across mammals, the rate at which teeth develop is closely related to how fast the brain grows and the age you mature. Teeth are good indicators of life history because their growth is less related to the environment and nutrition than is the growth of the skeleton.

A more decisive piece of evidence came last year, when researchers in France and Spain published their findings from a study of Neanderthal teeth. Neanderthals had much faster tooth growth than *Homo erectus* who went before them, and hence, possibly, a shorter childhood. Lead researcher Fernando Ramirez-Rozzi thinks Neanderthals died young – about 25 years old – primarily because of the cold, harsh environment they had to endure in glacial Europe. They evolved to grow up quicker than their immediate ancestors. Neanderthals and *Homo erectus* probably had to reach adulthood fairly quickly, without delaying for an adolescent growth spurt. So it still looks as though we are the original teenagers.

Action plan reminder

Multiple choice

1 What do you have to choose?

2 How many correct options are there for each question?

3 Are the questions in the same order as the ideas in the text?

4 If this is the first task, what should you do before you look at the questions?
  3

5 Should you read and answer each question in turn?

6 How much of the text should you read for each question?

7 Can you answer the questions using your general knowledge?

 Page 38 *Test 1 Reading Passage 3 Action plan*

Questions 27–30

Choose the correct letter, **A**, **B**, **C** or **D**.

Write the correct letter in boxes 27–30 on your answer sheet.

27   In the first paragraph, why does the writer say 'This is not merely an academic debate'?

   A   Anthropologists' theories need to be backed up by practical research.

   B   There have been some important misunderstandings among anthropologists.

   C   The attitudes of anthropologists towards adolescence are changing.

   D   The work of anthropologists could inform our understanding of modern adolescence.

> **Tip!** Read the text quickly. Then read it more carefully as you answer each question in turn. Some paragraphs don't have a multiple-choice question on them.

> **Advice**
> **27** Some questions tell you which paragraph to look at. You need to find the quoted sentence and then read the whole paragraph to find the answer.

28   What was Susan Anton's opinion of the Turkana boy?

   A   He would have experienced an adolescent phase had he lived.

   B   His skull showed he had already reached adulthood.

   C   His skeleton and teeth could not be compared to those from a more modern age.

   D   He must have grown much faster than others alive at the time.

29   What point does Steven Leigh make?

   A   Different parts of the human skeleton develop at different speeds.

   B   The growth period of many apes is confined to times when there is enough food.

   C   Humans have different rates of development from each other depending on living conditions.

   D   The growth phase in most apes lasts longer if more food is available.

30   What can we learn from a mammal's teeth?

   A   A poor diet will cause them to grow more slowly.
   B   They are a better indication of lifestyle than a skeleton.
   C   Their growing period is difficult to predict accurately.
   D   Their speed of growth is directly related to the body's speed of development.

Action plan reminder

Yes/No/Not given

1 What do the statements focus on?

2 What must you decide?

3 How can you get an idea of who or what the text is about?

4 Should you worry about words you don't understand?

5 Are the statements in the same order as the text?

6 Look at the questions. What will you do before you look for the answers?

◄ **Page 37** *Test 1 Reading Passage 3 Action plan*

Questions 31–36

Do the following statements agree with the claims of the writer in Reading Passage 3?

In boxes 31–36 on your answer sheet, write

YES	*if the statement agrees with the claims of the writer*
NO	*if the statement contradicts the claims of the writer*
NOT GIVEN	*if it is impossible to say what the writer thinks about this*

31 It is difficult for anthropologists to do research on human fossils because they are so rare.

32 Modern methods mean it is possible to predict the age of a skeleton with accuracy.

33 Susan Anton's conclusion about the Turkana boy reinforces an established idea.

34 Steven Leigh's ideas are likely to be met with disbelief by many anthropologists.

35 Researchers in France and Spain developed a unique method of analysing teeth.

36 There has been too little research comparing the brains of *Homo erectus* and Neanderthals.

Tip! For each question, find the key words (or paraphrases of them) in the text, then read that part carefully to see what the writer claims.

Advice

31 What do you find out about human fossils from the words 'sparse' and 'minuscule'?

34 What does 'a step too far' mean? Is this what many anthropologists think?

35 What does the text say about the methods used by researchers in France and Spain?

Action plan reminder

Matching sentence endings

1 How will you find the information you need?

2 Is the information in one part of the passage only?

3 Are the sentence beginnings in the same order as the information in the text?

4 Can you use a sentence ending more than once?

 Page 39 *Test 1 Reading Passage 3 Action plan*

Questions 37–40

*Complete each sentence with the correct ending, **A–G**, below.*

*Write the correct letter, **A–G**, in boxes 37–40 on your answer sheet.*

Tip! For each sentence beginning, underline the important words and find the part of the text you need to read.

37 Until recently, delayed growth in humans until adolescence was felt to be due to

38 In her research, Margaret Clegg discovered

39 Steven Leigh thought the existence of adolescence is connected to

40 Research on Neanderthals suggests that they had short lives because of

Tip! When you have finished, read the whole sentences and make sure they say the same as the text.

A	inconsistencies between height, skeleton and dental evidence.
B	the fact that human beings walk on two legs.
C	the way teeth grew.
D	a need to be dependent on others for survival.
E	difficult climatic conditions.
F	increased quantities of food.
G	the existence of much larger brains than previously.

Review

1 What information is Writing Task 1 based on?
2 How do you have to express the information?
3 Does it matter whether you use an informal style?
4 Are grammar, spelling and punctuation tested?
5 How long should you spend on this task?

6 How many words must you write?
7 Which parts of the data must you write about?
8 Should you make comparisons?
9 What should you draw attention to and interpret?

Useful language: the introduction

1 Read carefully these five introductions (1–5) to the task on page 87 written by IELTS candidates. Then answer questions a and b for each introduction.

 a **Does the candidate give enough information about the table?**
 b **Does the candidate describe the information in the table accurately?**

 1 In the table we can see some information about students enrolled at Bristol University from the year 1928 till 2008.
 2 The table shows the numbers of student enrolments at Bristol University, covering the number of students, the percentages of female and male, and where they came from, in three different years.
 3 This table shows the number of people who are studying at Bristol University and the number of people of each gender as well. Also, it shows the distance that students come from, divided into two categories: within 30 miles of Bristol and overseas.
 4 The table illustrates some information about student enrolments at Bristol University. The table shows the percentages of male and female students and how many students came from overseas or within 30 miles of Bristol in 1928, 1958 and 2008.
 5 The table gives information about Bristol University student enrolments, the percentages of males and females and what area they came from, in the years 1928, 1958 and 2008.

2 **Suggest any improvements you could make to the content of each introduction. (There are no language errors.)**

3 **Underline any useful words or phrases drawing attention to important data that you might use when writing about other topics.**

Useful language: drawing attention to important data

1 ⊙ These sentences were written by IELTS candidates to describe different graphs and tables. Underline the words in each one that you could use in writing about other topics.

1 *Also noteworthy is the low government expenditure on education.*

2 *This graph shows a striking difference between the younger age group and the older one.*

3 *The most striking feature of the graph is the sudden increase in the popularity of computer games.*

4 *Another fact worth noticing in the table is that females are more numerous than males.*

5 *The most remarkable point is that the number of males with a criminal record increased dramatically.*

6 *It is noticeable that expenditure on photography remained stable from 1992 to 2000.*

2 Using the sentences in Exercise 1 as models, expand these notes into full sentences.

1 noteworthy / fall in graduate numbers
2 striking similarity / teenagers in the USA / teenagers in South America
3 most striking feature / sudden decline / birth rate
4 fact worth noticing / high cost / fossil fuels
5 most remarkable / growth rate / increased suddenly
6 noticeable / few schools / swimming pools

Useful language: numbers and percentages

1 ⊙ Be careful to use the appropriate nouns to report different kinds of number. Choose the correct word in these IELTS candidates' answers.

1 In 1997 the employment *figure/number* was two million.
2 The data shows the difference between the *percentage/percentages* of men and women doing full-time jobs.
3 In future the *size/number* of the population will increase sharply.
4 In Britain people spent the smallest *number/amount* of money on personal stereos.
5 Cinemas expect an increasing *level/number* of attendance in the future across all ages.
6 Going out to restaurants decreased dramatically to seven *percentage/per cent*.
7 The *number/quantity* of people who came to Australia started to drop after 1994.
8 The graph shows that the *percentage/per cent* of 14- to 24-year-olds who are cinema-goers is higher than other groups.
9 We can also see that the *rate/proportion* of males gaining diplomas was higher than that of females.
10 A small *part/proportion* of graduates are self-employed.
11 It can be seen that the majority of prisoners are male as the *percentage/share* of prisoners who are female is only 4%.
12 The number of books published depends on the literacy *rate/figure*.

2 Write sentences using phrases 1–7 and the words in brackets.

◀ **Page 45** *Test 1 Writing Task 1 for useful verbs*

1 the rate of unemployment (1979 and 1985)

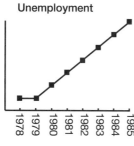

2 the proportion of the population (computers)

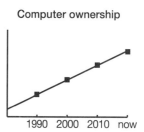

3 the amount of energy (industry)

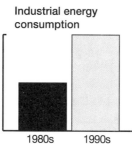

4 the number of cars (public transport)

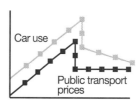

5 the level of literacy (change of government)

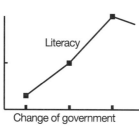

6 the quantity of food (affluent parts of the world)

7 the share of global resources (the poorest countries)

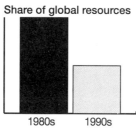

Useful language: spelling

◉ These sentences contain 22 of the most common spelling mistakes made by IELTS candidates. How fast can you find and correct them?

Give yourself one mark for spotting each mistake, another mark for putting it right correctly and deduct one mark for any changes you make to words that were not wrong!

1 Nowdays, knowladge about the enviroment is essencial and many goverments understand the benifits of educating childen to be aware of how they can contribute to this.

2 In my experiense, becouse sociaty is in some respects organised diffrently in other contries, foriegners find it relaxing to visit this part of the world.

3 It is my oppinion that few people beleive the information wich is given in advertisments.

4 Teenagers shoud not be allowed to have there own cars untill they are prepared to accept responsability for the affect that bad driving can have on other road users.

Useful language: finishing your summary

Here are four ways (1–4) used by IELTS candidates to finish their summaries for the task on page 87. Although there are no language errors, three of them are unsatisfactory for various reasons. Read the comments in the box and match them to the paragraphs.

---

a Not an accurate description of what the table shows.
b Statements should be supported by figures from the table.
c Too vague. It is unclear what part of the data is referred to, and offers no conclusion.
d A useful contrast, well supported by data from the table.

---

1 In conclusion, the percentage increased in different ways until 2008 and fell in other ways.

2 It is clear that the number of foreign students increased whereas the students who came from within 30 miles of Bristol decreased. Furthermore, in 2008 the number of female students who enrolled at the university was much higher than in 1928.

3 Finally, the figures for student enrolment at Bristol University changed dramatically. The number of students reached a peak in 1958 but went down again between the years 1958 and 2008. Overall, the number of foreign students remained almost the same between 1928 and 1958. However, it rose sharply in the next 50 years.

4 Lastly, there is an important difference in the proportion of students who come from within 30 miles of Bristol and those who come from overseas: at the beginning there were few students coming from overseas and more coming from near the city, while by 2008 the percentage of 'local' students had really decreased (from 50% to 1–2%), whereas the percentage of overseas students had increased from only 5% to 28%.

Test 2 Exam practice Writing Task 1

Action plan reminder

1 Look at Writing Task 1 below.
- What does the first part of the question tell you?
- What three things does the rest of the question remind you to do?

2 Look at the table in Writing Task 1 below.
- What do you learn from the title of this table?
- What do the headings of the three columns tell you?
- What information does the table contain?
- What do the numbers in the first row represent?
- Why is the second row divided into two smaller rows?
- Why do the bottom two rows not add up to 100%?

Before you write

3 Select data and highlight or make notes before you begin to write your summary.

4 Write your summary.
- What should you avoid copying word for word?
- Should you try to write about all the data?
- Should you challenge the data?

After you write

5 What should you check for when you have finished?

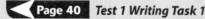

Page 40 *Test 1 Writing Task 1*

You should spend about 20 minutes on this task.

Tip! Remember you'll need more time for Task 2 than Task 1.

The table below gives information about student enrolments at Bristol University in 1928, 1958 and 2008.

Summarise the information by selecting and reporting the main features, and make comparisons where relevant.

Write at least 150 words.

Tip! Don't lose marks by writing too little.

Bristol University student enrolments

	1928	1958	2008
How many new students enrolled?	218	1,046	6,377
What percentage were female?	42%	32%	54%
What percentage were male?	58%	68%	46%
What percentage came from within 30 miles of Bristol?	50%	14%	1–2%
What percentage came from overseas?	5% from 3 countries	6% from 27 countries	28% from 98 countries

Advice

Between which years was the increase in enrolments greater?

When was the percentage of female enrolments lowest?

When did the percentage of overseas students change most markedly?

Review

1 What is Writing Task 2?

2 Which of these things does it test?
   - general knowledge
   - expressing ideas
   - having the correct opinions
   - evaluating ideas
   - academic knowledge
   - appropriate style
   - grammar
   - spelling
   - punctuation
   - paragraphing

3 How many words must you write?

4 How should you support your opinion?

5 How should you conclude your essay?

Useful language: conditionals

1 ⊙ **Choose the correct form of the verbs in italics in these sentences written by IELTS candidates.**

   1 If people *would have / had* fun doing shopping, more people *will do / would do* it.

   2 If shopping *was / would be* a routine domestic task in earlier times, this *could be / had been* because there was no interesting shopping to do.

   3 This change *may be regarded / is regarded* as positive if we *will analyse / analyse* why it has happened.

   4 People *spend / are spending* less time shopping if they *have / had* more enjoyable activities to do.

2 **Match these descriptions to the sentences in Exercise 1.**

   a offering an explanation for a possible situation in the past

   b imagining the necessary conditions for something to happen

   c stating a generally accepted fact

   d describing the possible result of doing something

3 ⊙ **Here are some sentences written by IELTS candidates. Put the verbs in brackets into the correct form. (Sometimes more than one answer is possible.)**

   1 Human beings .... (have) the right to express their own ideas, unless they break the rules of our society.

   2 Therefore, if I were a mother I .... (not give) my children money.

   3 It would be better if sports professionals .... (not earn) a lot of money from other activities.

   4 If they .... (be) richer, they could have afforded health care.

   5 I wondered whether the people in the disaster area .... (deal) better with the situation if they had experienced hardships growing up.

   6 Children may think that if they .... (bring up) by rich parents, they could get what they want very easily.

   7 Had anyone given him the chance to rest, he .... (be) more relaxed in mind and body.

Useful language: referring to people

⊙ These are some examples of language written by IELTS candidates. Choose the correct word in italics in each sentence. After checking your answers, use the other word in each pair in a sentence of your own.

1 If the company's *consumers/customers* are satisfied, they are likely to come back.

2 Successful businessmen and women have to do better than their *contestants/ competitors* on their way to the top.

3 The ancient city of the Incas, Machu Picchu, limits the number of *visitors/passengers* to 2,000 per day in order to reduce damage.

4 Providing for the needs of every *member/participant* of the family can be very difficult.

5 It will be better for everyone if doctors can show concern for their *clients/patients* as well as treating them.

6 *Individuals/Humans* raised in an environment where everything is done for them may be too reliant on others.

Useful language: positive and negative comments

1 ⊙ Here are some examples of positive and negative comments made by IELTS candidates.
Match the beginning and end of each sentence.

1 The first advantage of international tourism	a are compelling.
2 The benefits of computer use in education	b is that it brings in foreign currency.
3 One of the disadvantages of radio	c is that tourist attractions can be developed.
4 The negative aspect of the freedom to express your own ideas	d is that it is only an audio source.
5 Another positive result of increasing visitor numbers	e is the fact that some people abuse this privilege.

2 Complete the sentences below, expressing your own ideas about some of the topics in the box, or others that interest you.

> cheap public transport   living in a village   studying abroad   access to the Internet
> large families   working for a large company   using credit cards   large supermarkets

1 The first disadvantage ...

2 The main benefit ...

3 The negative aspect ...

4 One of the advantages ...

5 Another negative result of ...

6 A major drawback ...

Action plan reminder

1 Look at Writing Task 2 below and answer these questions.

- How much of the task do you need to read?
- How long should you spend on this task?
- What must you include in your answer?
- What should you underline in the task?
- Do you have to agree with the opinion in the exam question?
- Will you lose marks if you copy the wording of the task exactly?

Before you write

2 Make notes before you begin to write your essay. What should your notes include?

After you write

3 Answer these questions.

- Should you spend time checking your essay when you have finished?
- Should you spend time rewriting your essay neatly?
- Which of the following should you check for?
  overall structure; paragraphing; clearly linked ideas; up-to-date information; clear handwriting; humour; formal or neutral style; subject-verb agreement; quotations from famous writers; spelling; capital letters at the beginning of sentences; verb tenses; your own habitual errors

 Page 54 *Test 1 Writing Task 2 Action Plan*

You should spend about 40 minutes on this task.

Write about the following topic:

In the past, shopping was a routine domestic task. Many people nowadays regard it as a hobby.

To what extent do you think this is a positive trend?

Give reasons for your answer and include any relevant examples from your own knowledge or experience.

Write at least 250 words.

Advice

Do you know a word that means 'routine domestic task'?

Do people spend time shopping instead of taking part in other activities?

Is there a connection between changes to the way people shop and the economic situation?

 Before the exam, make sure you know how much space you use for 250 words, then you won't need to spend time counting during the exam.

Speaking Part 1

Review

1 What must you remember to take to the exam room?

2 What do you have to answer questions about?

3 Will the questions all be about the same topic?

4 Do you get a separate mark for Speaking Part 1?

Tip! You can use the preparation ideas in this test to help you when you practise other IELTS speaking tests.

◀ **Page 55** *Test 1 Speaking Part 1*

Useful language: work and studying

 Correct the one or two mistakes in these sentences written by IELTS candidates.

1 I went to Canada for studying engineering.

2 I am learning history at university.

3 I would like study oversea.

4 I have been study English for half a year.

5 I have classes at the daytime and I work in the evening.

6 I have a part-time work in a restaurant.

7 I am hoping to get a good employment when I graduate.

8 I finish my work at five o'clock.

9 There are lots of foreign pupils at my university.

10 I want to gain a lot of money.

Useful language: tenses

1 **Look at these questions about a job. Think about what tense you would use in the answer and underline the verbs that help you decide.**

1 What is your job?

2 How long have you been working there?

3 What do you enjoy about your job?

4 What job did you want to do when you were a child?

5 Do you think you will do a different job one day?

2 **Which question(s):**

1 ask about now? What tense is used?

2 ask about the past? What tense will you use in your answer?

3 ask about the future? Think of three different ways of beginning an answer.

4 ask about a length of time? What tense is used?

Tip! Listen carefully to the tense in the question so you give the right kind of answer.

3 **Look at the questions about work/studying on page 96 and answer them about yourself.**

Useful language: food vocabulary

1   Think about a place where you like to go if you eat out. Tick (✓) the
things below that are most important to you. Add any other reasons
you could give for choosing a restaurant or a café.

delicious/tasty food   family run   vegetarian
reasonably priced   part of a chain   traditional recipes
fresh ingredients   home-made dishes   lively atmosphere
fast service   plenty of choice

2   Look at the questions about food and restaurants on page 96 and the
Useful language below.

> Where I come from, …
> In my country we usually …
> When I'm at home, …
> Compared to my parents, …
> Until I came here, I …
> If I have something to celebrate, …
> My favourite restaurant …

3   Practise saying your answers. Record yourself answering the questions.
Listen to what you said and think about how to improve it. Did you
speak clearly? Did you use a range of grammatical structures and
vocabulary?

Speaking Part 2

Review

1 What does the examiner give you?

2 How long do you have to make notes?

3 Where should you write your notes?

4 How long do you talk for?

 Page 57 *Test 1 Speaking Part 2*

STRATEGIES

Making notes: spider diagrams

1   Look at this exam task and the completed spider diagram on the next
page.

> **Describe your favourite TV programme.**
> **You should say:**
>   **the name of the programme and where it is set**
>   **what kind of programme it is**
>   **what it is about**
> **and explain why you enjoy it.**

Tip! If you never eat in a
restaurant, imagine
one where you would
like to eat. You can do
this in the test, too, if
you don't have much
personal experience of
something.

Tip! Add some details
to each answer and
try to use a range of
grammatical structures
and vocabulary.

Tip! Read the card carefully.
Make sure you keep to
the topic.

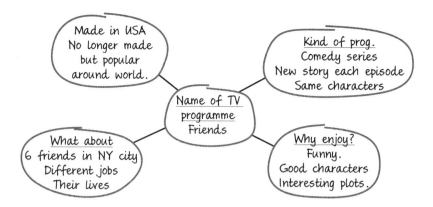

2 Now look at the task about a film on page 96 and write similar notes on the spider diagram below.

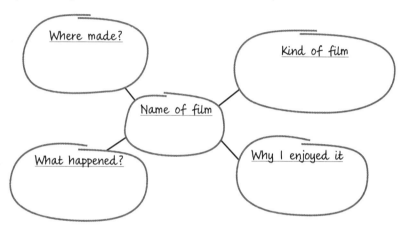

Useful language: giving a talk

1 Use your notes and record yourself talking about a film for two minutes. Use a clock.

> For me, the best part was ...
> It was one of the best films I've seen because of ...
> What stood out for me was ...
> I particularly liked ...
> Compared to other films, I felt ...

Tip! Although it doesn't matter what order you give the information asked for, make sure that what you say is logical.

2 Listen to what you said and think about how to improve it. Think about these questions.

Did you introduce the topic?

Did you use the correct tenses?

Did you use a range of vocabulary?

Did you connect your sentences?

Did you cover all the points on the card (not necessarily in that order)?

Did you speak clearly?

3 Look at the two follow-up questions on page 96 and think of your answers.

Speaking Part 3

Review

1 Will the questions be about a new topic?

2 Will they be about your own personal experience?

◄ Page 59 *Test 1 Speaking Part 3*

Useful language: starting sentences with *-ing*

1 ◉ **People often start sentences with the *-ing* form when they want to make a general point about an activity. Rewrite these sentences so they begin with an *-ing* word.**

1 More effort is required to read than watch TV.
   ..Reading requires.. more effort than watching TV.

2 The best way to learn is by doing, especially with children.
   .... works best, especially with children.

3 It improves people's level of confidence if they do some kind of paid work.
   .... improves people's level of confidence.

4 The most important thing for children is that they are loved.
   .... the most important thing for children.

5 People can suffer from stress when they are faced with a lot of financial problems.
   .... a lot of financial problems can be very stressful.

6 It is still considered a luxury to own a car in some parts of the world.
   .... is still considered a luxury in some parts of the world.

2 **Finish these sentences about films.**

1 Going to the cinema nowadays is ....

2 Watching a lot of violent films can ....

3 Invading the privacy of film stars ....

4 Watching films in English ....

3 **Look at the questions on page 96 about films and the cinema and think about what you would say. Practise saying your answers.**

Useful language: talking about the future

Do you agree with the statements below? Use an expression from the box with each statement to give your opinion.

It's likely that ...	It's doubtful whether ...
It seems probable that ...	I feel it's unlikely that ...
I'm not sure whether ...	I'd say that ...
I'm fairly certain that ...	I cannot imagine that ...

1   People will always enjoy occasional visits to the cinema rather than watch films at home.

2   The international film industry will continue to be dominated by the USA.

3   Watching films will become more popular than watching other kinds of programme on TV.

4   Less money will be available to the film industry.

5   There will be more computer-animated films.

6   More films will be made which have a family appeal.

7   Film stars will earn less money in future.

Useful language: making general statements

Answer these questions by making a general statement followed by your own opinion.

Tip! It is a good idea to talk about general opinions before giving your own.

1   Do you think fashion plays too big a part in our lives today?

2   How can tourism help people to understand other cultures?

3   Are people in your country interested in recycling?

4   How likely is it that people will stop reading books in the future?

General statement	Your opinion
For the most part, ...	but in fact ...
In general, ...	but I (don't) think ...
It's widely acknowledged that ...	but in my experience ...
Most people recognise that ...	but in my country ...
That depends.	and I agree that ...
That can vary according to the situation.	and because of that ...
In some circumstances, ...	For instance, I have noticed that ...
For some people ...	However, I believe ...

Speaking Part 1

The examiner will ask you some questions about yourself.

Let's talk about your studies (or your job).

Are you a full-time student at the moment?
Where do you study?
How long have you studied there?
Is it far from your home?
What job would you like to have in the future?

OR

What is your job?
How long have you been working there?
What do you enjoy about your job?
What job did you want to do when you were a child?
Do you think you will do a different job one day?

The examiner will then ask you some questions about one or two other topics, for example:

Now let's talk about food and restaurants.

Do you often eat out in restaurants, cafés and so on?
How do you choose where to go when you want to eat out?
Are fast-food restaurants such as burger bars popular in your country?
Do you ever cook for yourself, or other people?
Can you recommend a restaurant in your home town?

> **Tip!** Speak clearly. You will be marked on your pronunciation and how easy you are to understand.

Speaking Part 2

The examiner will give you a topic on a card like the one on the right and ask you to talk about it for one to two minutes. Before you talk you have one minute to think about what you're going to say. The examiner will give you some paper and a pencil so you can make notes if you want to.

The examiner may ask one or two more questions when you have finished, for example:

Do you often go to the cinema?
Do you think watching films in English is useful?

> **Describe a film you enjoyed.**
> **You should say:**
>   **the name of the film and where it was made**
>   **what kind of film it was**
>   **what happened in the film**
> **and explain why you enjoyed it.**

Speaking Part 3

The examiner will ask some more general questions which follow on from the topic in Part 2.

Is going to the cinema more or less popular than it used to be, do you think?
What are the most popular types of film among people you know?
Do you think there's too much violence in films?
Should there be more films made for children?
Do films influence other things – fashion, for example?
Do you think the media invade the privacy of film stars or put them under too much pressure?
Do you think films will continue to be an important form of entertainment?

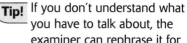

> **Tip!** If you don't understand what you have to talk about, the examiner can rephrase it for you.

> **Tip!** The examiner will notice if you try to use an answer you have learnt by heart and you will lose marks.

Questions 1–10

Complete the notes below.

*Write **NO MORE THAN TWO WORDS AND/OR A NUMBER** for each answer.*

Midbury Drama Club

Background

Example	*Answer*
• club started in	......1957........

- prize recently won by **1** .... section

- usually performs **2** .... plays

Meetings

- next auditions will be on Tuesday, **3** ....

- help is needed with **4** .... and ....

- rehearsals take place in the **5** .... hall

- nearest car park for rehearsals is in Ashburton Road opposite

  the **6** ....

Costs

- annual membership fee is **7** £........................

- extra payment for **8** ....

Contact

- secretary's name is Sarah **9** ....

- secretary's phone number is **10** ....

17 *Questions 11–15*

Choose the correct letter, **A**, **B** *or* **C**.

11   What does the charity *Forward thinking* do?

   A   It funds art exhibitions in hospitals.
   B   It produces affordable materials for art therapy.
   C   It encourages the use of arts projects in healthcare.

12   What benefit of *Forward thinking's* work does Jasmine mention?

   A   People avoid going to hospital.
   B   Patients require fewer drugs.
   C   Medical students do better in tests.

13   When did the organisation become known as *Forward thinking*?

   A   1986
   B   in the 1990s
   C   2005

14   Where does *Forward thinking* operate?

   A   within Clifton city
   B   in all parts of London
   C   in several towns and villages near Clifton

15   Jasmine explains that the Colville Centre is

   A   a school for people with health problems.
   B   a venue for a range of different activities.
   C   a building which needs repairing.

Who can take part in each of the classes?

*Write the correct letter **A**, **B** or **C** next to questions 16–20.*

Class participants		
A	children and teenagers	
B	adults	
C	all ages	

16   Learn Salsa!   ....

17   Smooth Movers   ....

18   Art of the Forest   ....

19   The Money Maze   ....

20   Make a Play   ....

Questions 21–26

Complete the flow-chart below.

*Choose **SIX** answers from the box and write the correct letter, **A–I**, next to questions 21–26.*

A	air quality
B	journey times
C	land use
D	leisure facilities
E	means of transport
F	parking facilities
G	number of pedestrians
H	places of employment
I	traffic flow

CITY CENTRE FIELD TRIP

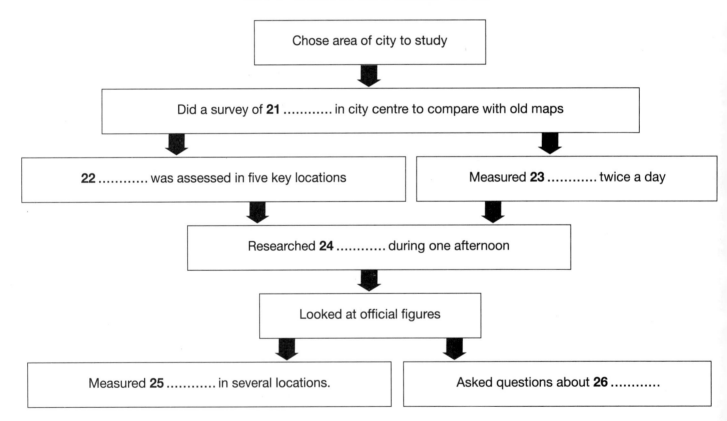

Chose area of city to study

Did a survey of **21** .... in city centre to compare with old maps

22 .... was assessed in five key locations

Measured **23** .... twice a day

Researched **24** .... during one afternoon

Looked at official figures

Measured **25** .... in several locations.

Asked questions about **26** ....

Who will be responsible for each task?

A	Stefan
B	Lauren
C	both Stefan and Lauren

Write the correct letter next to questions 27–30.

27 draw graphs and maps   ....

28 choose photographs   ....

29 write report   ....

30 do presentation   ....

🎧19 **Questions 31–35**

Complete the sentences below.

*Write **ONLY ONE WORD** for each answer.*

Manufacturing in the English Midlands

31 In the eighteenth century, the ....characteristics........... still determined how most people made a living.
land *land*

32 In the ground were minerals which supported the many .... of the region.
industries *industry* *majority population public*

33 Since the late sixteenth century the French settlers had made ....glass........... .
燧石 flint . iron . ore . clay . lead 铅 . limestone . considerable . numerous . plenty of . a wide range of *a variety of*

34 In Cheshire ....salt........ was mined and transported on the river Mersey. 被动
dig – dug

35 Potters worked in a few ....villages........ situated on the small hills of North Staffordshire.
开采

🎧19 **Questions 36–40**

Complete the notes below.

*Write **ONE WORD** for each answer.*

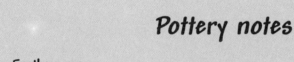

Pottery notes

Earthenware

advantages:

- potters used 36 ....local........ clay
- saved money on 37 .....fuel........... *timber . gas . coal*

disadvantages: *on the other hand* 窑

- needed two firings in the kiln to be 38 ....waterproof.... 防水的
- fragility led to high 39 .....break....breakable.... during manufacturing
  wastage

Stoneware

- more expensive but better
- made from a 40 .....combination..... of clay and flint
  mixture

Test 3   Reading Passage 1

You should spend about 20 minutes on **Questions 1–13**, which are based on Reading Passage 1 below.

Seed vault guards resources for the future

Fiona Harvey paid a visit to a building whose contents are very precious.

About 1,000 km from the North Pole, Svalbard is one of the most remote places on earth. For this reason, it is the site of a vault that will safeguard a priceless component of our common heritage – the seeds of our staple crops. Here, seeds from the world's most vital food crops will be locked away for hundreds or even thousands of years. If something goes wrong in the world, the vault will provide the means to restore farming. We, or our descendants, will not have to retread thousands of years of agriculture from scratch.

Deep in the vault at the end of a long tunnel, are three storage vaults which are lined with insulated panels to help maintain the cold temperatures. Electronic transmitters linked to a satellite system monitor temperature, etc. and pass the information back to the appropriate authorities at Longyearbyen and the Nordic Gene Bank which provide the technical information for managing the seed vaults. The seeds are placed in sealed boxes and stored on shelves in the vaults. The minimal moisture level and low temperature ensure low metabolic activity. The remote location, as well as the rugged structure, provide unparalleled security for the world's agricultural heritage.

The three vaults are buried deep in the hillside. To reach them, it is necessary to proceed down a long and surprisingly large corridor. At 93.3 metres in length, it connects the 26-metre long entrance building to the three vaults, each of which extends a further 27 metres into the mountain. Towards the end of this tunnel, after about 80 metres, there are several small rooms on the right-hand side. One is a transformer room to which only the power company officials have access – this houses the equipment needed to transform the incoming electrical current down to 220 volts. A second is an electrical room housing controls for the compressor and other equipment. The other room is an office which can be heated to provide comfortable working conditions for those who will make an inventory of the samples in and out of the vault.

Anyone seeking access to the seeds has to pass through four locked doors: the heavy steel entrance doors, a second door approximately 90 metres down the tunnel and finally the two keyed doors separated by an airlock, from which it is possible to proceed directly into the seed vaults. Keys are coded to allow access to different levels of the facility.

A work of art will make the vault visible for miles around. The vault entrance is filled with highly reflective sheets of steel and mirrors which form an installation acting as a beacon. It reflects polar light in the summer months, while in the winter, a network of 200 fibre-optic cables will give the piece a muted greenish-turquoise and white light.

Cary Fowler, the mastermind behind the vault, stands inside the echoing cavern. For him, this is the culmination of nearly 30 years of work. 'It's an insurance policy,' he explains, 'a very cheap insurance policy when you consider what we're insuring – the earth's biological diversity.'

Seeds are being brought here from all over the world, from seed banks created by governments, universities and private institutions. Soon, there will be seed varieties from at least 100 crops in the Svalbard vault – extending to examples of all of the 1.5 million known crop seed varieties in the world. If any more are unearthed, either in the wild or found in obscure collections, they can be added, too – the vault has room for at least 4.5 million samples.

Inside the entrance area it is more than 10° C below freezing, but in the chambers where the seeds are kept, refrigerators push down the temperature even further, to –18° C. At this temperature, which will be kept constant to stop the seeds germinating or rotting, the wheat seeds will remain viable for an estimated 1,700 years, the barley for 2,000 years and the sorghum for 20,000 years.

Svalbard's Arctic conditions will keep the seeds cold. In order to maintain the temperature at a constant –10° C to –20° C, the cold Arctic air will be drawn into the vault during the winter, automatically and without human intervention. The surrounding rock will maintain the temperature requirements during the extremely cold season and, during warmer periods, refrigeration equipment will engage. Looking out across the snow-covered mountains of Svalbard, it is hard not to feel respect for the 2,300 or so people who live here, mainly in Longyearbyen, a village a few miles away. There are three months without light in winter.

Svalbard is intended as the seed bank of last resort. Each sample is made up of a few hundred seeds, sealed inside a watertight package which will never be tampered with while it is in the vault. The packages of seeds remain the property of the collections they have come from. Svalbard will disburse samples 'only if all the other seeds in other collections around the world are gone,' explains Fowler. If seeds do have to be given out, those who receive them are expected to germinate them and generate new samples, to be returned to the vault.

Questions 1–6

Label the diagram below.

Choose **NO MORE THAN TWO WORDS OR A NUMBER** from the passage for each answer.

Write your answers in boxes 1–6 on your answer sheet.

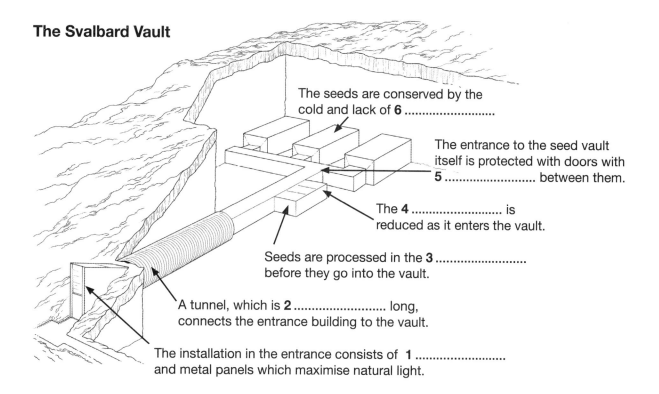

The Svalbard Vault

The seeds are conserved by the cold and lack of **6** ....

The entrance to the seed vault itself is protected with doors with **5** .... between them.

The **4** .... is reduced as it enters the vault.

Seeds are processed in the **3** .... before they go into the vault.

A tunnel, which is **2** .... long, connects the entrance building to the vault.

The installation in the entrance consists of **1** .... and metal panels which maximise natural light.

Questions 7–13

Do the following statements agree with the information given in Reading Passage 1?

In boxes 7–13 on your answer sheet, write

TRUE	if the statement agrees with the information
FALSE	if the statement contradicts the information
NOT GIVEN	if there is no information on this

7   The vault has the capacity to accommodate undiscovered types of seed at a later date.

8   There are different levels of refrigeration according to the kinds of seeds stored.

9   During winter, the flow of air entering the vault is regularly monitored by staff.

10   There is a back-up refrigeration system ready to be switched on if the present one fails.

11   The people who work at Svalbard are mainly locals.

12   Once a seed package is in the vault, it remains unopened.

13   If seeds are sent from Svalbard to other banks, there is an obligation for the recipient to send replacements back.

*You should spend about 20 minutes on **Questions 14–26**, which are based on Reading Passage 2 below.*

WHAT COOKBOOKS REALLY TEACH US

A Shelves bend under their weight of cookery books. Even a medium-sized bookshop contains many more recipes than one person could hope to cook in a lifetime. Although the recipes in one book are often similar to those in another, their presentation varies wildly, from an array of vegetarian cookbooks to instructions on cooking the food that historical figures might have eaten. The reason for this abundance is that cookbooks promise to bring about a kind of domestic transformation for the user. The daily routine can be put to one side and they liberate the user, if only temporarily. To follow their instructions is to turn a task which has to be performed every day into an engaging, romantic process. Cookbooks also provide an opportunity to delve into distant cultures without having to turn up at an airport to get there.

B The first Western cookbook appeared just over 1,600 years ago. *De re coquinara* (it means 'concerning cookery') is attributed to a Roman gourmet named Apicius. It is probably a compilation of Roman and Greek recipes, some or all of them drawn from manuscripts that were later lost. The editor was sloppy, allowing several duplicated recipes to sneak in. Yet Apicius's book set the tone of cookery advice in Europe for more than a thousand years. As a cookbook it is unsatisfactory with very basic instructions. Joseph Vehling, a chef who translated Apicius in the 1930s, suggested the author had been obscure on purpose, in case his secrets leaked out.

C But a more likely reason is that Apicius's recipes were written by and for professional cooks, who could follow their shorthand. This situation continued for hundreds of years. There was no order to cookbooks: a cake recipe might be followed by a mutton one. But then, they were not written for careful study. Before the 19th century few educated people cooked for themselves. The wealthiest employed literate chefs; others presumably read recipes to their servants. Such cooks would have been capable of creating dishes from the vaguest of instructions.

D The invention of printing might have been expected to lead to greater clarity but at first the reverse was true. As words acquired commercial value, plagiarism exploded. Recipes were distorted through reproduction. A recipe for boiled capon in *The Good Huswives Jewell*, printed in 1596, advised the cook to add three or four dates. By 1653, when the recipe was given by a different author in *A Book of Fruits & Flowers*, the cook was told to set the dish aside for three or four days.

E The dominant theme in 16th and 17th century cookbooks was order. Books combined recipes and household advice, on the assumption that a well-made dish, a well-ordered larder and well-disciplined children were equally important. Cookbooks thus became a symbol of dependability in chaotic times. They hardly seem to have been affected by the English civil war or the revolutions in America and France.

F   In the 1850s Isabella Beeton published *The Book of Household Management*. Like earlier cookery writers she plagiarised freely, lifting not just recipes but philosophical observations from other books. If Beeton's recipes were not wholly new, though, the way in which she presented them certainly was. She explains when the chief ingredients are most likely to be in season, how long the dish will take to prepare and even how much it is likely to cost. Beeton's recipes were well suited to her times. Two centuries earlier, an understanding of rural ways had been so widespread that one writer could advise cooks to heat water until it was a little hotter than milk comes from a cow. By the 1850s Britain was industrialising. The growing urban middle class needed details, and Beeton provided them in full.

G   In France, cookbooks were fast becoming even more systematic. Compared with Britain, France had produced few books written for the ordinary householder by the end of the 19th century. The most celebrated French cookbooks were written by superstar chefs who had a clear sense of codifying a unified approach to sophisticated French cooking. The 5,000 recipes in Auguste Escoffier's *Le Guide Culinaire* (The Culinary Guide), published in 1902, might as well have been written in stone, given the book's reputation among French chefs, many of whom still consider it the definitive reference book.

H   What Escoffier did for French cooking, Fannie Farmer did for American home cooking. She not only synthesised American cuisine; she elevated it to the status of science. 'Progress in civilisation has been accompanied by progress in cookery,' she breezily announced in *The Boston Cooking-School Cook Book*, before launching into a collection of recipes that sometimes resembles a book of chemistry experiments. She was occasionally over-fussy. She explained that currants should be picked between June 28th and July 3rd, but not when it is raining. But in the main her book is reassuringly authoritative. Its recipes are short, with no unnecessary chat and no unnecessary spices.

I   In 1950 *Mediterranean Food* by Elizabeth David launched a revolution in cooking advice in Britain. In some ways *Mediterranean Food* recalled even older cookbooks but the smells and noises that filled David's books were not mere decoration for her recipes. They were the point of her books. When she began to write, many ingredients were not widely available or affordable. She understood this, acknowledging in a later edition of one of her books that 'even if people could not very often make the dishes here described, it was stimulating to think about them.' David's books were not so much cooking manuals as guides to the kind of food people might well wish to eat.

Questions 14–16

Complete the summary below.

Choose **NO MORE THAN TWO WORDS** from the passage for each answer.

Write your answers in boxes 14–16 on your answer sheet.

Why are there so many cookery books?

There are a great number more cookery books published than is really necessary and it is their **14** .... which makes them differ from each other. There are such large numbers because they offer people an escape from their **15** .... and some give the user the chance to inform themselves about other **16** ....

Questions 17–21

Reading Passage 2 has nine paragraphs, **A–I**.

Which paragraph contains the following information?

Write the correct letter, **A–I**, in boxes 17–21 on your answer sheet.
NB You may use any letter more than once.

17   cookery books providing a sense of stability during periods of unrest

18   details in recipes being altered as they were passed on

19   knowledge which was in danger of disappearing

20   the negative effect on cookery books of a new development

21   a period when there was no need for cookery books to be precise

Questions 22–26

Look at the following statements (**Questions 22–26**) and list of books (**A–E**) below.

Match each statement with the correct book, **A–E**.

Write the correct letter, **A–E**, in boxes 22–26 on your answer sheet.

22 Its recipes were easy to follow despite the writer's attention to detail.

23 Its writer may have deliberately avoided passing on details.

24 It appealed to ambitious ideas people have about cooking.

25 Its writer used ideas from other books but added additional related information.

26 It put into print ideas which are still respected today.

List of cookery books

A *De re coquinara*
B *The Book of Household Management*
C *Le Guide Culinaire*
D *The Boston Cooking-School Cook Book*
E *Mediterranean Food*

---

*You should spend about 20 minutes on **Questions 27–40**, which are based on Reading Passage 3 below.*

Is there more to video games than people realise?

Many people who spend a lot of time playing video games insist that they have helped them in areas like confidence-building, presentation skills and debating. Yet this way of thinking about video games can be found almost nowhere within the mainstream media, which still tend to treat games as an odd mix of the slightly menacing and the alien. This lack of awareness has become increasingly inappropriate, as video games and the culture that surrounds them have become very big business indeed.

Recently, the British government released the Byron report into the effects of electronic media on children. Its conclusions set out a clear, rational basis for exploring the regulation of video games. The ensuing debate, however, has descended into the same old squabbling between partisan factions: the preachers of mental and moral decline, and the innovative game designers. In between are the gamers, busily buying and playing while nonsense is talked over their heads.

Susan Greenfield, renowned neuroscientist, outlines her concerns in a new book. Every individual's mind is the product of a brain that has been personalised by the sum total of their experiences; with an increasing quantity of our experiences from very early childhood taking place 'on screen' rather than in the world, there is potentially a profound shift in the way children's minds work. She suggests that the fast-paced, second-hand experiences created by video games and the Internet may inculcate a worldview that is less empathetic, more risk-taking and less contemplative than what we tend to think of as healthy.

Greenfield's prose is full of mixed metaphors and self-contradictions and is perhaps the worst enemy of her attempts to persuade. This is unfortunate, because however much technophiles may snort, she is articulating widely held fears that have a basis in fact. Unlike even their immediate antecedents, the latest electronic media are at once domestic and work-related, their mobility blurring the boundaries between these spaces, and video games are at their forefront. A generational divide has opened that is in many ways more profound than the equivalent shifts associated with radio or television, more alienating for those unfamiliar with new technologies, more absorbing for those who are. So how do our lawmakers regulate something that is too fluid to be fully comprehended or controlled?

Adam Martin, a lead programmer for an online games developer, says: 'Computer games teach and people don't even notice they're being taught.' But isn't the kind of learning that goes on in games rather narrow? 'A large part of the addictiveness of games does come from the fact that as you play you are mastering a set of challenges. But humanity's larger understanding of the world comes primarily through communication and experimentation, through answering the question "What if?" Games excel at teaching this too.'

Steven Johnson's thesis is not that electronic games constitute a great, popular art, but that the mean level of mass culture has been demanding steadily more intellectual engagement from consumers. Games, he points out, generate satisfaction via the complexity of their virtual worlds, not by their robotic predictability. Testing the nature and limits of the laws of such imaginary worlds has more in common with scientific methods than with a pointless addiction, while the complexity of the problems children encounter within games exceeds that of anything they might find at school.

Greenfield argues that there are ways of thinking that playing video games simply cannot teach. She has a point. We should never forget, for instance, the unique ability of books to engage and expand the human imagination, and to give us the means of more fully expressing our situations in the world. Intriguingly, the video games industry is now growing in ways that have more in common with an old-fashioned world of companionable pastimes than with a cyber-future of lonely, isolated obsessives. Games in which friends and relations gather round a console to compete at activities are growing in popularity. The agenda is increasingly being set by the concerns of mainstream consumers – what they consider acceptable for their children, what they want to play at parties and across generations.

These trends embody a familiar but important truth: games are human products, and lie within our control. This doesn't mean we yet control or understand them fully, but it should remind us that there is nothing inevitable or incomprehensible about them. No matter how deeply it may be felt, instinctive fear is an inappropriate response to technology of any kind.

So far, the dire predictions many traditionalists have made about the 'death' of old-fashioned narratives and imaginative thought at the hands of video games cannot be upheld. Television and cinema may be suffering, economically, at the hands of interactive media. But literacy standards have failed to decline. Young people still enjoy sport, going out and listening to music. And most research – including a recent $1.5m study funded by the US government – suggests that even pre-teens are not in the habit of blurring game worlds and real worlds.

The sheer pace and scale of the changes we face, however, leave little room for complacency. Richard Bartle, a British writer and game researcher, says 'Times change: accept it; embrace it.' Just as, today, we have no living memories of a time before radio, we will soon live in a world in which no one living experienced growing up without computers. It is for this reason that we must try to examine what we stand to lose and gain, before it is too late.

Questions 27–32

Do the following statements agree with the views of the writer in Reading Passage 3?

In boxes 27–32 on your answer sheet, write

YES	if the statement agrees with the views of the writer
NO	if the statement contradicts the views of the writer
NOT GIVEN	if it is impossible to say what the writer thinks about this

27 Much media comment ignores the impact that video games can have on many people's lives.

28 The publication of the Byron Report was followed by a worthwhile discussion between those for and against video games.

29 Susan Greenfield's way of writing has become more complex over the years.

30 It is likely that video games will take over the role of certain kinds of books in the future.

31 More sociable games are being brought out to satisfy the demands of the buying public.

32 Being afraid of technological advances is a justifiable reaction.

Questions 33–37

Choose the correct letter, *A*, *B*, *C* or *D*.

Write the correct letter, *A–D*, in boxes 33–37 on your answer sheet.

33 According to the writer, what view about video games does Susan Greenfield put forward in her new book?

A	They are exposing a child to an adult view of the world too soon.
B	Children become easily frightened by some of the situations in them.
C	They are changing the way children's view of the world develops.
D	Children don't learn from them because they are too repetitive.

34 According to the writer, what problems are faced when regulating video games?

A	The widespread and ever-changing use of games makes it difficult for lawmakers to control them.
B	The appeal of the games to a younger generation isn't really understood by many lawmakers.
C	The lawmakers try to apply the same rules to the games as they did to radio and television.
D	Many lawmakers feel it is too late for the regulations to have much effect on the use of games.

35 What main point does Adam Martin make about video games?

A	People are learning how to avoid becoming addicted to them.
B	They enable people to learn without being aware of it happening.
C	They satisfy a need for people to compete with each other.
D	People learn a narrow range of skills but they are still useful.

36 Which of the following does Steven Johnson disagree with?

    A   the opinion that video games offer educational benefits to the user
    B   the attitude that video games are often labelled as predictable and undemanding
    C   the idea that children's logic is tested more by video games than at school
    D   the suggestion that video games can be compared to scientific procedures

37 Which of the following is the most suitable subtitle for Reading Passage 3?

    A   A debate about the effects of video games on other forms of technology.
    B   An examination of the opinions of young people about video games.
    C   A discussion of whether attitudes towards video games are outdated.
    D   An analysis of the principles behind the historical development of video games.

Questions 38–40

*Complete each sentence with the correct ending, **A–E**, below.*

*Write the correct letter, **A–E**, on your answer sheet.*

38 There is little evidence for the traditionalists' prediction that

39 A recent study by the US government found that

40 Richard Bartle suggests that it is important for people to accept the fact that

A	young people have no problem separating their own lives from the ones they play on the screen.
B	levels of reading ability will continue to drop significantly.
C	new advances in technology have to be absorbed into our lives.
D	games cannot provide preparation for the skills needed in real life.
E	young people will continue to play video games despite warnings against doing so.

Test 3   Writing

Writing Task 1

You should spend about 20 minutes on this task.

> *The graph below gives information about international tourist arrivals in different parts of the world.*
>
> *Summarise the information by selecting and reporting the main features, and make comparisons where relevant.*

Write at least 150 words.

International tourist arrivals

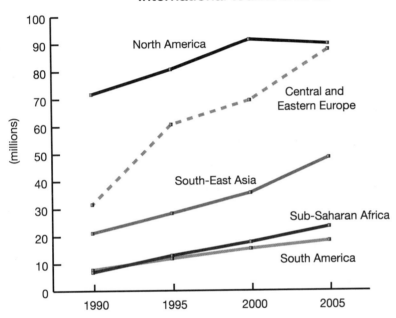

Based on data published by the United Nations World Tourism Organization, 2008.

Writing Task 2

You should spend about 40 minutes on this task.

Write about the following topic:

> *Some people argue that it is more important to have an enjoyable job than to earn a lot of money. Others disagree and think that a good salary leads to a better life.*
>
> *Discuss both these views and give your own opinion.*

Give reasons for your answer and include any relevant examples from your own knowledge or experience.

Write at least 250 words.

Speaking Part 1

The examiner will ask you some questions about yourself, your home, work or studies and familiar topics.

> *Let's talk about your studies (or your job).*
> *Are you studying or do you have a job?*
>
> *Where are you studying?*
> *How many hours do you spend there in a week?*
> *Tell me something about the place where you study.*
> *What are your favourite subjects?*

OR

> *What is your job?*
> *How long have you been doing that job?*
> *Which part of your job do you enjoy the most? Why?*
> *Tell me about the place where you work.*

The examiner will then ask you some questions about one or two other topics, for example:

> *Now let's talk about your free time.*
> *Do you spend a lot of time with your friends?*
> *Do you go out much in the evening?*
> *How much television do you watch?*
> *Do you do any sports?*

Speaking Part 2

The examiner will give you a topic on a card like the one on the right and ask you to talk about it for one to two minutes. Before you talk you'll have one minute to think about what you're going to say. The examiner will give you some paper and a pencil so you can make notes if you want to.

The examiner may ask one or two more questions when you have finished, for example:

> *Do you enjoy travelling?*
> *Are you good at remembering things that happened a long time ago?*

Describe a journey you remember well.
You should say:
     how you travelled
     where you went
     what happened
and explain why the journey was memorable for you.

Speaking Part 3

The examiner will ask some more general questions which follow on from the topic in Part 2.

> *Do you think too many people are dependent on cars as a means of transport?*
> *Why do people prefer to travel by car? Is there a way of changing this attitude?*
> *How could public transport systems be improved?*
> *How can the amount of air travel be reduced throughout the world?*
> *How will people travel in the future, do you think?*

20 *Questions 1–5*

Complete the form below.

Write **ONE WORD AND/OR A NUMBER** *for each answer.*

MEGEQUIP CUSTOMER DETAILS

Example	Answer
Order from	..winter.. catalogue

Name	**1** .... Greening
Address	**2** .... York Terrace
Delivery address	5, York **3** ....
Payment method	**4** .... in advance
Reason for discount	address within the **5** ....

20 *Questions 6–10*

Complete the table below.

Write **NO MORE THAN ONE WORD AND/OR A NUMBER** *for each answer.*

MEGEQUIP CUSTOMER ORDER				
Item	**Catalogue no.**	**Catalogue section**	**Colour**	**Delivery notes**
desk lamp	664	**6**	slate	customer will **7** ....
chair	131	Home Office	**8**	our van
filing cabinet two drawers with **9**	153	Commercial	grey	direct from London no later than **10** ....

Questions 11 and 12

Choose TWO letters, A–E.

Which **TWO** things make the museum unusual?

    A   the guides

    B   the events

    C   the animals

    D   the buildings

    E   the objects

 Questions 13 and 14

Choose TWO letters, A–E.

Which **TWO** things can visitors do at the museum?

    A   buy home-made bread

    B   ride a horse

    C   ride on a tram

    D   buy copies of original posters

    E   go down a coal mine

21

Questions 15–20

Label the map below.

*Write the correct letter, **A–I**, next to questions 15–20.*

15	The exhibition centre	....
16	The High Street	....
17	The farmhouse	....
18	The coal mine	....
19	The Manor House	....
20	The Railway Station	....

Brampton open-air museum

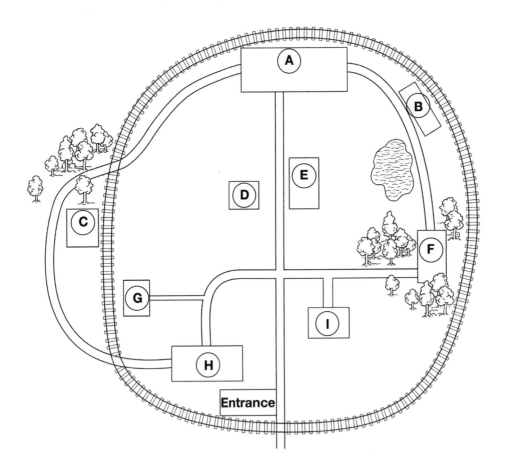

🎧22 *Questions 21–26*

Which attitude is associated with the following people during the conversation?

*Choose **SIX** answers from the box and write the correct letter, **A–H**, next to questions 21–26.*

Attitudes	
A	amused
B	critical
C	forgetful
D	impatient
E	polite
F	relaxed
G	sympathetic
H	unrealistic

People

21   Cressida's fellow students   ....

22   Cressida   ....

23   Ainsley Webb   ....

24   Dr Erskine   ....

25   Professor Jenkins   ....

26   TV news centre staff   ....

*Choose the correct letter, **A**, **B** or **C**.*

27   What was Cressida asked to do at the beginning of her placement?

     A   go out to buy things for the production team
     B   run errands to other parts of the TV news centre
     C   meet visitors and escort them to the studio

28   What was fortunate for Cressida?

     A   She was familiar with a piece of equipment.
     B   She spent a lot of time in the editing suite.
     C   She was given a chance to interview someone.

29   What does Cressida feel she needs to improve?

     A   her understanding of business
     B   her organisational skills
     C   her ability to work in a team

30   What has given her an idea for her final assignment?

     A   a meeting with a public relations professional
     B   seeing a politician speaking to an audience
     C   a disagreement with one of the TV presenters

 **23** *Questions 31–40*

Complete the table below.

Write **NO MORE THAN TWO WORDS** *for each answer.*

THE HISTORY OF THE ELECTRIC GUITAR			
DATE	MAKER	NAME OF GUITAR	FEATURES
1890s	Orville Gibson	no name	similar in shape to a **31** ....
1925	John Dopyera	The National Guitar	made of metal, good for playing **32** .... music
1930s	C. F. Martin Company	The Dreadnought	strings made of **33** ....
1931	George Beauchamp	The **34**	used two **35** .... shaped like horseshoes to increase sound
1935	Adolph Rickenbacker	The Rickenbacker Electro Spanish	made from **36** ....
1941	Les Paul	The Log	the first to be completely **37** ....
1950	Leo Fender	The Fender Broadcaster	its simplicity made it ideal for **38** ....
1951	Leo Fender	The **39**	easy to carry around
1952	Ted McCarty	The Gibson Les Paul	**40** .... in colour
1954	Leo Fender	The Fender Stratocaster	double cutaway design

*You should spend about 20 minutes on **Questions 1–13**, which are based on Reading Passage 1 below.*

Can animals count?

Prime among basic numerical faculties is the ability to distinguish between a larger and a smaller number, says psychologist Elizabeth Brannon. Humans can do this with ease – providing the ratio is big enough – but do other animals share this ability? In one experiment, rhesus monkeys and university students examined two sets of geometrical objects that appeared briefly on a computer monitor. They had to decide which set contained more objects. Both groups performed successfully but, importantly, Brannon's team found that monkeys, like humans, make more errors when two sets of objects are close in number. 'The students' performance ends up looking just like a monkey's. It's practically identical,' she says.

Humans and monkeys are mammals, in the animal family known as primates. These are not the only animals whose numerical capacities rely on ratio, however. The same seems to apply to some amphibians. Psychologist Claudia Uller's team tempted salamanders with two sets of fruit flies held in clear tubes. In a series of trials, the researchers noted which tube the salamanders scampered towards, reasoning that if they had a capacity to recognise number, they would head for the larger number. The salamanders successfully discriminated between tubes containing 8 and 16 flies respectively, but not between 3 and 4, 4 and 6, or 8 and 12. So it seems that for the salamanders to discriminate between two numbers, the larger must be at least twice as big as the smaller. However, they could differentiate between 2 and 3 flies just as well as

between 1 and 2 flies, suggesting they recognise small numbers in a different way from larger numbers.

Further support for this theory comes from studies of mosquitofish, which instinctively join the biggest shoal* they can. A team at the University of Padova found that while mosquitofish can tell the difference between a group containing 3 shoal-mates and a group containing 4, they did not show a preference between groups of 4 and 5. The team also found that mosquitofish can discriminate between numbers up to 16, but only if the ratio between the fish in each shoal was greater than 2:1. This indicates that the fish, like salamanders, possess both the approximate and precise number systems found in more intelligent animals such as infant humans and other primates.

While these findings are highly suggestive, some critics argue that the animals might be relying on other factors to complete the tasks, without considering the number itself. 'Any study that's claiming an animal is capable of representing number should also be controlling for other factors,' says Brannon. Experiments have confirmed that primates can indeed perform numerical feats without extra clues, but what about the more primitive animals? To consider this possibility, the mosquitofish tests were repeated, this time using varying geometrical shapes in place of fish. The team arranged these shapes so that they had the same overall surface area and luminance even though they contained a different number of objects. Across hundreds of trials

* a group of fish

on 14 different fish, the team found they consistently discriminated 2 objects from 3. The team is now testing whether mosquitofish can also distinguish 3 geometric objects from 4.

Even more primitive organisms may share this ability. Entomologist Jurgen Tautz sent a group of bees down a corridor, at the end of which lay two chambers – one which contained sugar water, which they like, while the other was empty. To test the bees' numeracy, the team marked each chamber with a different number of geometrical shapes – between 2 and 6. The bees quickly learned to match the number of shapes with the correct chamber. Like the salamanders and fish, there was a limit to the bees' mathematical prowess – they could differentiate up to 4 shapes, but failed with 5 or 6 shapes.

These studies still do not show whether animals learn to count through training, or whether they are born with the skills already intact. If the latter is true, it would suggest there was a strong evolutionary advantage to a mathematical mind. Proof that this may be the case has emerged from an experiment testing the mathematical ability of three- and four-day-old chicks. Like mosquitofish, chicks prefer to be around as many of their siblings as possible, so they will always head towards a larger number of their kin. If chicks spend their first few days surrounded by certain objects, they become attached to these objects as if they were family. Researchers placed each chick in the middle of a platform and showed it two groups of balls of paper. Next, they hid the two piles behind screens, changed the quantities and revealed them to the chick. This forced the chick to perform simple computations to decide which side now contained the biggest number of its "brothers". Without any prior coaching, the chicks scuttled to the larger quantity at a rate well above chance. They were doing some very simple arithmetic, claim the researchers.

Why these skills evolved is not hard to imagine, since it would help almost any animal forage for food. Animals on the prowl for sustenance must constantly decide which tree has the most fruit, or which patch of flowers will contain the most nectar. There are also other, less obvious, advantages of numeracy. In one compelling example, researchers in America found that female coots appear to calculate how many eggs they have laid – and add any in the nest laid by an intruder – before making any decisions about adding to them. Exactly how ancient these skills are is difficult to determine, however. Only by studying the numerical abilities of more and more creatures using standardised procedures can we hope to understand the basic preconditions for the evolution of number.

Questions 1–7

Complete the table below.

*Choose **NO MORE THAN THREE WORDS** from the passage for each answer.*

Write your answers in boxes 1–7 on your answer sheet.

ANIMAL NUMERACY		
Subjects	**Experiment**	**Results**
Mammals and birds		
rhesus monkeys and humans	looked at two sets of geometrical objects on computer screen	performance of two groups is almost **1** ....
chicks	chose between two sets of **2** .... which are altered	chicks can do calculations in order to choose larger group
coots	behaviour of **3** .... birds was observed	bird seems to have ability to count eggs
Amphibians, fish and insects		
salamanders	offered clear tubes containing different quantities of **4**	salamanders distinguish between numbers over four if bigger number is at least two times larger
5	shown real shoals and later artificial ones of geometrical shapes; these are used to check influence of total **6** .... and brightness	subjects know difference between two and three and possibly three and four, but not between four and five
bees	had to learn where **7** .... was stored	could soon choose correct place

Questions 8–13

Do the following statements agree with the information given in Reading Passage 1?

In boxes 8–13 on your answer sheet, write

      TRUE   *if the statement agrees with the information*
      FALSE   *if the statement contradicts the information*
      NOT GIVEN   *if there is no information on this*

8   Primates are better at identifying the larger of two numbers if one is much bigger than the other.

9   Jurgen Tautz trained the insects in his experiment to recognise the shapes of individual numbers.

10   The research involving young chicks took place over two separate days.

11   The experiment with chicks suggests that some numerical ability exists in newborn animals.

12   Researchers have experimented by altering quantities of nectar or fruit available to certain wild animals.

13   When assessing the number of eggs in their nest, coots take into account those of other birds.

You should spend about 20 minutes on **Questions 14–26**, which are based on Reading Passage 2 below.

Questions 14–18

Reading Passage 2 has five paragraphs **A–E**.

*Choose the correct heading for each paragraph, **A–E**, from the list of headings below.*

*Write the correct number, **i–viii**, in boxes 14–18 on your answer sheet.*

	List of Headings
i	A lack of consistent policy
ii	Learning from experience
iii	The greatest advantage
iv	The role of research
v	A unique material
vi	An irrational anxiety
vii	Avoiding the real challenges
viii	A sign of things to come

14 Paragraph **A**

15 Paragraph **B**

16 Paragraph **C**

17 Paragraph **D**

18 Paragraph **E**

Is it time to halt the rising tide of plastic packaging?

A Close up, plastic packaging can be a marvellous thing. Those who make a living from it call it a forgotten infrastructure that allows modern urban life to exist. Plastics have helped society defy natural limits such as the seasons, the rotting of food and the distance most of us live from where our food is produced. And yet we do not like it. Partly we do not like waste, but plastic waste, with its hydrocarbon roots and industrial manufacture, is especially galling. In 2008, the UK, for example, produced around two million tonnes of plastic waste, twice as much as in the early 1990s. The very qualities of plastic – its cheapness, its indestructible aura – make it a reproachful symbol of an unsustainable way of life. The facts, however, do not justify our unease. All plastics are, at least theoretically, recyclable. Plastic packaging makes up just 6 to 7 per cent of the contents of British dustbins by weight and less than 3 per cent of landfill. Supermarkets and brands, which are under pressure to reduce the quantity of packaging of all types that they use, are finding good environmental reasons to turn to plastic: it is lighter, so requires less energy for transportation than glass, for example; it requires relatively little energy to produce; and it is often re-usable. An Austrian study found that if plastic packaging were removed from the supply chain, other packaging would have to increase fourfold to make up for it.

B So are we just wrong about plastic packaging? Is it time to stop worrying and learn to love the disposable plastic wrapping around sandwiches? Certainly there are bigger targets for environmental savings such as improving household insulation and energy emissions. Naturally, the plastics industry is keen to point them out. What's more, concern over plastic packaging has produced a squall of conflicting initiatives from retailers, manufacturers and local authorities. It's a squall that dies down and then blows harder from one month to the next. 'It is being left to the individual conscience and supermarkets playing the market,' says Tim Lang, a professor specialising in food policy. 'It's a mess.'

C Dick Searle of the Packaging Federation points out that societies without sophisticated packaging lose half their food before it reaches consumers and that in the UK, waste in supply chains is about 3 per cent. In India, it is more than 50 per cent. The difference comes later: the British throw out 30 per cent of the food they buy – an environmental cost in terms of emissions equivalent to a fifth of the cars on their roads. Packagers agree that cardboard, metals and glass all have their good points, but there's nothing quite like plastic. With more than 20 families of polymers to choose from and then sometimes blend, packaging designers and manufacturers have a limitless variety of qualities to play with.

D But if there is one law of plastic that, in environmental terms at least, prevails over all others, it is this: a little goes a long way. This means, first, that plastic is relatively cheap to use – it represents just over one-third of the UK packaging market by value but it wraps more than half the total number of items bought. Second, it means that even though plastic encases about 53 per cent of products bought, it only makes up 20 per cent by weight of the packaging consumed. And in the packaging equation, weight is the main issue because the heavier something is, the more energy you expend moving it around. In view of this, righteous indignation against plastic can look foolish.

E One store commissioned a study to find precise data on which had less environmental impact: selling apples loose or ready-wrapped. Helene Roberts, head of packaging, explains that in fact they found apples in fours on a tray covered by plastic film needed 27 per cent less packaging in transportation than those sold loose. Steve Kelsey, a packaging designer, finds the debate frustrating. He argues that the hunger to do something quickly is diverting effort away from more complicated questions about how you truly alter supply chains. Rather than further reducing the weight of a plastic bottle, more thought should be given to how packaging can be recycled. Helene Roberts explains that their greatest packaging reduction came when the company switched to re-usable plastic crates and stopped consuming 62,000 tonnes of cardboard boxes every year. Plastic packaging is important, and it might provide a way of thinking about broader questions of sustainability. To target plastic on its own is to evade the complexity of the issues. There seems to be a universal eagerness to condemn plastic. Is this due to an inability to make the general changes in society that are really required? 'Plastic as a lightweight food wrapper is now built in as the logical thing,' Lang says. 'Does that make it an environmentally sound system of packaging? It only makes sense if you have a structure such as exists now. An environmentally driven packaging system would look completely different.' Dick Searle put the challenge another way. 'The amount of packaging used today is a reflection of modern life.'

Questions 19–23

Look at the following statements (Questions 19–23) and the list of people below.

Match each statement to the correct person **A–D**.

Write the correct letter, **A–D**, in boxes 19–23 on your answer sheet.

NB You may use any letter more than once.

19   Comparison of two approaches to packaging revealed an interesting result.

20   People are expected to do the right thing.

21   Most food reaches UK shops in good condition.

22   Complex issues are ignored in the search for speedy solutions.

23   It is merely because of the way societies operate that using plastic seems valid.

People
A   Tim Lang
B   Dick Searle
C   Helene Roberts
D   Steve Kelsey

Questions 24–26

Complete the summary below.

Write **NO MORE THAN ONE WORD** from the text for each answer.

Write your answers in boxes 24–26 on your answer sheet.

A revolutionary material

Plastic packaging has changed the way we consume food. However, we instinctively dislike it, partly because it is the product of **24** .... processes, but also because it seems to be **25** .... so we feel it is wasteful. Nevertheless, it is thanks to plastic that for many people their choice of food is no longer restricted by the **26** .... in which it is available or the location of its source.

Reading Passage 2

*You should spend about 20 minutes on **Questions 27–40**, which are based on Reading Passage 3 below.*

The growth of intelligence

No one doubts that intelligence develops as children grow older. Yet the concept of intelligence has proved both quite difficult to define in unambiguous terms and unexpectedly controversial in some respects. Although, at one level, there seem to be almost as many definitions of intelligence as people who have tried to define it, there is broad agreement on two key features. That is, intelligence involves the capacity not only to learn from experience but also to adapt to one's environment. However, we cannot leave the concept there. Before turning to what is known about the development of intelligence, it is necessary to consider whether we are considering the growth of one or many skills. That question has been tackled in rather different ways by psychometricians and by developmentalists.

The former group has examined the issue by determining how children's abilities on a wide range of tasks intercorrelate, or go together. Statistical techniques have been used to find out whether the patterns are best explained by one broad underlying capacity, general intelligence, or by a set of multiple, relatively separate, special skills in domains such as verbal and visuospatial ability. While it cannot be claimed that everyone agrees on what the results mean, most people now accept that for practical purposes it is reasonable to suppose that both are involved. In brief, the evidence in favour of some kind of general intellectual capacity is that people who are superior (or inferior) on one type of task tend also to be superior (or inferior) on others. Moreover, general measures of intelligence tend to have considerable powers to predict a person's performance on a wide range of tasks requiring special skills. Nevertheless, it is plain that it is not at all uncommon for individuals to be very good at some sorts of task and yet quite poor at some others.

Furthermore the influences that affect verbal skills are not quite the same as those that affect other skills.

This approach to investigating intelligence is based on the nature of the task involved, but studies of age-related changes show that this is not the only, or necessarily the most important, approach. For instance, some decades ago, Horn and Cattell argued for a differentiation between what they termed 'fluid' and 'crystallised' intelligence. Fluid abilities are best assessed by tests that require mental manipulation of abstract symbols. Crystallised abilities, by contrast, reflect knowledge of the environment in which we live and past experience of similar tasks; they may be assessed by tests of comprehension and information. It seems that fluid abilities peak in early adult life, whereas crystallised abilities increase up to advanced old age.

Developmental studies also show that the interconnections between different skills vary with age. Thus in the first year of life an interest in perceptual patterns is a major contributor to cognitive abilities, whereas verbal abilities are more important later on. These findings seemed to suggest a substantial lack of continuity between infancy and middle childhood. However, it is important to realise that the apparent discontinuity will vary according to which of the cognitive skills were assessed in infancy. It has been found that tests of coping with novelty do predict later intelligence. These findings reinforce the view that young children's intellectual performance needs to be assessed from their interest in and curiosity about the environment, and the extent to which this is applied to new situations, as well as by standardised intelligence testing.

These psychometric approaches have focused on children's increase in cognitive skills as they grow older. Piaget brought about a revolution in the approach to cognitive development through his arguments (backed up by observations) that the focus should be on the thinking processes involved rather than on levels of cognitive achievement. These ideas of Piaget gave rise to an immense body of research and it would be true to say that subsequent thinking has been heavily dependent on his genius in opening up new ways of thinking about cognitive development. Nevertheless, most of his concepts have had to be so radically revised, or rejected, that his theory no longer provides an appropriate basis for thinking about cognitive development. To appreciate why that is so, we need to focus on some rather different elements of Piaget's theorising.

The first element, which has stood the test of time, is his view that the child is an active agent of learning and of the importance of this activity in cognitive development. Numerous studies have shown how infants actively scan their environment; how they prefer patterned to non-patterned objects, how they choose novel over familiar stimuli, and how they explore their environment as if to see how it works. Children's questions and comments vividly illustrate the ways in which they are constantly constructing schemes of what they know and trying out their ideas of how to fit new knowledge into those schemes or deciding that the schemes need modification. Moreover, a variety of studies have shown that active experiences have a greater effect on learning than comparable passive experiences. However, a second element concerns the notion that development proceeds through a series of separate stages that have to be gone through step-by-step, in a set order, each of which is characterised by a particular cognitive structure. That has turned out to be a rather misleading way of thinking about cognitive development, although it is not wholly wrong.

Questions 27–30

Choose the correct letter, A, B, C or D.

Write your answers in boxes 27–30 on your answer sheet.

27   Most researchers accept that one feature of intelligence is the ability to

      A   change our behaviour according to our situation.
      B   react to others' behaviour patterns.
      C   experiment with environmental features.
      D   cope with unexpected setbacks.

28   What have psychometricians used statistics for?

      A   to find out if cooperative tasks are a useful tool in measuring certain skills
      B   to explore whether several abilities are involved in the development of intelligence
      C   to demonstrate that mathematical models can predict test results for different skills
      D   to discover whether common sense is fundamental to developing children's abilities

29   Why are Horn and Cattell mentioned?

      A   They disagreed about the interpretation of different intelligence tests.
      B   Their research concerned both linguistic and mathematical abilities.
      C   They were the first to prove that intelligence can be measured by testing a range of special skills.
      D   Their work was an example of research into how people's cognitive skills vary with age.

30 What was innovative about Piaget's research?

    A   He refused to accept that children developed according to a set pattern.

    B   He emphasised the way children thought more than how well they did in tests.

    C   He used visually appealing materials instead of traditional intelligence tests.

    D   He studied children of all ages and levels of intelligence.

Questions 31–36

Do the following statements agree with the views of the writer in Reading Passage 3?

In boxes 31–36 on your answer sheet, write

    YES   *if the statement agrees with the views of the writer*

    NO   *if the statement contradicts the views of the writer*

    NOT GIVEN   *if it is impossible to say what the writer thinks about this*

31 A surprising number of academics have come to the same conclusion about what the term intelligence means.

32 A general test of intelligence is unlikely to indicate the level of performance in every type of task.

33 The elderly perform less well on comprehension tests than young adults.

34 We must take into account which skills are tested when comparing intelligence at different ages.

35 Piaget's work influenced theoretical studies more than practical research.

36 Piaget's emphasis on active learning has been discredited by later researchers.

Questions 37–40

*Complete the summary using the list of words, **A–I**, below.*
*Write the correct letter, **A–I**, in boxes 37–40 on your answer sheet.*

Researchers investigating the development of intelligence have shown that **37** .... skills become more significant with age. One good predictor of **38** .... intelligence is the degree to which small children are **39** .... about their surroundings and how much interest they show on finding themselves in an **40** .... setting.

A	adult	**B**	practical	**C**	verbal
D	spatial	**E**	inquisitive	**F**	uncertain
G	academic	**H**	plentiful	**I**	unfamiliar

Writing Task 1

You should spend about 20 minutes on this task.

The graph below gives information about how much people in the United States and the United Kingdom spend on petrol.

Summarise the information by selecting and reporting the main features, and make comparisons where relevant.

Write at least 150 words.

How much do drivers spend on petrol?

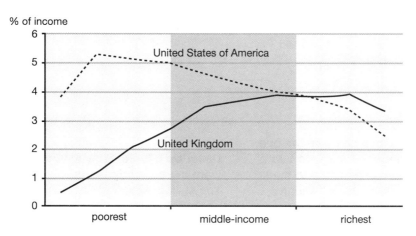

Writing Task 2

You should spend about 40 minutes on this task.

Write about the following topic:

It is generally believed that the Internet is an excellent means of communication but some people suggest that it may not be the best place to find information.

Discuss both these views and give your own opinion.

Give reasons for your answer and include any relevant examples from your own knowledge or experience.

Write at least 250 words.

Speaking Part 1

The examiner will ask you some questions about yourself, your home, work or studies and familiar topics.

Let's talk about your home town.

Where is your home town?
Can you describe the area you come from?
What facilities are there in your area for children/teenagers?
Is it a place where tourists go?

The examiner will then ask you some questions about one or two other topics, for example:

Now let's talk about how you travel.

How do you get to college/school/work?
Do you travel alone or with friends?
What do you do during your journey?
Do you ever have any problems with your transport?
How could your journey be improved?

Speaking Part 2

The examiner will give you a topic on a card like the one on the right and ask you to talk about it for one to two minutes. Before you talk you'll have one minute to think about what you're going to say. The examiner will give you some paper and a pencil so you can make notes if you want to.

The examiner may ask one or two more questions when you have finished, for example:

Do you like to have a routine to your day?
Do you like spending some time alone?

> **Describe a typical day in your life when you were in your early teens.**
> **You should say:**
>   **what you did**
>   **who you spent time with**
>   **how you felt about the things you had to do**
> **and explain what was the best and worst part of the day for you.**

Speaking Part 3

The examiner will ask some more general questions which follow on from the topic in Part 2.

In what way is the relationship between parents and teenagers different from the relationship between parents and younger children?
What causes the most arguments between parents and teenagers?
Do teenagers have more independence in your country than they used to?
Who are the role models for teenagers in your country? Do you think they are good ones?

 **Questions 1–10**

Complete the notes below.

Write **NO MORE THAN TWO WORDS AND/OR A NUMBER** *for each answer.*

Costwise Car Hire

Example	*Answer*
Number of offices in Sydney:	..............3..............

Booking reference number: **1** ....

Office just by **2** .... terminal.

Opening hours: **3** .... to ....

After-hours charge: **4** $ ....

Cheapest model of car available: **5** ....

Information needed when booking: **6** .... number

Length of hire period: **7** ....

Reduce cost by driving under **8** .... km per week.

Insurance does not cover: **9** ....

After hours put keys in box near the office on the **10** ....

🎧 **25** *Questions 11–15*

The following are essential requirements for which jobs?

*Write the correct letter, **A**, **B** or **C**, next to questions 11–15.*

Essential requirements
A foreign languages
B willingness to travel abroad
C professional qualification

11 conference organiser ....

12 catering manager ....

13 housekeeper ....

14 fitness centre staff ....

15 reservations assistant ....

Choose **FIVE** *answers from the box and write the correct letter,* **A–G**, *next to questions 16–20.*

A	CV
B	names of referees
C	work permit
D	recruitment seminar
E	evidence of qualifications
F	conditions of employment
G	initial interview

INTERNATIONAL FINEST GROUP
RECRUITMENT PROCEDURES

register interest in working for International Finest Group

⬇

receive personal code and check **16** ....

⬇

download application form

⬇

send in form and attach **17** ....

⬇

receive reply and confirm **18** ....

⬇

send in **19** ....

⬇

attend **20** ....

🎧26 **Questions 21 and 22**

*Choose **TWO** letters, **A–E**.*

Which **TWO** possible objections to a roof garden are discussed?

    A   problems of access

    B   the cost of construction

    C   the time needed to install it

    D   who will look after it

    E   how to support the weight of it

🎧26 **Questions 23 and 24**

*Choose **TWO** letters, **A–E**.*

Which **TWO** recent developments in roof-garden building are mentioned?

    A   waterproof barrier materials

    B   drainage systems

    C   tank designs

    D   lightweight construction materials

    E   watering systems

🎧26 **Questions 25–30**

Label the diagram below.

*Write the correct letter, **A–H**, next to questions 25–30.*

25	wall	....
26	electric wire	....
27	fibre optic cable	....
28	wooden post	....
29	glass cap	....
30	acrylic rod	....

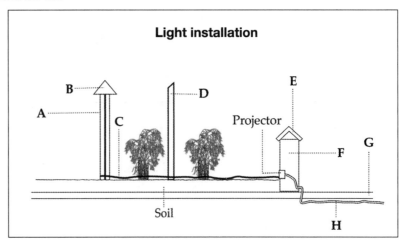

Light installation

Complete the notes below.

Write **NO MORE THAN TWO WORDS** *for each answer.*

The Argus system

Developed by Rob Holman in N. Carolina with other researchers.

Research is vital for understanding of **31** ....

Matches information from under the water with information from a

32 .... According to S. Jeffress Williams, useful because can make

observations during a **33** ....

Dr Holman's sand collection

Dr H. has samples from every **34** ....

Used in teaching students of **35** ....

 e.g. US East Coast display:

 grains from south are small, light-coloured and **36** .... in shape

27 **Questions 37–40**

Complete the flow-chart below.

Write **NO MORE THAN THREE WORDS** *for each answer.*

Taking samples when travelling

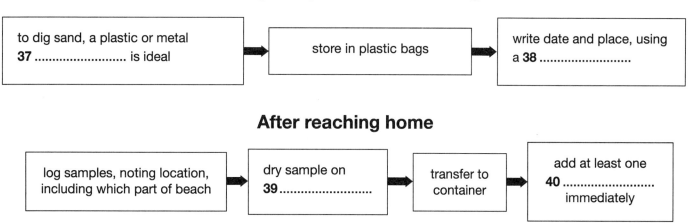

| to dig sand, a plastic or metal **37** .... is ideal | → | store in plastic bags | → | write date and place, using a **38** .... |

After reaching home

| log samples, noting location, including which part of beach | → | dry sample on **39** .... | → | transfer to container | → | add at least one **40** .... immediately |

You should spend about 20 minutes on **Questions 1–13**, which are based on Reading Passage 1 below.

NATURE ON DISPLAY IN AMERICAN ZOOS

by Elizabeth Hanson

The first zoo in the United States opened in Philadelphia in 1874, followed by the Cincinnati Zoo the next year. By 1940 there were zoos in more than one hundred American cities. The Philadelphia Zoo was more thoroughly planned and better financed than most of the hundreds of zoos that would open later but in its landscape and its mission – to both educate and entertain – it embodied ideas about how to build a zoo that stayed consistent for decades. The zoos came into existence in the late nineteenth century during the transition of the United States from a rural and agricultural nation to an industrial one. The population more than doubled between 1860 and 1900. As more middle-class people lived in cities, they began seeking new relationships with the natural world as a place for recreation, self-improvement, and spiritual renewal. Cities established systems of public parks, and nature tourism – already popular – became even more fashionable with the establishment of national parks. Nature was thought to be good for people of all ages and classes. Nature study was incorporated into school curricula, and natural history collecting became an increasingly popular pastime.

At the same time, the fields of study which were previously thought of as 'natural history' grew into separate areas such as taxonomy, experimental embryology and genetics, each with its own experts and structures. As laboratory research gained prestige in the zoology departments of American universities, the gap between professional and amateur scientific activities widened. Previously, natural history had been open to amateurs and was easily popularized, but research required access to microscopes and other equipment in laboratories, as well as advanced education.

The new zoos set themselves apart from traveling animal shows by stating their mission as education and the advancement of science, in addition to recreation. Zoos presented zoology for the non-specialist, at a time when the intellectual distance between amateur naturalists and laboratory-oriented zoologists was increasing. They attracted wide audiences and quickly became a feature of every growing and forward-thinking city. They were emblems of civic pride on a level of importance with art museums, natural history museums and botanical gardens.

Most American zoos were founded and operated as part of the public parks administration. They were dependent on municipal funds, and they charged no admission fee. They tended to assemble as many different mammal and bird species as possible, along with a few reptiles, exhibiting one or two specimens of each, and they competed with each other to become the first to display a rarity, like a rhinoceros. In the constant effort to attract the public to make return visits, certain types of display came in and out of fashion; for example, dozens of zoos built special islands for their large populations of monkeys. In the 1930s, the Works Progress Administration funded millions of dollars of construction at dozens of zoos. For the most part, the collections of animals were organised by species in a combination of enclosures according to a fairly loose classification scheme.

Although many histories of individual zoos describe the 1940s through the 1960s as a period of stagnation, and in some cases there was neglect, new zoos continued to be set up all over the country. In the 1940s and 1950s, the first zoos designed specifically for children were built, some with the appeal of farm animals. An increasing number of zoos tried new ways of organizing their displays. In addition to the traditional approach of exhibiting like kinds together, zoo planners had a new approach of putting animals in groups according to their continent of origin and designing exhibits showing animals of particular habitats, for example, polar, desert, or forest. During the 1960s, a few zoos arranged some displays according to animal behavior; the Bronx Zoo, for instance, opened its World of Darkness exhibit of nocturnal animals. Paradoxically, at the same time as zoo displays began incorporating ideas about the ecological relationships between animals, big cats and primates continued to be displayed in bathroom-like cages lined with tiles.

By the 1970s, a new wave of reform was stirring. Popular movements for environmentalism and animal welfare called attention to endangered species and to zoos that did not provide adequate care for their animals. More projects were undertaken by research scientists and zoos began hiring full-time vets as they stepped up captive breeding programs. Many zoos that had been supported entirely by municipal budgets began recruiting private financial support and charging admission fees. In the prosperous 1980s and 1990s, zoos built realistic 'landscape immersion' exhibits, many of them around the theme of the tropical rainforest and, increasingly, conservation moved to the forefront of zoo agendas.

Although zoos were popular and proliferating institutions in the United States at the turn of the twentieth century, historians have paid little attention to them. Perhaps zoos have been ignored because they were, and remain still, multi-purpose institutions, and as such they fall between the categories of analysis that historians often use. In addition, their stated goals of recreation, education, the advancement of science, and protection of endangered species have often conflicted. Zoos occupy a difficult middle ground between science and showmanship, high culture and low, remote forests and the cement cityscape, and wild animals and urban people.

Questions 1–7

Do the following statements agree with the information given in Reading Passage 1?

In boxes 1–7 on your answer sheet, write

      TRUE   *if the statement agrees with the information*
      FALSE   *if the statement contradicts the information*
      NOT GIVEN *if there is no information on this*

1   The concepts on which the Philadelphia Zoo was based soon became unfashionable.

2   The opening of zoos coincided with a trend for people to live in urban areas.

3   During the period when many zoos were opened, the study of natural history became more popular in universities than other scientific subjects.

4   Cities recognised that the new zoos were as significant an amenity as museums.

5   Between 1940 and 1960 some older zoos had to move to new sites in order to expand.

6   In the 1970s new ways of funding zoos were developed.

7   There has been serious disagreement amongst historians about the role of the first zoos.

Questions 8–13

Complete the notes below.

Choose **NO MORE THAN ONE WORD** from the passage for each answer.

Write your answers in boxes 8–13 on your answer sheet.

- *Up to 1940*   More mammals and birds exhibited than **8** ....
  9 .... were very popular animals in many zoos at one time.

- *1940s and 1950s*   Zoos started exhibiting animals according to their
  10 .... and where they came from.

- *1960s*   Some zoos categorised animals by **11** ....

- *1970s*   **12** .... were employed following protests about animal care.

- *1980s onwards*   The importance of **13** .... became greater.

---

*You should spend about 20 minutes on **Questions 14–26**, which are based on Reading Passage 2 below.*

Can we prevent the poles from melting?

A growing number of scientists are looking to increasingly ambitious technological fixes to halt the tide of global warming. **Mark Rowe** reports.

A Such is our dependence on fossil fuels, and such is the volume of carbon dioxide we have already released into the atmosphere, that most climate scientists agree that significant global warming is now inevitable – the best we can hope to do is keep it at a reasonable level, and even that is going to be an uphill task. At present, the only serious option on the table for doing this is cutting back on our carbon emissions, but while a few countries are making major strides in this regard, the majority are having great difficulty even stemming the rate of increase, let alone reversing it. Consequently, an increasing number of scientists are beginning to explore the alternatives. They all fall under the banner of geoengineering – generally defined as the intentional large-scale manipulation of the environment.

B Geoengineering has been shown to work, at least on a small, localised scale, for decades. May Day parades in Moscow have taken place under clear blue skies, aircraft having deposited dry ice, silver iodide and cement powder to disperse clouds. Many of the schemes now suggested look to do the opposite, and reduce the amount of sunlight reaching the planet. One scheme focuses on achieving a general cooling of the Earth and involves the concept of releasing aerosol sprays into the stratosphere above the Arctic to create clouds of sulphur dioxide, which would, in turn, lead to a global dimming. The idea is modelled on historical volcanic explosions, such as that of Mount Pinatubo in the Philippines in 1991, which led to a short-term cooling of global temperatures by 0.5°C. The aerosols could be delivered by artillery, high-flying aircraft or balloons.

C Instead of concentrating on global cooling, other schemes look specifically at reversing the melting at the poles. One idea is to bolster an ice cap by spraying it with water. Using pumps to carry water from below the sea ice, the spray would come out as snow or ice particles, producing thicker sea ice with a higher albedo (the ratio of sunlight reflected from a surface) to reflect summer radiation. Scientists have also scrutinised whether it is possible to block icefjords in Greenland with cables which have been reinforced, preventing icebergs from moving into the sea. Veli Albert Kallio, a Finnish scientist, says that such an idea is impractical, because the force of the ice would ultimately snap the cables and rapidly release a large quantity of frozen ice into the sea. However, Kallio believes that the sort of cables used in suspension bridges could potentially be used to divert, rather than halt, the southward movement of ice from Spitsbergen. 'It would stop the ice moving south, and local currents would see them float northwards,' he says.

D   A number of geoengineering ideas are currently being examined in the Russian Arctic. These include planting millions of birch trees: the thinking, according to Kallio, is that their white bark would increase the amount of reflected sunlight. The loss of their leaves in winter would also enable the snow to reflect radiation. In contrast, the native evergreen pines tend to shade the snow and absorb radiation. Using ice-breaking vessels to deliberately break up and scatter coastal sea ice in both Arctic and Antarctic waters in their respective autumns, and diverting Russian rivers to increase cold-water flow to ice-forming areas, could also be used to slow down warming, Kallio says. 'You would need the wind to blow the right way, but in the right conditions, by letting ice float free and head north, you would enhance ice growth.'

E   But will such ideas ever be implemented? The major counter-arguments to geoengineering schemes are, first, that they are a 'cop-out' that allow us to continue living the way we do, rather than reducing carbon emissions; and, second, even if they do work, would the side-effects outweigh the advantages? Then there's the daunting prospect of upkeep and repair of any scheme as well as the consequences of a technical failure. 'I think all of us agree that if we were to end geoengineering on a given day, then the planet would return to its pre-engineered condition very rapidly, and probably within 10 to 20 years,' says Dr Phil Rasch, chief scientist for climate change at the US-based Pacific Northwest National Laboratory. 'That's certainly something to worry about. I would consider geoengineering as a strategy to employ only while we manage the conversion to a non-fossil-fuel economy.' 'The risk with geoengineering projects is that you can "overshoot",' says Dr Dan Lunt, from the University of Bristol. 'You may bring global temperatures back to pre-industrial levels, but the risk is that the poles will still be warmer than they should be and the tropics will be cooler than before industrialisation.'

F   The main reason why geoengineering is countenanced by the mainstream scientific community is that most researchers have little faith in the ability of politicians to agree – and then bring in – the necessary carbon cuts. Even leading conservation organisations believe the subject is worth exploring. As Dr Martin Sommerkorn, a climate change advisor says, 'But human-induced climate change has brought humanity to a position where it is important not to exclude thinking thoroughly about this topic and its possibilities despite the potential drawbacks. If, over the coming years, the science tells us about an ever-increased climate sensitivity of the planet – and this isn't unrealistic – then we may be best served by not having to start our thinking from scratch.'

Questions 14–18

Reading Passage 2 has six paragraphs, **A–F**.

Which paragraph contains the following information?

Write the correct letter, **A–F**, in boxes 14–18 on your answer sheet. You may use any letter more than once.

14 the existence of geoengineering projects distracting from the real task of changing the way we live

15 circumstances in which geoengineering has demonstrated success

16 maintenance problems associated with geoengineering projects

17 support for geoengineering being due to a lack of confidence in governments

18 more success in fighting climate change in some parts of the world than others

Questions 19–23

Complete the summary below.

Choose **NO MORE THAN TWO WORDS** from the passage for each answer.

Write your answers in boxes 19–23 on your answer sheet.

Geoengineering projects

A range of geoengineering ideas has been put forward, which aim either to prevent the melting of the ice caps or to stop the general rise in global temperatures. One scheme to discourage the melting of ice and snow involves introducing **19** .... to the Arctic because of their colour. The build-up of ice could be encouraged by dispersing ice along the coasts using special ships and changing the direction of some **20** .... but this scheme is dependent on certain weather conditions. Another way of increasing the amount of ice involves using **21** .... to bring water to the surface. A scheme to stop ice moving would use **22** .... but this method is more likely to be successful in preventing the ice from travelling in one direction rather than stopping it altogether. A suggestion for cooling global temperatures is based on what has happened in the past after **23** .... and it involves creating clouds of gas.

Questions 24–26

Look at the following people (Questions 24–26) and the list of opinions below.

Match each person with the correct opinion, **A–E**.

Write the correct letter, **A–E**, in boxes 24–26 on your answer sheet.

24 Phil Rasch

25 Dan Lunt

26 Martin Sommerkorn

	List of opinions
A	The problems of geoengineering shouldn't mean that ideas are not seriously considered.
B	Some geoengineering projects are more likely to succeed than others.
C	Geoengineering only offers a short-term solution.
D	A positive outcome of geoengineering may have a negative consequence elsewhere.
E	Most geoengineering projects aren't clear in what they are aiming at.

*You should spend about 20 minutes on **Questions 27–40**, which are based on Reading Passage 3 below.*

America's oldest art?

Set within treacherously steep cliffs, and hidden away in the secluded valleys of northeast Brazil, is some of South America's most significant and spectacular rock-art. Most of the art so far discovered from the ongoing excavations comes from the archaeologically-important National Park of the Serra da Capivara in the state of Piaui, and it is causing quite a controversy. The reason for the uproar? The art is being dated to around 25,000 or perhaps, according to some archaeologists, even 36,000 years ago. If correct, this is set to challenge the widely held view that the Americas were first colonised from the north, via the Bering Straits from eastern Siberia at around 10,000 BC, only moving down into Central and South America in the millennia thereafter.

Prior to the designation of 130,000 hectares as a National Park, the rock-art sites were difficult to get to, and often dangerous to enter. In ancient times, this inaccessibility must have heightened the importance of the sites, and indeed of the people who painted on the rocks. Wild animals and human figures dominate the art, and are incorporated into often-complex scenes involving hunting, supernatural beings, fighting and dancing. The artists depicted the animals that roamed the local ancient brushwood forest. The large mammals are usually painted in groups and tend to be shown in a running stance, as though trying to escape from hunting parties. Processions – lines of human and animal figures –

also appear of great importance to these ancient artists. Might such lines represent family units or groups of warriors? On a number of panels, rows of stylised figures, some numbering up to 30 individual figures, were painted using the natural undulating contours of the rock surface, so evoking the contours of the surrounding landscape. Other interesting, but very rare, occurrences are scenes that show small human figures holding on to and dancing around a tree, possibly involved in some form of a ritual dance.

Due to the favourable climatic conditions, the imagery on many panels is in a remarkable state of preservation. Despite this, however, there are serious conservation issues that affect their long-term survival. The chemical and mineral qualities of the rock on which the imagery is painted is fragile and on several panels it is unstable. As well as the secretion of sodium carbonate on the rock surface, complete panel sections have, over the ancient and recent past, broken away from the main rock surface. These have then become buried and sealed into sometimes-ancient floor deposits. Perversely, this form of natural erosion and subsequent deposition has assisted archaeologists in dating several major rock-art sites. Of course, dating the art is extremely difficult given the non-existence of plant and animal remains that might be scientifically dated. However, there are a small number of sites in the Serra da Capivara that are giving up their secrets through good systematic excavation. Thus, at Toca do Boqueirao da Pedra Furada, rock-art researcher Niéde Guidon managed to obtain a number of dates. At different levels of excavation, she located fallen painted rock fragments, which she was able to date to at least 36,000 years ago. Along with the painted fragments, crude stone tools were found. Also discovered were a series of scientifically datable sites of fireplaces, or hearths, the earliest dated to 46,000 BC, arguably the oldest dates for human habitation in the Americas.

However, these conclusions are not without controversy. Critics, mainly from North America, have suggested that the hearths may in fact be a natural phenomenon, the result of seasonal brushwood fires. Several North American researchers have gone further and suggested that the rock-art from this site dates from no earlier than about 3,730 years ago, based on the results of limited radiocarbon dating. Adding further fuel to the general debate is the fact that the artists in the area of the National Park tended not to draw over old motifs (as often occurs with rock-art), which makes it hard to work out the relative chronology of the

images or styles. However, the diversity of imagery and the narrative the paintings create from each of the many sites within the National Park suggests different artists were probably making their art at different times, and potentially using each site over many thousands of years.

With fierce debates thus raging over the dating, where these artists originate from is also still very much open to speculation. The traditional view ignores all the early dating evidence from the South American rock-art sites. In a revised scenario, some palaeo-anthropologists are now suggesting that modern humans may have migrated from Africa using the strong currents of the Atlantic Ocean some 60,000 years or more ago, while others suggest a more improbable colonisation coming from the Pacific Ocean. Yet, while either hypothesis is plausible, there is still no supporting archaeological evidence between the South American coastline and the interior. Rather, it seems possible that there were a number of waves of human colonisation of the Americas occurring possibly over a 60,000–100,000 year period, probably using the Bering Straits as a land-bridge to cross into the Americas.

Despite the compelling evidence from South America, it stands alone: the earliest secure human evidence yet found in the state of Oregon in North America only dates to 12,300 years BC. So this is a fierce debate that is likely to go on for many more years. However, the splendid rock-art and its allied archaeology of northeast Brazil, described here, is playing a huge and significant role in the discussion.

Questions 27–29

*Choose the correct letter, **A**, **B**, **C** or **D**.*

Write the correct letter in boxes 27–29 on your answer sheet.

27 According to the first paragraph, the rock-art in Serra da Capivara may revolutionise accepted ideas about

     A   the way primitive people lived in North America.

     B   the date when the earliest people arrived in South America.

     C   the origin of the people who crossed the Bering Straits.

     D   the variety of cultures which developed in South America.

28 How did the ancient artists use the form of the rock where they painted?

     A   to mimic the shape of the countryside nearby

     B   to emphasise the shape of different animals

     C   to give added light and shade to their paintings

     D   to give the impression of distance in complex works

29 In the fourth paragraph, what does the writer say is unusual about the rock-artists of Serra da Capivara?

     A   They had a very wide range of subject-matter.

     B   Their work often appears to be illustrating a story.

     C   They tended to use a variety of styles in one painting.

     D   They rarely made new paintings on top of old ones.

Questions 30–36

In boxes 30–36 on your answer sheet, write

     YES   *if the statement agrees with the claims of the writer*

     NO   *if the statement contradicts the claims of the writer*

     NOT GIVEN   *if it is impossible to say what the writer thinks about this*

30 Archaeologists have completed their survey of the rock-art in Piaui.

31 The location of the rock-art suggests that the artists had a significant role in their society.

32 The paintings of animals show they were regarded as sacred by the ancient humans.

33 Some damage to paintings is most likely due to changes in the weather of the region.

34 The fact that some paintings were buried is useful to archaeologists.

35 The tools found near some paintings were probably used for hunting animals.

36 The North American researchers have confirmed Niéde Guidon's dating of the paintings.

Questions 37–40

*Complete each sentence with the correct ending, **A–F**, below.*

*Write the correct letter, **A–F**, on your answer sheet.*

37   Materials derived from plants or animals

38   The discussions about the ancient hearths

39   Theories about where the first South Americans originated from

40   The finds of archaeologists in Oregon

A	are giving rise to a great deal of debate among palaeo-anthropologists.
B	do not support the earliest dates suggested for the arrival of people in America.
C	are absent from rock-art sites in the Serra da Capivara.
D	have not been accepted by academics outside America.
E	centre on whether or not they are actually man-made.
F	reflect the advances in scientific dating methods.

Writing Task 1

You should spend about 20 minutes on this task.

The diagrams below give information about the manufacture of frozen fish pies.

Summarise the information by selecting and reporting the main features, and make comparisons where relevant.

Write at least 150 words.

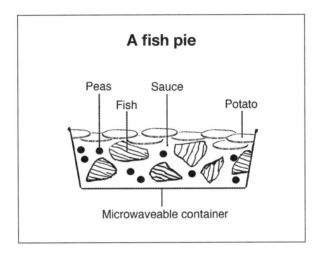

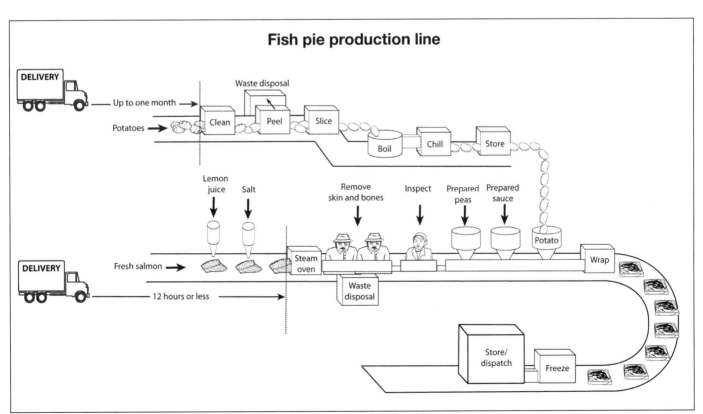

Writing Task 2

You should spend about 40 minutes on this task.

Write about the following topic:

> *In some countries it is thought advisable that children begin formal education at four years old, while in others they do not have to start school until they are seven or eight.*
>
> *How far do you agree with either of these views?*

Give reasons for your answer and include any relevant examples from your own knowledge or experience.

Write at least 250 words.

Speaking Part 1

The examiner will ask you some questions about yourself, your home, work or studies and familiar topics.

Let's talk about your home town.

Do you live in a town or a city?
Have your family always lived there?
Do you like living there?
Do many tourists visit your area? (What do they come to see?)
Do you think your home town/city will change much in the future?

The examiner will then ask you some questions about one or two other topics, for example:

Now let's talk about music.

What kind of music do you like?
What do you like about it?
Are your friends interested in the same kind of music?
Where do you usually listen to music?
Do you ever go to concerts?
Do you play or would you like to play an instrument?

Speaking Part 2

The examiner will give you a topic on a card like the one on the right and ask you to talk about it for one to two minutes. Before you talk you'll have one minute to think about what you're going to say. The examiner will give you some paper and a pencil so you can make notes if you want to.

The examiner may ask one or two more questions when you have finished, for example:

Do you throw things away when you don't need them any more?
Do you sometimes buy something and then regret it?

> **Describe one of your possessions which you couldn't live without.**
> **You should say:**
>   **what it is**
>   **why you first bought it / how you got it**
>   **when and how often you use it**
> **and explain why it is so special.**

Speaking Part 3

The examiner will ask some more general questions which follow on from the topic in Part 2.

Do you think some people spend too much money on things they don't need? What sort of things?
Is it worth trying to repair things which break rather than throwing them away? Why do you think that?
Many people feel they must have lots of hi-tech gadgets these days. What do you think of this trend?
Do you think technology has made our lives easier or more stressful? Why?
Some people aren't interested in keeping up to date with new technology. Do you think that matters?

 Questions 1–10

Complete the table below.

Write **ONE WORD AND/OR A NUMBER** for each answer.

HOSTELS			
Name	**Location**	**Cost of double room**	**Notes**
Hostelling International West End	*Example* 10 minutes from downtown by *Answer* ....bus..........	$50 per night but only $1 .... for members	Membership card offers discount on entry to 2 .... Internet access costs $3 per 3 ....
4 .... Hostel	Near beach. Two-minute walk to 5	$62. Meals extra but only available in 6	Was built as a hotel in 7 .... Can hire 8 .... from hostel
Backpackers Hostel	In 9 .... district	$45 plus $5 for breakfast	A 10 .... on every floor for guests to use

29 *Questions 11–15*

Label the map below.

Choose **FIVE** *answers from the box and write the correct letter,* **A–H**, *next to questions 11–15.*

A	biography
B	fiction
C	magazines
D	newspapers
E	non-fiction
F	photocopiers
G	reference books
H	study area

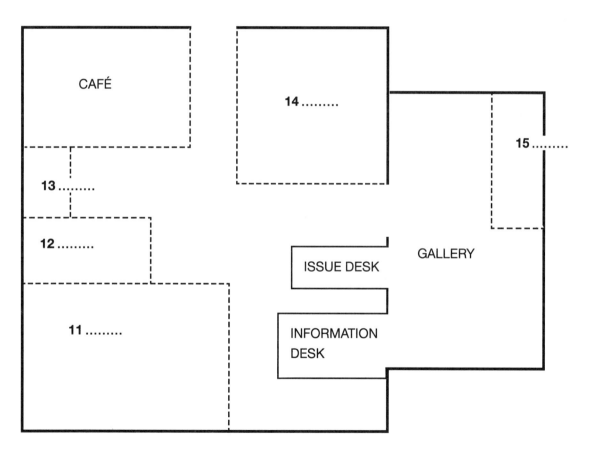

Choose the correct letter, A, B or C.

16 After two years, library members have to

> **A**   show proof of their current address.
> **B**   pay for a new membership card.
> **C**   bring a passport or identity card into the library.

17 What happens if you reserve a book?

> **A**   It will be available after five days.
> **B**   You can collect it a week later.
> **C**   You will be contacted when it is available.

18 Which materials can be borrowed for one week only?

> **A**   some reference books
> **B**   CD-ROMs
> **C**   children's DVDs

19 On which day does the library stay open later than it used to?

> **A**   Wednesday
> **B**   Saturday
> **C**   Sunday

20 Large bags should be left on the

> **A**   first floor.
> **B**   second floor.
> **C**   third floor.

Choose the correct letter, A, B or C.

21   Why did Anita and Lee choose to talk about John Chapman?

        A   He was Lee's childhood hero.
        B   They wanted to talk about the USA.
        C   He was relevant to the topic of their studies.

22   Where did the students record their sources of information?

        A   on their laptops
        B   on a handout
        C   on a database

23   The tutor claims she does not understand whether

        A   apples grew in America before Europeans arrived.
        B   the Native Americans had always eaten apples.
        C   American apples were first bred in Europe.

24   The tutor says the audience was particularly interested to hear about

        A   grafting techniques in ancient China.
        B   the cultivation of apples in Kazakhstan.
        C   the spread of apples along the Silk Route.

25   How will Anita and Lee present their follow-up work?

        A   on the department website
        B   as a paper
        C   as a poster

What do Lee and Anita agree about their presentation skills with their tutor?

Write the correct letter, A, B or C, next to questions 26–30.

A   excellent

B   acceptable

C   poor

Presentation skills

26   use of equipment   ....

27   handling software   ....

28   timing of sections   ....

29   design of handout   ....

30   clarity of speech   ....

Questions 31–40

Complete the table below.

Write **NO MORE THAN ONE WORD** *for each answer.*

INVESTIGATING TASTE		
Procedure	**Result**	**Cause**
more yellow added to green colour of **31**	subjects believed extra **32** .... added to drink	brain influenced by product presentation
gum chewed until it is **33** .... then again with sugar	mint flavour **34**	sweetness necessary for mintiness
same drink tasted cold and at room temperature	**35** .... drink seems sweeter	temperature affects sweetness
crisps eaten in rooms which were **36**	with louder crunch, subjects believed crisps taste **37**	sound affects taste perceptions
variety of cheese sauces prepared	subjects believed some sauces tasted less strong	**38** .... affects taste perceptions
two different flavoured **39** .... tasted together	subjects still tasted **40** .... when no longer there	brain is filling the taste 'gap'

*You should spend about 20 minutes on **Questions 1–13**, which are based on Reading Passage 1 below.*

Communicating in Colour

There are more than 160 known species of chameleons. The main distribution is in Africa and Madagascar, and other tropical regions, although some species are also found in parts of southern Europe and Asia. There are introduced populations in Hawaii and probably in California and Florida too.

New species are still discovered quite frequently. Dr Andrew Marshall, a conservationist from York University, was surveying monkeys in Tanzania, when he stumbled across a twig snake in the Magombera forest which, frightened, coughed up a chameleon and fled. Though a colleague persuaded him not to touch it because of the risk from venom, Marshall suspected it might be a new species, and took a photograph to send to colleagues, who confirmed his suspicions. *Kinyongia magomberae*, literally "the chameleon from Magombera", is the result, and the fact it was not easy to identify is precisely what

made it unique. The most remarkable feature of chameleons is their ability to change colour, an ability rivalled only by cuttlefish and octopi in the animal kingdom. Because of this, colour is not the best thing for telling chameleons apart and different species are usually identified based on the patterning and shape of the head, and the arrangement of scales. In this case it was the bulge of scales on the chameleon's nose.

Chameleons are able to use colour for both communication and camouflage by switching from bright, showy colours to the exact colour of a twig within seconds. They show an extraordinary range of colours, from nearly black to bright blues, oranges, pinks and greens, even several at once. A popular misconception is that chameleons can match whatever background they are placed on, whether a chequered red and yellow shirt or a Smartie* box. But each species has a characteristic set of cells containing pigment distributed over their bodies in a specific pattern, which determines the range of colours and patterns they can show. To the great disappointment of many children, placing a chameleon on a Smartie box generally results in a stressed, confused, dark grey or mottled chameleon.

Chameleons are visual animals with excellent eyesight, and they communicate with colour. When two male dwarf chameleons encounter

---

*Smarties™ are sugar-coated chocolates in a range of bright colours.

each other, each shows its brightest colours. They puff out their throats and present themselves side-on with their bodies flattened to appear as large as possible and to show off their colours. This enables them to assess each other from a distance. If one is clearly superior, the other quickly changes to submissive colouration, which is usually a dull combination of greys or browns. If the opponents are closely matched and both maintain their bright colours, the contest can escalate to physical fighting and jaw-locking, each trying to push each other along the branch in a contest of strength. Eventually, the loser will signal his defeat with submissive colouration.

Females also have aggressive displays used to repel male attempts at courtship. When courting a female, males display the same bright colours that they use during contests. Most of the time, females are unreceptive and aggressively reject males by displaying a contrasting light and dark colour pattern, with their mouths open and moving their bodies rapidly from side to side. If the male continues to court a female, she often chases and bites him until he retreats. The range of colour change during female displays, although impressive, is not as great as that shown by males.

Many people assume that colour change evolved to enable chameleons to match a greater variety of backgrounds in their environment. If this was the case, then the ability of chameleons to change colour should be associated with the range of background colours in the chameleon's habitat, but there is no evidence for such a pattern. For example, forest habitats might have a greater range of brown and green background colours than grasslands, so forest-dwelling species might be expected to have greater powers of colour change. Instead, the males whose display colours are the most eye-catching show the greatest colour change. Their displays are composed of colours that contrast highly with each other as well as with the background vegetation. This suggests that the species that evolved the most impressive capacities for colour change did so to enable them to intimidate rivals or attract mates rather than to facilitate camouflage.

How do we know that chameleon display colours are eye-catching to another chameleon – or, for that matter, to a predatory bird? Getting a view from the perspective of chameleons or their bird predators requires information on the chameleon's or bird's visual system and an understanding of how their brains might process visual information. This is because the perceived colour of an object depends as much on the brain's wiring as on the physical properties of the object itself. Luckily, recent scientific advances have made it possible to obtain such measurements in the field, and information on visual systems of a variety of animals is becoming increasingly available.

The spectacular diversity of colours and ornaments in nature has inspired biologists for centuries. But if we want to understand the function and evolution of animal colour patterns, we need to know how they are perceived by the animals themselves – or their predators. After all, camouflage and conspicuousness are in the eye of the beholder.

Questions 1–4

Answer the questions below.

Choose **NO MORE THAN THREE WORDS** from the passage for each answer.

Write your answers in boxes 1–4 on your answer sheet.

1   What kind of climate do most chameleons live in?

2   Which animal caught a chameleon from an undiscovered species?

3   What was the new species named after?

4   Which part of the body is unique to the species *Kinyongia magomberae*?

Questions 5–13

Do the following statements agree with the information given in Reading Passage 1?

In boxes 5–13 on your answer sheet, write

> **TRUE**   if the statement agrees with the information
> **FALSE**   if the statement contradicts the information
> **NOT GIVEN**   if there is no information on this

5   Few creatures can change colour as effectively as cuttlefish.

6   Chameleons can imitate a pattern provided there are only two colours.

7   Chameleons appear to enjoy trying out new colours.

8   Size matters more than colour when male chameleons compete.

9   After a fight, the defeated male hides among branches of a tree.

10   Females use colour and movement to discourage males.

11   The popular explanation of why chameleons change colour has been proved wrong.

12   There are more predators of chameleons in grassland habitats than in others.

13   Measuring animals' visual systems necessitates removing them from their habitat.

*You should spend about 20 minutes on **Questions 14–26**, which are based on Reading Passage 2 below.*

The Pursuit of Happiness

A

In the late 1990s, psychologist Martin Seligman of the University of Pennsylvania urged colleagues to observe optimal moods with the same kind of focus with which they had for so long studied illnesses: we would never learn about the full range of human functions unless we knew as much about mental wellness as we do about mental illness. A new generation of psychologists built up a respectable body of research on positive character traits and happiness-boosting practices. At the same time, developments in neuroscience provided new clues to what makes us happy and what that looks like in the brain. Self-appointed experts took advantage of the trend with guarantees to eliminate worry, stress, dejection and even boredom. This happiness movement has provoked a great deal of opposition among psychologists who observe that the preoccupation with happiness has come at the cost of sadness, an important feeling that people have tried to banish from their emotional repertoire. Allan Horwitz of Rutgers laments that young people who are naturally weepy after

breakups are often urged to medicate themselves instead of working through their sadness. Wake Forest University's Eric Wilson fumes that the obsession with happiness amounts to a "craven disregard" for the melancholic perspective that has given rise to the greatest works of art. "The happy man," he writes, "is a hollow man."

B

After all, people are remarkably adaptable. Following a variable period of adjustment, we bounce back to our previous level of happiness, no matter what happens to us. (There are some scientifically proven exceptions, notably suffering the unexpected loss of a job or the loss of a spouse. Both events tend to permanently knock people back a step.) Our adaptability works in two directions. Because we are so adaptable, points out Professor Sonja Lyubomirsky of the University of California, we quickly get used to many of the accomplishments we strive for in life, such as landing the big job or getting married. Soon after we reach a milestone, we start to feel that something is missing. We begin coveting another worldly possession or eyeing a social advancement. But such an approach keeps us tethered to a treadmill where happiness is always just out of reach, one toy or one step away. It's possible to get off the treadmill entirely by focusing on activities that are dynamic, surprising, and attention-absorbing, and thus less likely to bore us than, say, acquiring shiny new toys.

C

Moreover, happiness is not a reward for escaping pain. Russ Harris, the author of *The Happiness Trap*, calls popular conceptions of happiness dangerous because they set people up for a "struggle against reality". They don't acknowledge that real life is full of disappointments, loss, and inconveniences. "If you're going to live a rich and meaningful life," Harris says, "you're going to feel a full range of emotions." Action toward goals other than happiness makes people happy. It is not crossing the finish line that is most rewarding, it is anticipating achieving the goal. University of Wisconsin neuroscientist Richard Davidson has found that working hard toward a goal, and making progress to the point of expecting a goal to be realised, not only activates positive feelings but also suppresses negative emotions such as fear and depression.

D

We are constantly making decisions, ranging from what clothes to put on, to whom we should marry, not to mention all those flavors of ice cream. We base many of our decisions on whether we think a particular preference will increase our well-being. Intuitively, we seem convinced that the more choices we have, the better off we will ultimately be. But our world of unlimited opportunity imprisons us more than it makes us happy. In what Swarthmore psychologist Barry Schwartz calls "the paradox of choice," facing many possibilities leaves us stressed out – and less satisfied with whatever we do decide. Having too many choices keeps us wondering about all the opportunities missed.

E

Besides, not everyone can put on a happy face. Barbara Held, a professor of psychology at Bowdoin College, rails against "the tyranny of the positive attitude". "Looking on the bright side isn't possible for some people and is even counterproductive," she insists. "When you put pressure on people to cope in a way that doesn't fit them, it not only doesn't work, it makes them feel like a failure on top of already feeling bad." The one-size-fits-all approach to managing emotional life is misguided, agrees Professor Julie Norem, author of *The Positive Power of Negative Thinking*. In her research, she has shown that the defensive pessimism that anxious people feel can be harnessed to help them get things done, which in turn makes them happier. A naturally pessimistic architect, for example, can set low expectations for an upcoming presentation and review all of the bad outcomes that she's imagining, so that she can prepare carefully and increase her chances of success.

F

By contrast, an individual who is not living according to their values, will not be happy, no matter how much they achieve. Some people, however, are not sure what their values are. In that case Harris has a great question: "Imagine I could wave a magic wand to ensure that you would have the approval and admiration of everyone on the planet, forever. What, in that case, would you choose to do with your life?" Once this has been answered honestly, you can start taking steps toward your ideal vision of yourself. The actual answer is unimportant, as long as you're living consciously. The state of happiness is not really a state at all. It's an ongoing personal experiment.

Questions 14–19

Reading Passage 2 has six paragraphs, **A–F**.

Which paragraph mentions the following?

*Write the correct letter, **A–F**, in boxes 14–19 on your answer sheet.*
***NB** You may use any letter more than once.*

14   the need for individuals to understand what really matters to them

15   tension resulting from a wide variety of alternatives

16   the hope of success as a means of overcoming unhappy feelings

17   people who call themselves specialists

18   human beings' capacity for coping with change

19   doing things which are interesting in themselves

Questions 20 and 21

*Choose **TWO** letters, **A–E**.*

Write the correct letters in boxes 20 and 21 on your answer sheet.

Which **TWO** of the following people argue against aiming for constant happiness?

A	Martin Seligman
B	Eric Wilson
C	Sonja Lyubomirsky
D	Russ Harris
E	Barry Schwartz

Questions 22 and 23

*Choose **TWO** letters, **A–E**.*

Write the correct letters in boxes 22 and 23 on your answer sheet.

Which **TWO** of the following beliefs are identified as mistaken in the text?

A	Inherited wealth brings less happiness than earned wealth.
B	Social status affects our perception of how happy we are.
C	An optimistic outlook ensures success.
D	Unhappiness can and should be avoided.
E	Extremes of emotion are normal in the young.

Questions 24–26

Complete the sentences below.

*Choose **NO MORE THAN ONE WORD** from the passage for each answer.*

Write your answers in boxes 24–26 on your answer sheet.

24   In order to have a complete understanding of how people's minds work, Martin Seligman
     suggested that research should examine our most positive .... as closely as it does our
     psychological problems.

25   Soon after arriving at a .... in their lives, people become accustomed to what they have
     achieved and have a sense that they are lacking something.

26   People who are .... by nature are more likely to succeed if they make thorough preparation
     for a presentation.

*You should spend about 20 minutes on **Questions 27–40**, which are based on Reading Passage 3 below.*

The Deep Sea

At a time when most think of outer space as the final frontier, we must remember that a great deal of unfinished business remains here on earth. Robots crawl on the surface of Mars, and spacecraft exit our solar system, but most of our own planet has still never been seen by human eyes. It seems ironic that we know more about impact craters on the far side of the moon than about the longest and largest mountain range on earth. It is amazing that human beings crossed a quarter of a million miles of space to visit our nearest celestial neighbor before penetrating just two miles deep into the earth's own waters to explore the Midocean Ridge. And it would be hard to imagine a more significant part of our planet to investigate – a chain of volcanic mountains 42,000 miles long where most of the earth's solid surface was born, and where vast volcanoes continue to create new submarine landscapes.

The figure we so often see quoted – 71% of the earth's surface – understates the oceans' importance. If you consider instead three-dimensional volumes, the land-dwellers' share of the planet shrinks even more toward insignificance: less than 1% of the total. Most of the oceans' enormous volume, lies deep below the familiar surface. The upper sunlit layer, by one estimate, contains only 2 or 3% of the total space available to life. The other 97% of the earth's biosphere lies deep beneath the water's surface, where sunlight never penetrates.

Until recently, it was impossible to study the deep ocean directly. By the sixteenth century, diving bells allowed people to stay underwater for a short time: they could swim to the bell to breathe air trapped underneath it rather than return all the way to the surface. Later, other devices, including pressurized or armored suits, heavy metal helmets, and compressed air supplied through hoses from the surface, allowed at least one diver to reach 500 feet or so.

It was 1930 when a biologist named William Beebe and his engineering colleague Otis Barton sealed themselves into a new kind of diving craft, an invention that finally allowed humans to penetrate beyond the shallow sunlit layer of the sea and the history of deep-sea exploration began. Science then was largely incidental – something that happened along the way. In terms of technical ingenuity and human bravery, this part of the story is every bit as amazing as the history of early aviation. Yet many of these individuals, and the deep-diving vehicles that they built and tested, are not well known.

It was not until the 1970s that deep-diving manned submersibles were able to reach the Midocean Ridge and begin making major contributions to a wide range of scientific questions. A burst of discoveries followed in short order. Several of these profoundly changed whole fields of science, and their implications are still not fully understood. For example, biologists may now be seeing – in the strange communities of microbes and animals that live around deep volcanic vents – clues to the origin of life on earth. No one even knew that these communities existed before explorers began diving to the bottom in submersibles.

Entering the deep, black abyss presents unique challenges for which humans must carefully prepare if they wish to survive. It is an unforgiving environment, both harsh and strangely beautiful, that few who have not experienced it firsthand can fully appreciate. Even the most powerful searchlights penetrate only tens of feet. Suspended particles scatter the light and water itself is far less transparent than air; it absorbs and scatters light. The ocean also swallows other types of electromagnetic radiation, including radio signals. That is why many deep sea vehicles dangle from tethers. Inside those tethers, copper wires or fiber optic strands transmit signals that would dissipate and die if broadcast into open water.

Another challenge is that the temperature near the bottom in very deep water typically hovers just four degrees above freezing, and submersibles rarely have much insulation. Since water absorbs heat more quickly than air, the cold down below seems to penetrate a diving capsule far more quickly than it would penetrate, say, a control van up above, on the deck of the mother ship.

And finally, the abyss clamps down with crushing pressure on anything that enters it. This force is like air pressure on land, except that water is much heavier than air. At sea level on land, we don't even notice 1 atmosphere of pressure, about 15 pounds per square inch, the weight of the earth's blanket of air. In the deepest part of the ocean, nearly seven miles down, it's about 1,200 atmospheres, 18,000 pounds per square inch. A square-inch column of lead would crush down on your body with equal force if it were 3,600 feet tall.

Fish that live in the deep don't feel the pressure, because they are filled with water from their own environment. It has already been compressed by abyssal pressure as much as water can be (which is not much). A diving craft, however, is a hollow chamber, rudely displacing the water around it. That chamber must withstand the full brunt of deep-sea pressure – thousands of pounds per square inch. If seawater with that much pressure behind it ever finds a way to break inside, it explodes through the hole with laserlike intensity.

It was into such a terrifying environment that the first twentieth-century explorers ventured.

Questions 27–30

*Write the correct letter, **A**, **B**, **C** or **D**, in boxes 27–30 on your answer sheet.*

27   In the first paragraph, the writer finds it surprising that

    A   we send robots to Mars rather than to the sea bed.
    B   we choose to explore the least accessible side of the moon.
    C   people reached the moon before they explored the deepest parts of the earth's oceans.
    D   spaceships are sent beyond our solar system instead of exploring it.

28   The writer argues that saying 71% of the earth's surface is ocean is not accurate because it

    A   ignores the depth of the world's oceans.
    B   is based on an estimated volume.
    C   overlooks the significance of landscape features.
    D   refers to the proportion of water in which life is possible.

29   How did the diving bell help divers?

    A   It allowed each diver to carry a supply of air underwater.
    B   It enabled piped air to reach deep below the surface.
    C   It offered access to a reservoir of air below the surface.
    D   It meant that they could dive as deep as 500 feet.

30   What point does the writer make about scientific discoveries between 1930 and 1970?

    A   They were rarely the primary purpose of deep sea exploration.
    B   The people who conducted experiments were not professional scientists.
    C   Many people refused to believe the discoveries that were made.
    D   They involved the use of technologies from other disciplines.

Questions 31–36

Do the following statements agree with the views of the writer in Reading Passage 3?

In boxes 31–36 on your answer sheet, write

YES	if the statement agrees with the views of the writer
NO	if the statement contradicts the views of the writer
NOT GIVEN	if it is impossible to say what the writer thinks about this

31 The Midocean Ridge is largely the same as when the continents emerged.

32 We can make an approximate calculation of the percentage of the ocean which sunlight penetrates.

33 Many unexpected scientific phenomena came to light when exploration of the Midocean Ridge began.

34 The number of people exploring the abyss has risen sharply in the 21st century.

35 One danger of the darkness is that deep sea vehicles become entangled in vegetation.

36 The construction of submersibles offers little protection from the cold at great depths.

Questions 37–40

Complete the summary using the list of words, **A–I**, below.

Deep diving craft

A diving craft has to be **37** .... enough to cope with the enormous pressure of the

abyss, which is capable of crushing almost anything. Unlike creatures that live there, which are

not **38** .... because they contain compressed water, a submersible is filled with **39** ....

If it has a weak spot in its construction, there will be a **40** .... explosion of water into the craft.

A	ocean	**B**	air	**C**	deep
D	hollow	**E**	sturdy	**F**	atmosphere
G	energetic	**H**	violent	**I**	heavy

Writing Task 1

You should spend about 20 minutes on this task.

> *The charts below give information about weather in two Brazilian cities.*
>
> *Summarise the information by selecting and reporting the main features, and make comparisons where relevant.*

Write at least 150 words.

Rainfall

No. of wet days

▌ average mm per month

Temperature

▌ average daily high/low

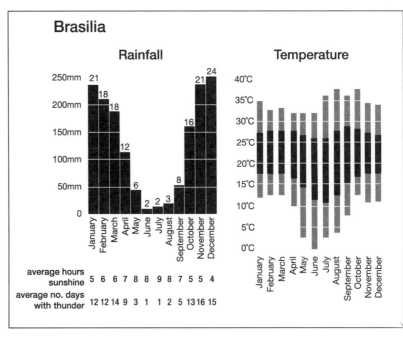

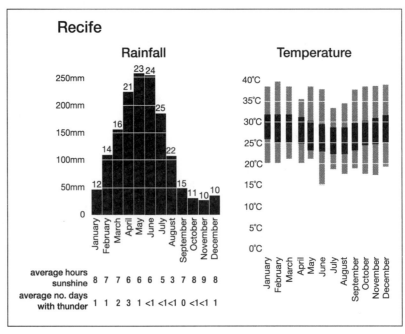

Writing Task 2

You should spend about 40 minutes on this task.

Write about the following topic:

> **Some people choose to eat no meat or fish.**
>
> **They believe that this is not only better for their own health but also benefits the world as a whole.**
>
> **Discuss this view and give your own opinion.**

Give reasons for your answer and include any relevant examples from your own knowledge or experience.

Write at least 250 words.

Speaking Part 1

The examiner will ask you some questions about yourself, your home, work or studies and familiar topics.

Let's talk about your free time.

Do you have a lot of free time?
What do you like to do when you are at home?
Do you spend more time with your family or with friends?
Where do you go when you go out?
Is there enough to do in your home town?

The examiner will then ask you some questions about one or two other topics, for example:

Now let's talk about keeping fit.

Do you try to keep fit? How?
Do you think it's important for young people to keep fit?
Is sport compulsory for schoolchildren in your country?
Do you do any sports? Which do you like best?
Have you ever watched a sporting event live?

Speaking Part 2

The examiner will give you a topic on a card like the one on the right and ask you to talk about it for one to two minutes. Before you talk you have one minute to think about what you're going to say. The examiner will give you some paper and a pencil so you can make notes if you want to.

The examiner may ask one or two more questions when you have finished, for example:

Are you good at making decisions?
Do you think you usually make the right decisions?

> **Describe an important decision you had to make.**
> **You should say:**
> **what you had to decide**
> **what or who helped you decide**
> **if you made the right decision**
> **and explain why the decision was important.**

Speaking Part 3

The examiner will ask some more general questions which follow on from the topic in Part 2.

Do you think it's harder to make decisions nowadays because we have so many choices?
What are the disadvantages of asking for other people's advice when making a decision?
Why do you think some people are better at making decisions than others?
Do you think children should be given the opportunity to make their own decisions? What kind of decisions?
Some people say we only learn by making mistakes. Do you agree?

Test 1   Key

LISTENING SECTION 1

Training

Useful language: spelling

2 O R U and W don't fit in any of the columns.

A	E	I	S
H	C	Y	F
J	G		L
K	T		N
	V		X

3 1 B O R O U G H
   2 J A Y W I C K
   3 F R A V E L L I
   4 Q U A R R Y S I D E
   5 C H A R L E S W O R T H
   6 K I M M A R S H A L L

Useful language: numbers

1 391   2 48   3 07862 335201
4 1899   5 117   6 454.50

Useful language: dates

1 21(st) September* / September 21
2 1(st) February 1986 / February 1, 1986 / 01/02/86 / 02/01/86
3 31(st) March / March 31
4 14(th) December / December 14
5 11(th) January / January 11
6 7(th) August / August 7

the 21st of September, the 1st of February, etc. are also possible

Useful language: measurements

1 8,850 metres / meters / m
2 658 kilometres / kilometers / km
3 180 centimetres / centimeters / cm
4 150 grams / grammes / g
5 62 kilogram(me)s / kilos / kg
6 1 metre / meter / m 65 centimetres / centimeters / cm
   or 1.65 metres / meters / m

Useful language: deciding what to write in the gaps

Which gaps need ...	What tells you this?
a date? **1**	starts on
a distance? **3**	on average
only numbers? Example; **2**	lasts; days; years
a price? **5**	costs; £
a website address? **8**	www.; .com
• a meal or kind of food? **6**	food
• a place? **9**	spent ... in the
• a facility? **7**	Camp site has a
• clothes or a piece of equipment? **4**	Hats provided
• an event? **10**	take place

Exam practice

Questions 1–10

Example The two holidays last fourteen and ten days. The woman chooses the ten-day holiday. She says: 'I think the ten-day trip is better.'

1 **17th April / 17 April / April 17**
Distraction 27th April and 10th April. They are wrong because the man says that the trip 'finishes' on 27th April and the woman says she '**can't leave work**' before the 10th of April.

2 **16 / sixteen**
Distraction The man mentions '12' and '14'. 12 is wrong because that is the number of people booked on the trip 'at the moment'; 14 is wrong because that will be the number with the woman and her sister. Neither is the maximum possible number. The woman asks, 'Is it a big group?'; 'the maximum number [= no more than]'.

3 **45 km / forty-five km / kilometres / kilometers**
Distraction The man mentions '35 km' and '50 km'. The shortest distance is 35 km and the longest distance is 50 km but neither is the 'average'.
'distances' tells you that you will soon hear the answer; 'approximately ... a day [= on average]'.

4 **(swimming) pool**
Distraction 'restaurants' and 'en-suite facilities' are mentioned but the man says 'all' the hotels (not just 'some') have these; 'gym' is wrong because 'none of them' has one.

5 **1,013**
Distraction 1,177 is wrong because this price includes flights.

6 **snacks**
Distraction 'breakfast', 'packed lunch' and 'dinner' are all mentioned but these are included in the price.

7 **(cycle) helmet**
Distraction 'lock', 'bell', 'lights', 'small bag' and 'pannier' are all mentioned but they 'come with the bike' so you don't need to bring them.
You know that the answer is coming when after listing what the holiday company provides, the man says '**But** we won't allow you to cycle unless you bring ...'.

8 **ballantyne** (you can write this in small or capital letters)

9 **route** [alterations = changes]
Distraction 'tracks' get muddy but they don't change.

10 **theatre / theater** 'a guide who'll take you round [= guided tour]'.
Distraction 'castles and museums' are visited but there aren't any other tours.

LISTENING SECTION 2

Training

Useful language: paraphrasing

1 e **2** c **3** a **4** g **5** i **6** b **7** d **8** f
9 j **10** h

Exam practice

Questions 11–14

11 A

Distraction B: 'It was originally … in front of the cathedral' but later 'it was moved'. It was never 'beside' the cathedral; C: 'at the beginning of the twentieth century it was moved to a site by the river' but John goes on to say it found another 'home' 'in the 1960s'. Although 'there are plans to move [the market] back …' these are for some time in the future, not now.

12 C

Distraction A: Antique furniture is sold on 'one new stall', not 'on only one day'; B: Local produce [= 'fresh fruit and vegetables, meat and cheese from the area'] is sold from 'Tuesday to Saturday'.

13 B

Distraction A: Ice cream is served with the cake in one café but the area isn't famous for the ice cream; C: John says 'Our fish is good of course but there isn't one particular dish that stands out'.

14 B

Distraction A: Fish can be bought from the fishermen but this isn't a change ('They've been doing that for as long as anyone can remember …'); C: There are more restaurants ('a couple of new ones have opened recently') not fewer.

Questions 15–20

15 D

Distraction C: The entertainment is in 'one of the cafés with live music' in the area.
Distraction F: 'it doesn't look out over the water', so it doesn't have good views.
Distraction G: It is in 'one of the busiest parts of the town', so it isn't a quiet location.
Distraction H: It doesn't have a wide menu – John just mentions 'delicious fresh fish and seafood'.

16 H

Distraction E: It's not good value because prices 'are from mid-range to fairly expensive'.
Distraction F: 'it also misses out on the sea view'.
Distraction G: It 'is on the main road' so it isn't in a 'quiet location'.

17 F

Distraction G: John says it 'is in the city centre' so it's not in a 'quiet location'.
Distraction D: 'you may have to wait to be served' so the service isn't 'excellent'.

18 G

Distraction B: John says 'You can't park your car there …';
E: 'It's not cheap'.

19 C

Distraction H: It serves 'beautifully prepared Greek dishes' so it doesn't have a 'wide menu'; D: 'Service can be slow' so it's not 'excellent'.

20 A

Distraction H: 'There are only a few dishes on the menu'.

LISTENING SECTION 3

Exam practice

Questions 21–26

21 C

Distraction 'equipment' is wrong because Reza says 'I'll make notes for myself about what lighting I'm going to need ... a good range of equipment, but I'll need to make a list for each location for my own reference' (he will decide on the lighting equipment himself so they won't discuss it).

22 E: The word 'roadworks' tells you when to listen for the answer to 22 but it does not come immediately.

23 G

24 A

25 H: The meaning of 'understudies' is given before you hear the word.

26 B

Distraction Mike mentions 'costumes' but points out they 'don't actually need' any.

Questions 27–30

27 B: It's outside the mill, by the window.
Distraction Helen mentions a mirror but says they decided not to use it.

28 A: They are on the inside, next to the wall behind the wheel.
Distraction Helen mentions torches but says the actors will be carrying them.

29 E: [wooden = made of wood]
Distraction Mike says the lights won't shine directly on the screen.

30 G: [huge = large]
Distraction Mike mentions the bike, but he is referring to how the girl arrives at the mill.

LISTENING SECTION 4

Training

Useful language: following the speaker

Suggested answers (other answers are possible)

1 D	**6** A	**11** A	**16** B
2 A	**7** B	**12** A	**17** D
3 C/D	**8** A/B	**13** B	**18** B
4 A/B	**9** D	**14** A/C	**19** A/C
5 A/B	**10** A	**15** A/C	**20** A/B

Exam practice

Questions 31–40

31 **(the) Atlantic (Ocean)**

32 **(luxury) food (source)**
Distraction Rabbits' 'fur' is mentioned but there is no suggestion they were imported for the fur to be 'used for' something.

33 **(in) gardens**
Distraction 'nests' are what the ants make, not their 'habitat' (which is what this column is about).

34 **earthworm / earth worm**

35 **soil (condition)**
Distraction 'natives', 'native species' and 'locals' are all mentioned but the pests 'displace' these, they do not improve them.

36 **North(-)west / north(-)west**
Distraction 'Scotland' and 'Iceland' are mentioned, but they are names of countries so they cannot be the adjective in front of 'Europe'.

37 **plant pots**
Distraction 'ornamental shrubs' are mentioned but the flatworms came in the earth in the pots, not the plants.

38 **seaweed(s) / sea weed(s)**

39 **United States / USA**

40 **(new) competitors**

READING PASSAGE 1
Exam practice

Questions 1–6

1 **TRUE**: The first paragraph says 'But Peter Falkingham has done little of that for a while now' ('that' refers back to 'field workers camped in the desert in the hot sun [= outdoor research]').

2 **TRUE**: The third paragraph talks about the model making 'several attempts': 'This, perhaps unsurprisingly, results almost without fail in the animal falling on its face. So the computer alters the activation pattern and tries again ... usually to similar effect' (Sellers and Manning are mentioned in the previous paragraph but there is nothing about a computer model).

3 **FALSE**: The text says speeds for humans on the computer model matched what they can do in real life: 'And indeed, using the same method for living animals (humans, emu and ostriches) similar top speeds were achieved on the computer as in reality'.

4 **NOT GIVEN**: The sentence at the end of the third paragraph says the Manchester team are 'confident in the results' (about how dinosaurs moved) but there is no mention of some palaeontologists expressing reservations.

5 **FALSE**: The fifth paragraph talks about modern-day trackers being able to analyse the tracks of wild animals and the next sentence compares this to analysing fossil tracks which is much harder to do: 'But a fossil track poses a more considerable challenge to interpret in the same way.'

6 **NOT GIVEN**: The sixth paragraph says Falkingham uses digital mud to simulate prehistoric mud but it doesn't say anything about the research being inaccurate.

Questions 7–9

7 **sail**: 'There are also those who believe that the spines acted as a support for a sail. Of these, ... and the other half think it was used as a temperature-regulating device [= control body heat].'
Distraction 'hump' is wrong because it is thought it 'stored fat and water', not that it controlled temperature.

8 **narrow**: You need an adjective to describe the shape or size of the skull: 'The skull seems out of proportion with its thick, heavy body because it is so narrow ...'.
Distraction Its body is 'thick' and 'heavy' and its jaws are 'delicate and fine'.

9 **Locomotion**: 'It has a deep broad tail and powerful [= highly developed] leg muscles to aid [= make easier] locomotion.'

Questions 10–13

The sixth paragraph is about Peter Falkingham's computer model (title of the flow-chart).

10 **moisture**: 'Falkingham uses computational techniques to … and control the moisture content, consistency [= texture and thickness], and other conditions to simulate the mud of prehistoric times.'

11 **stress**: 'stress values [= levels of stress] can be extracted and calculated [= measured] from inside it'.

12 **ground**: 'By running hundreds of these simulations simultaneously [= multiple simulations] on supercomputers, Falkingham can start to understand … over a given kind of ground.'
Distraction 'tracks' is wrong because it means the same as 'footprints'.

13 **fossil tracks**: 'researchers can make sense of fossil tracks with greater confidence [= more accurate interpretation].' (Both words are necessary here as 'tracks' could mean any tracks.)

READING PASSAGE 2
Exam practice

Questions 14–20

14 **C**: Paragraphs C and D mention insects. Paragraph C mentions a specific insect – fruit flies: 'Meanwhile, a fruit fly, with a brain containing only a fraction of the computing power, can effortlessly navigate in three dimensions.'
Distraction Paragraph D is wrong because it talks about robots copying insects but not about a particular insect.

15 **D**: Paragraph D mentions robots learning from their mistakes [= bumping into things]: the text says '... the unorthodox idea of tiny "insectoid" robots that learned to walk by bumping into things instead of computing mathematically the precise position of their feet'.
Distraction The other paragraphs all talk about robots learning things and what they can't do but they don't mention them 'learning from their mistakes'.

16 B: Paragraph B mentions mathematicians and computer scientists who are 'optimistic [= not put off]' about the possibilities: the text says 'But a sizeable number of mathematicians and computer scientists, who are specialists in the area, [= many researchers] are optimistic about the possibilities. To them it is only a matter of time [= will eventually] before a thinking machine [= Artificial Intelligence] walks out of the laboratory [= be developed]'.
Distraction The researchers [= scientists] in Paragraph A are negative about the future. Paragraph D is about past research and Paragraph E mentions people who believe AI will be developed but they aren't 'many researchers'.

17 D: The text says 'He changed the course of research when he explored the unorthodox idea of tiny "insectoid" robots … Today many of the descendants of Brooks' insectoid robots are on Mars gathering data for NASA … For all their successes in mimicking the behaviour of insects, however …'.
Distraction In Paragraph C, robots are mentioned which had 'limited' success but the reference is to the past (whereas the approach in Paragraph D is still having some success on Mars).

18 A: Paragraph A says 'Physicist Roger Penrose of Oxford University and others [= some academics] believe that machines are physically incapable of human thought [= doubt the possibility of creating Artificial Intelligence]'.
Distraction Paragraphs B, E and F talk about creating Artificial Intelligence in the future as something very possible, not something that is in doubt; Paragraph D says that there are problems creating Artificial Intelligence but it talks about partial successes.

19 F: Paragraph F says 'There is no universal consensus [= generally accepted agreement] as to …, in human terms, what consciousness means [= what our brains do]'.
Distraction Paragraph B says 'the basic laws of intelligence remain a mystery' (there is no mention of a lack of agreement).

20 C: The text says that humans learn by extending what we already know but 'Robots know only what has been programmed into them'.
Distraction Paragraph D is about robots being unable to copy the behaviour patterns of higher mammals [= humans] rather than about them extending their own intelligence.

Questions 21–23

21 D: Colin McGinn says Artificial Intelligence 'is like sheep trying to do complicated psychoanalysis. They just don't have the conceptual equipment …'.
Distraction A is wrong because although McGinn mentions psychoanalysis, he is using it as an example of how intelligent humans are compared to machines (he is not referring to feelings).

22 C: Marvin Minsky says 'But then we started to try to make machines that could answer questions about simple children's stories. There's no machine today that can do that'.
Distraction B is wrong because although Minsky talks about different parts of the brain, he doesn't say that different kinds of people use different parts.

23 A: Hans Moravec says 'Without emotions to guide them, [brain-damaged people] debate endlessly over their options … as robots become more intelligent and are able to make choices, they could likewise become paralysed with indecision. To aid them, robots of the future might need to have emotions hardwired into their brains'.
Distraction E is wrong because Moravec says robots will be programmed to feel fear but doesn't mention whether people should be frightened of them or not.

Questions 24–26

Suggested words to underline: early robots; 'top-down' approach; unable to recognise; Rodney Brooks; collecting information

The summary is about the second half of Paragraph B, and Paragraphs C and D.

'Prototype robots' (in Paragraph C) tells you that part of the text is about early robots.

'Weaknesses' in the summary means 'shortcomings' which is in Paragraph C. The previous paragraph mentions the 'top-down approach' so you need to read that as well.

24 disc: 'top-down approach' is at the end of Paragraph B so that is where the answer is (the instructions allow only one word per gap, so 'single disc' is not correct).
Distraction 'computer' is wrong because the disc is put into the robot. The computer is used to program the disc.

25 patterns: Paragraph C says 'Our brains, like the fruit fly's, unconsciously recognise what we see by performing countless calculations. This unconscious awareness of patterns is exactly what computers are missing.'
Distraction 'what we see' doesn't make sense and is more than one word; 'common sense' is wrong because you can't 'recognise' common sense; it is also two words.

26 Mars: Paragraph D says 'Today many of the descendants of Brooks' insectoid robots [= robots similar to those invented by Brooks] are on Mars gathering data [= collecting information] for NASA'.
Distraction 'NASA' is wrong because that is where the information is sent, not where the robots are.

READING PASSAGE 3
Exam practice
Questions 27–32

27 YES: The first paragraph refers to the ideas: 'By 2050 only a small number [= a handful of] languages will be flourishing [= almost all humans will speak one of a handful of megalanguages (mega = big)].'

28 NO: The words 'too limited' suggest an attitude towards the work ['efforts' = what they have done] of the Australian linguists. This implies they should have done more, so it is critical of them: the writer is positive about Australian linguists' work, not critical, saying they 'achieved a great deal in terms of preserving traditional languages', and adds that the 'initiative' by the Australian government 'has resulted in good documentation of most … Aboriginal languages'.

29 YES: 'the use of technology' in the text is digital recording and storage, and internet and mobile phone technologies. The writer mentions these methods, as an example of what he says in the previous sentence: 'there is growing evidence that not all approaches to the preservation of languages will be particularly helpful [= unsatisfactory]'. He then describes how these technologies encourage an unsatisfactory method of research: 'the "quick dash" style of recording trip ... That's not quite what some endangered-language specialists have been seeking for more than 30 years ... Michael Krauss ... has often complained that linguists are playing with non-essentials while most of their raw data is disappearing'. *NOTE It's important to read all round the relevant part of the text when you are looking for the answer.*

30 NOT GIVEN: 'overshadowed' implies that Chomsky's political views have been more important or better known than his academic work. Although he refers to both, the writer does not compare Chomsky's political views with his academic work in terms of their importance or fame: 'Chomsky ... has been the great man of theoretical linguistics for far longer than he has been known as a political commentator'; there is no suggestion that one has 'overshadowed' the other.

31 YES: 'documentary linguists observe ... Such work calls for persistent [= long-term] funding [= financial support]'.

32 NO: The writer tells us about Chomsky's attitude to disappearing languages ('He has recently begun to speak in support of language preservation'), but he does not suggest Chomsky is 'too emotional' about it. In fact he thinks Chomsky's reasons are 'unsentimental', which means the opposite.

Questions 33–36

33 D: 'Worried about the loss of rainforests and the ozone layer? Well, neither of those is doing any worse than a large majority of the 6,000 to 7,000 languages that remain in use on Earth.' *Distraction* A: The writer doesn't dismiss concern about environmental issues as unfounded; B: He doesn't say anything about the attitudes of academics in relation to 'the loss of rainforests and the ozone layer'; C: The text talks about different kinds of linguists but not academics in other subjects.

34 A: In the second paragraph Evans says 'speakers become less able to express the wealth of knowledge that has filled ancestors' lives with meaning [= ideas are part of their culture]'. *Distraction* B: Evans suggests that the lost language has a better vocabulary for the landscape than the creole, but he does not mention speakers of a creole not understanding older members of the community; C: The 'few words' are mentioned to illustrate how the range of vocabulary in the creole is poorer than the original language, not that it is clearer or more concise; D: The writer doesn't mention accessing practical information.

35 C: In the third paragraph the writer says '... language-loss hotspots such as West Africa and South America'. (The metaphor 'hotspot' can mean somewhere where there is a lot of activity, so a 'language-loss hotspot' is a place experiencing severe problems with language loss.) *Distraction* A: The text refers to the training of linguists in England as well as these places; it doesn't mention the language used by linguists in these countries; B: Austin, who heads the programme, is Australian, but 'programme' implies other trainers

as well, whose nationality is not mentioned. Therefore we don't know that the linguists were all trained by Australians; D: The fact that 'many documentary linguists' have been trained there does not tell us how many undocumented languages there are.

36 A: The fourth paragraph says 'Michael Krauss ... has often complained that linguists are playing with non-essentials [= technologies] while most of their raw data is disappearing'. *Distraction* B: Krauss is one of the 'endangered-language specialists' who do not think this use of technology is needed; C: It is the 'raw data' that is declining. Krauss's opinion about the numbers of people interested in studying linguistics is not mentioned; D: Krauss's opinion about funding in universities is not mentioned.

Questions 37–40

37 C: Austin is mentioned in both paragraph three and paragraph seven. Only paragraph seven describes Austin's beliefs about language. 'Austin and Co.' means Austin and others like him. (Used like this, 'and Co.' is an informal expression.) Paragraph seven says that 'Austin and Co. are in no doubt that ... languages are unique, even if they ... have common underlying features'. *Distraction* A: This makes grammatical sense, but 'every' language is not 'in danger'; B, D, G: These endings fit grammatically, but are not mentioned in the text.

38 A: The seventh paragraph says that Evans talks about language communities which may 'oppose efforts to preserve' their languages. Because they are described as 'endangered' we know that they are 'in danger of disappearing'. *Distraction* D: The communities described believe that retaining their languages may actually have disadvantages. 'They may have given up using the language with their children, believing they will benefit from speaking a more widely understood one'; G: It is not realising 'what is involved', it is the people's existing attitude to their language; B, C, E, F: These endings fit grammatically, but are not mentioned in the text.

39 F: The opposite of 'practical' in this context is 'theoretical', and the text mentions the 'emphasis on theory'. There are two options which mention theory (B) or theoretical linguistics (F) [prevalence = widespread influence / popularity / dominance]. The eighth paragraph says 'Plenty of students continue to be drawn to the intellectual thrill of linguistics field work'. *Distraction* A: Field work is not 'in danger of disappearing' even if students' enthusiasm is gradually worn down; B: cannot be the correct answer because 'the linguistics profession's emphasis on theory gradually wears down the enthusiasm of linguists who work in communities'; G: It is not realising 'what is involved' [harsh and even hazardous places] that 'wears down the enthusiasm', it is the 'emphasis on theory'; C, D, E: These endings fit grammatically, but do not make sense.

40 B: The eighth paragraph says 'Chomsky ... believes that good descriptive work requires thorough theoretical understanding [= a strong basis in theory]'. *Distraction* A: There is no mention of field work being in danger of disappearing; E: He does not mention 'drawbacks'; F: Chomsky's view about this is not mentioned in the text; D: This works grammatically, but Chomsky's 'interests are mostly theoretical', not 'practical'.

WRITING TASK 1

Training

STRATEGIES

Before you write

A Reading the question

1 The first part of the question tells you what the data is about – the percentage of the population living in urban areas in the whole world and in different parts of the world.

The rest of the question reminds you to (1) select and (2) report the main features and (3) to make comparisons.

2 The title of this bar chart tells you that it shows changes in the percentage of the world's population living in cities.

3 The three bars represent three years, 1950, 2007 and 2030. The chart shows changes that have already taken place as well as predicting future changes.

4 The numbers represent percentages.

5 The bar chart contains information about the world as a whole and about five regions of the world.

B Understanding the data

1 ✓

2 ✗ This bar chart gives information about the percentage of the population living in urban areas in **five** regions of the world **and the world as a whole**, in three different years, 1950, 2007 and 2030.

3 ✓

4 ✗ According to the chart, ~~more~~ a higher percentage of North Americans already live in cities than the rest of the world. ('more' suggests the actual number is greater, but the chart does not give us numbers, only percentages, so we cannot be sure.)

5 ✓

6 ✗ According to this chart, ~~there will be twice as many~~ the percentage of Latin Americans and Caribbeans living in cities in 2030 ~~as there were~~ will be twice what it was eighty years earlier (the chart does not give information about population growth or actual numbers, only about the percentage of the population in cities).

7 ✓

C Selecting from the data

1 2

2 7

3 Three from 1, 3, 4, 5, 6

D Writing a summary

1 1 shows

2 compares

3 doubled

4 marked

5 whereas

6 greatest

7 smaller

8 in spite of

2 The longest part of the answer is the comparisons and contrasts.

After you write

E Checking your answer

1 'approximatly' instead of 'approximately' (line 10)

2 a 1 area > areas;
    2 result > results (see Corrected summary for repeated errors)
  b those
  c 4 *there isn't any* > there is no (contracted forms are informal and therefore inappropriate; the style should be neutral or formal) *that* > where (relative pronoun)
    5 *is also seen* > can also be seen (impersonal structure)
    6 *the Latin America* > Latin America (the definite article is only used in the names of countries and regions before descriptors such as 'united', e.g. The United Arab Emirates, or in structures with 'of', e.g. The People's Republic of China, not before North, South, etc.)
    7 *By comparing* > In terms of / When we compare 'By comparing' should relate to the subject of the finite verb 'have'. But that subject is 'Europe, Asia and Africa', so that does not make sense.
  d 'region(s)'

Corrected IELTS candidate's summary

This answer is only one possible interpretation of the task. Other approaches are also valid.

In the chart we can see the percentage of the population who live in urban **areas** in the years 1950, 2007 and 2030. The first three columns show us the **results** in the whole world and the other columns show the **results** in different parts of the world.

What is very obvious from the chart is that the number of people living in urban **areas** and also **those** moving to urban **areas** is growing quite fast in all **regions** of the world and there **is no region where** the percentage has come down. It **can also be seen** that in North America and **Latin America** this percentage is higher than other parts. **In terms of** the proportion of people in cities in the rest of the world, Europe, Asia and Africa respectively have the highest percentages.

The increase in the number of people in urban **areas** is such that it is estimated that in the year 2030, **approximately** 60% of the people in the world will be living in urban **areas**.

This writer's first language influences him/her when s/he forgets to use plural forms.

Useful language: contrasting facts and ideas

1 The profits of both companies declined, so the candidate should not have used a contrastive structure (On the other hand …). The sentences could be joined with 'and'.

2 This is a real contrast, but the candidate has made a grammatical mistake because s/he has started a new sentence with 'Whereas'.

3 **a** However   **b** whereas

4 **1** while   **2** On the other hand   **3** By contrast
  4 whereas   **5** However

5 *Possible answers*
  1 For the workforce, working conditions have always been more important than wages, whereas profitability has been the main concern of the management.
  2 In the United States, people tend to eat early in the evening. By contrast, in Spain, few people eat before nine o'clock.
  3 These two sentences do not give contrasting information.
  Suggested answer:
  Both the students at the state university and those attending a private college showed an improved performance in the tests.
  4 Home computers were a rarity in the 1980s while the majority of families have at least one computer now.
  5 Car ownership has risen sharply in rural areas. On the other hand, the provision of public transport has declined.
  6 A sense of humour is rated as essential by 90% of women who are looking for a partner. However, only 70% of women say they want to meet someone wealthy.

Useful language: expressing percentages, proportions and quantities

ten percent (of)   a small/low percentage (of)   a/one tenth (of)
one out of ten   a small minority of   few (of)   hardly any (of)

Useful language: talking about numbers as they get bigger and smaller

1 **1** e   **2** a   **3** f   **4** b   **5** c   **6** d

2 **1** rise, increase, go up, grow, double, decrease, shrink, halve, fall, go down
  2 grow, expand, shrink, contract
  3 rise, increase, go up, double, decrease, halve, fall, go down

3 **1** will decrease/shrink/will go down/will fall
  2 has risen/increased/gone up
  3 halved
  4 has risen/increased/grown/gone up/expanded
  5 doubled
  6 will decrease/fall/go down

Useful language: writing about information in a chart or graph

1 **a** It can be seen that

2 **b** It is clear that

3 **b** It is easy to see that

4 **b** The pie chart shows

5 **b** The graphs provide information about

6 **b** From the charts we can see

Exam practice

Model answer
This answer is only one possible interpretation of the task. Other approaches are also valid.

> This bar chart compares the growth in the percentage of the population living in urban areas in six different regions of the world.
> According to the chart, between 1950 and 2007 the percentage of the population living in cities in Latin America and the Caribbean almost doubled, from 42% to 76%, whereas in Europe it only increased by 21%. However, in Europe over half the people already lived in cities in 1950.
> When we compare the projected increases in Asia and Europe by 2050 we see that in Asia the percentage will continue to grow at the same speed, with a further increase of 25%, whereas in Europe the change will be even slower than before, increasing by only 12%. By 2050, the vast majority (around 90%) of people in Latin America, the Caribbean and North America will live in cities. Even in Africa, more than half the population (62%) will live in urban areas by then.

WRITING TASK 2
Training
STRATEGIES
Before you write

A   Reading the question

1 40 minutes. You should spend at least five minutes planning, and allow five minutes for checking, so you need to write your answer in half an hour.

2 continuous coverage of sport on television

3 discourages the young from taking part in any sport

4 You can decide whether you agree completely, partly, or not at all. As long as what you write is relevant, you can say what you like.

5 Reasons for your opinion and relevant examples

6 At least 250 words. You will lose marks if you write less, but you will not gain marks for a much longer answer unless it is all relevant and the language is accurate.

7 *Suggested answers*
  non-stop/24-hour/round-the-clock broadcasting/transmission

8 *Suggested answers*
  makes young people/teenagers less keen on/enthusiastic about / dissuades young people/teenagers from / puts young people/teenagers off participating in/engaging in/getting involved in

B   Planning your answer

b Stage 1

c Stage 2

d Stage 3

C Developing a clearly structured argument

1 1 b 2 a 3 c 4 e 5 d 6 j 7 f 8 h 9 i 10 g

2 Stage 3 takes more than one paragraph. This is the writer's opinion, the main part of the essay.

Useful language: style

1 B is a more suitable style for an essay, which should be written in a formal or neutral style.

2 1 I've 2 kids are getting; grown-ups 3 – here means 'for example' or 'that is to say' 4 I think; I've seen; let; do nothing 5 more and more 6 And
Note: Nothing in A is incorrect in informal writing or speech.

3 1 In my opinion [= I think]; adult behaviour [= the way grown-ups behave] 2 are permitted 3 it is noticeable that 4 remain inactive 5 should 6 Moreover

4 1 people dislike; they are unlikely to 2 As I see it; make no difference 3 television; rarely played

Useful language: impersonal structures

1 1 It is true that
2 It is obviously necessary to
3 It is no doubt true that
4 It is a fact that

2 *Possible answers*
1 It is unlucky / a pity / a shame that
2 No one can deny that
3 It is clear why
4 Most people agree that
5 It is unlucky / a pity / a shame that
6 People often say/maintain that
7 People tend to believe that
8 I accept that

3 *Possible answers*
1 It is understandable that children prefer watching cartoons to doing their homework.
2 It is often assumed that music is a universal language.
3 It is no doubt true that careless driving is the cause of many serious accidents.

Useful language: *the* and no article

1 the (followed by 'of'); – ('wealth' is uncountable, and mentioned generally in this sentence)

2 the (there is only one Internet); the ('necessary' shows this is some particular information, not general)

3 – – – ('money', 'love' and 'good teaching' are all uncountable nouns, talking about these things in general)

4 – (uncountable, general); the (followed by 'of'); – (uncountable, general)

5 the (followed by 'of'); – (uncountable); the (followed by 'of' although this is implied, not actually stated)

6 – ('governments' is plural, and are mentioned in general); – (uncountable, general); the (referring to the particular children already mentioned); – (uncountable)

Useful language: giving reasons

1 a This is not true <u>for</u> a number of reasons.

2 b Some people have a wide knowledge of the world <u>as a result of</u> travelling.

3 b In society today, <u>because of</u> the advance of science and technology, people know more than they used to.

4 b They gave free educational materials to the children <u>so that</u> the children were more likely to attend classes.

5 b I assume <u>the reason for this</u> is that media companies are producing better films nowadays.

6 a In those countries women's rights are more developed <u>and, as a consequence,</u> women are more fairly treated there.

Useful language: paragraphing

This answer is only one possible interpretation of the task. Other approaches are also valid.

These days, it is noticeable that young people are becoming less interested in team games, sports and other forms of exercise. It is my belief that this is mainly because of our everyday work, which is increasingly sedentary. Besides, I think every person would admit that sitting and relaxing is much easier than moving and running and sweating.
[She has introduced the topic and now starts to question it.]
new para The question is, how much of this laziness is because of the sports programmes on television? From one point of view it could be true that these programmes make young people lazy. However, this may be because some people who like sport, and also like watching sports, are attracted to the television programmes and spend so much time watching sport that there is no spare time for them to participate themselves.
[She is now going to look at another aspect of the matter.]
new para By contrast, watching sport may encourage some other young people to take up sport, as these individuals might like that sport and consequently want to try it to see how it feels. Watching such programmes on television can make us feel that we want to be active, want to play basketball, or go swimming and so on. Thus, I would suggest that there are positive aspects of watching sports programmes.
[She is now going to explain the conclusion she has reached.]
new para In my opinion, the fundamental issue is the reason why we like sport. Does an individual like sport merely as a spectator or as a participant? If the reason is simply the pleasure of watching other people playing volleyball or football or even dancing, that person will never want to be among those who take part. However, if a person enjoys being active and joining in, then sports programmes will never prevent this.

Exam practice

Model answer
See corrected answer above.

SPEAKING PART 1

Training

Useful language: adding information to your answers

1 1 For six years. ('for' is correct because six years is a period of time. You can use 'since' with a point of time in the past, e.g. since 2002 / last summer.)

2 Yes, they do. (The present simple is needed here because it is a fact. The short answer needs to agree with the auxiliary verb in the question – 'do'.)

3 They were fun. ('funny' is used to talk about something that made you laugh, like a film or a joke.)

4 I studied Spanish until I was 14. ('until I was 14' means it is now finished so the present perfect cannot be used.)

5 Go to a class. (not a particular one)

2 **a** 5   **b** 2   **c** 4   **d** 1   **e** 3

SPEAKING PART 2

Training

Useful language: adjectives for describing people

a a creative person – imaginative, inventive

b a funny person – amusing, entertaining, witty

c a kind person – considerate, sympathetic

d a positive person – cheerful, encouraging, optimistic

e a strong person – courageous, determined, reliable

SPEAKING PART 3

Training

Useful language: giving opinions

1 **In** my opinion,

2 As far as I am **concerned,**

3 There are several reasons **for** my opinion.

4 I strongly disagree **with** the idea that …

5 I ~~am~~ completely agree **with** this opinion.

6 From ~~the~~ **my** point of ~~my~~ view, …

7 ✓

8 You can say 'According to my father / the latest research', etc., but not '~~According to my point of view~~'. You can say 'My point of view is …' or 'From my point of view, …'

9 ✓

10 You can say 'In my opinion' but not '~~In my own opinion~~'. Also, you don't need to say 'I think' when you have already said 'In my opinion'.

11 ✓

12 ✓

13 See 8 above. You can use 'According to' with a noun, e.g. 'the President', or pronoun, e.g. 'him', but not ~~me~~ or ~~myself~~.

Useful language: easily confused words and expressions

1 1 **strict**: If someone is 'strict' they limit the behaviour of others; 'restricted' is used to say something is limited, e.g. a view, a menu, membership, etc.

2 **brought up**: People 'grow up' but they are 'brought up' by others, usually parents.

3 **extended**: Aunts, uncles, cousins, grandparents, etc. are your extended family; 'joint' is used for something shared between two or more people, e.g. a bank account.

4 **elderly**: The adjective 'elderly' is used as a respectful way to say 'old'; 'elder' is used to talk about people in one family, e.g. 'My elder brother'.

5 **single**: In a 'single-parent family' the children live with their father or mother but not both; 'sole' is used to mean 'single' before nouns like 'purpose', 'responsibility', 'concern'.

6 **behaviour**: We say 'bad/good behaviour'; 'behaving' is part of a verb.

7 **allow**: 'allow' is followed by an object ('them') and the *to*-infinitive, 'let' is not. We can say 'let them do' but not '~~let them to do~~'.

8 **society**: We don't need 'the' as we are talking about society in general, not one particular society.

TEST 1   TRANSCRIPT

Spelling

🎧 **02** 1 A   E   I   S

🎧 **03** 2 C F G H J K L N O R T U V W X Y

🎧 **04** 3

1 My address is 23 Borough Road. That's <u>B–O–R–O–U–G–H.</u>
2 Send your application to Jaywick Ltd. That's <u>J–A–Y–W–I–C–K.</u>
3 My name is Anna Fravelli. I'll spell that for you.
   <u>F–R–A–V–E double L–I.</u>
4 We'll meet outside Quarryside School. That's
   <u>Q–U–A double R–Y–S–I–D–E.</u>
5 You need to get a bus to my village. It's Charlesworth. That's
   <u>C–H–A–R–L–E–S–W–O–R–T–H.</u>
6 Have a look at my website. It's www dot kimmarshall dot com.
   That's <u>K–I double M–A–R–S–H–A double L.</u>

🎧 **05** **Numbers**

1 I live at <u>391</u> King Street.
2 A family ticket is cheaper. It's only <u>$48.</u>
3 You can ring me on my mobile. The number is <u>07862 335201.</u>
4 The theatre, which is very old, has been open since <u>1899.</u>
5 Take the application to the secretary who is in Room <u>117.</u>
6 Your flight will be <u>£454.50</u> including taxes.

🎧 **06** **Dates**

1 The first day of the course is the <u>21st of September.</u>
2 I was born on the <u>1st of February 1986.</u>
3 I have an appointment with Dr Andrews on the <u>31st of March.</u>
4 We're getting married in <u>December.</u> On the <u>14th.</u>
5 I will fly into New York on the <u>11th of January.</u>
6 You need to come for an interview on the <u>7th of August.</u>

🎧 **07** **Measurements**

1 Mount Everest is <u>8,850 metres</u> high.
2 It's <u>658 kilometres</u> from Wellington to Auckland.
3 John is <u>180 centimetres</u> tall.
4 Mix the sugar with <u>150 grams</u> of flour.
5 I weigh <u>62 kilograms.</u>
6 The desk I bought is <u>1 metre 65 centimetres</u> across.

🎧 **08** **LISTENING SECTION 1**

You will hear a telephone conversation between a woman and a man who works for a holiday company, about a holiday she would like to go on. First you have some time to look at questions 1 to 6.

[Pause the recording for 30 seconds.]

You will see that there is an example that has been done for you. On this occasion only, the conversation relating to this will be played first.

Man: 'Holidays for You'. Sean speaking. Can I help you?

Woman: Oh hi. I've been looking at your website. Um, I'm interested in a cycling holiday in Austria in April.

Man: Ah! We have two trips in April – one lasts fourteen days and the other ten days.

Woman: Mm … I think the **(Example)** <u>10</u>-day trip is better. So let's see. I've got a calendar here. What are the dates?

The length of the trip that the woman chooses is 10 days, so '10' has been written in the space. Now we shall begin. You should answer the questions as you listen because you will not hear the recording a second time. Listen carefully and answer questions 1 to 6.

[repeat]

Man: Well, that trip is in the middle of the month. **(1)** <u>It starts on</u> the <u>17th of April</u> and it finishes on the 27th.

Woman: That suits me. I can't leave work before the 10th of April.

Man: Let me see if there are any spaces. Is it just for yourself?

Woman: Myself and my sister – so two of us.

Man: Um, yes. We have spaces.

Woman: Is it a big group?

Man: At the moment there are 12 people booked on this trip and with you two that will be 14. **(2)** <u>The maximum number is 16</u> so it's almost fully booked. We can't go over that because it's hard to keep a larger group together.

Woman: I need to check that I'm fit enough for this but the distances look OK. The website says **(3)** <u>we'll ride approximately 45km a day. Is that right?</u>

Man: <u>That's correct</u> and I've got the exact distances here. It really depends on which part of the trip. Some days are only 35km and some are more. But you'll never have to cycle more than 50km in one day.

Woman: Oh, OK. I can manage that. And we stay in hotels?

Man: Yes. They all have restaurants and the rooms have en-suite facilities.

Woman: And do they have pools? It's how I relax after a long day.

Man: There is a **(4)** <u>swimming pool in a few of the hotels</u> but none of them has a gym.

Woman: I don't think we'll need a gym after all that cycling! I'd better find out how much the holiday costs before I get too excited.

Man: Including flights it's £1,177 for one person.

Woman: Oh, we'll book our own flights on the Internet.

Man: Ah, that's just £ **(5)** <u>1,013</u> then. And we can book insurance for you if you want.

Woman: Mm … and which meals are included in that price?

Man: Well, er, breakfast of course. And the hotels will provide you with a packed lunch each day. We do stop during the afternoon in a village somewhere for a rest, so **(6)** <u>any snacks you buy then are extra.</u> Then dinner will be in the hotel every evening and that's included in the price of the holiday.

Before you hear the rest of the conversation, you have some time to look at questions 7 to 10.

[Pause the recording for 30 seconds.]

....

Now listen and answer questions 7 to 10.

Woman: And you provide the bicycles of course. What else?

Man: A lock and a bell come with the bike as well as lights, although you shouldn't need to cycle in the dark. There's a small bag, or pannier, on the front of the bike, where you can put the things you want to take with you during the day like water or fruit. **(7)** <u>But we won't allow you to cycle unless you bring a helmet.</u> We don't provide these locally because, like walking boots on a walking holiday, it's really important it fits properly.

Woman: OK.

Man: If there's any special gear you need for your holiday, we recommend a particular website and you can get a discount by quoting your booking reference.

Woman: Great. What is it?

Man: It's www.ballantyne.com. That's all one word, and I'll spell it for you: www dot **(8)** <u>B–A double L–A–N–T–Y–N–E</u> dot com.

Woman: Good. I've got that down. I've been looking at your website while we've been talking. I see we cycle along the river Danube?

Man: Yes, it's one of Europe's most well-known areas for cycling.

Woman: It looks fascinating – lots of beautiful countryside and things to see.

Man: I should warn you that we do reserve the right to make some <u>alterations</u> to the **(9)** <u>route</u> if the weather is bad. Some of the tracks sometimes get very muddy.

Woman: OK. Well, hopefully it won't rain too much! I know we stop in towns and villages but do we get a chance to look around? Because I'm really interested in history.

Man: Oh yes, you get opportunities to explore. Is there something in particular you want to see?

Woman: There's a **(10)** <u>theatre</u> in a town called Grein. A friend of mine went there last year and said it was amazing.

Man: Let's see. Um, ah yes, <u>there's a guide who'll take you round the building.</u> We don't have any other tours arranged but you can visit several castles and museums on the holiday.

Woman: Well, thank you for all that information. I'd like to book that then.

Man: Right. Well, I'll just …

That is the end of section 1. You now have half a minute to check your answers.

[Pause the recording for 30 seconds.]

🎧09 **LISTENING SECTION 2**

You will hear someone talking on the radio about food and restaurants in the local area. First you have some time to look at questions 11 to 14.

[Pause the recording for 30 seconds.]

Now listen and answer questions 11 to 14.

Announcer: And now we have our 'Know your town' section where we look at what's on offer in our area. Today John Munroe is going to tell us about local food and eating out. John.

John: Well, most of us buy our food in supermarkets these days but we're very lucky having a wonderful market here. It was originally on the piece of land in front of the cathedral but at the beginning of

the twentieth century it was moved to a site by the river. **(11)** <u>When the new shopping centre was built in the 1960s, it found a home beneath the multi-storey car park where it still is,</u> but there are plans to move it back to its previous home by the river.

The market is now open six days a week. On Tuesday to Saturday you can buy fresh fruit and vegetables, meat and cheese from the area, as well as a whole range of imported produce. **(12)** <u>But if you come on a Sunday, you'll find a different market, where craftspeople sell what they have made – things like bags, cards, clothes.</u> During the week there are a few stalls selling more everyday utensils like saucepans and cleaning products alongside the fruit and vegetables – as well as one new stall selling antique furniture which is proving to be very popular.

People often ask what our local dish is. As we're by the sea, they expect it to be some kind of fish recipe. Our fish is good of course but there isn't one particular dish that stands out. **(13)** <u>What we do have is an apple cake that isn't really made anywhere else.</u> There's a new café in the High Street: Barton's, which bakes them fresh every morning and serves them with delicious home-made ice cream in a choice of flavours.

Now, the harbour is obviously the place to buy fresh fish. Every morning there's a stall where local fishermen sell a selection of the day's catch before the rest goes to London or abroad. They've been doing that for as long as anyone can remember of course, but the harbour itself looks very different from a few years ago. **(14)** <u>Most of the restaurants used to be at the far end, but that part was redeveloped and the restaurants had to relocate to the other end.</u> Many of them are simply the old ones in new premises but a couple of new ones have opened recently so there's a good range now both in the harbour and the town itself. I'm now going to give you my 'Top Six Places to Eat' in different parts of the town.

Before you hear the rest of the talk, you have some time to look at questions 15 to 20.

[Pause the recording for 30 seconds.]

....

Now listen and answer questions 15 to 20.

So Number 1 for me is Merrivales, which is in one of the busiest parts of the town leading down to the harbour. It's in a side street so it doesn't look out over the water but it's very close, so you can take a walk after your meal and find one of the cafés with live music. At Merrivales you can enjoy delicious fresh fish and seafood. **(15)** <u>The friendly staff offer very attentive service</u> and a really enjoyable evening.

The Lobster Pot is on the main road going down to the harbour so it also misses out on the sea view, but the food makes up for that. **(16)** <u>It serves a huge range of fish and seafood as well as vegetarian and meat dishes so there's something for everyone.</u> Prices are from mid-range to fairly expensive so it's really only for a special occasion.

Elliots is in the city centre and is a very upmarket restaurant in the evening but during the day it serves lunch and coffee. **(17)** <u>It's on the twentieth floor above some offices and it's a great place to sit for a while as you can see most of the city spread out from there.</u> It does get very busy though and you may have to wait to be served.

Not far from the city centre is The Cabin which is on the canal bank. You can't park your car there – it's a fifteen-minute walk from the nearest car park – but **(18)** <u>it's very peaceful, a good place to relax away from the traffic.</u> It's not cheap but it's an ideal place for a long lunch.

The Olive Tree is a family-run restaurant in the city centre offering beautifully prepared Greek dishes. It's well known locally and very popular. Service can be slow when it's busy as all the food is freshly made. There's plenty of room and on Friday and Saturday nights, **(19)** the wooden floors resound with live music and dancing which is certainly worth going for.

The last place I want to recommend has only just opened in a converted school building. The Old School Restaurant has been very cleverly renovated. **(20)** The use of mirrors, plants and the colours on the walls makes you feel as though you're in a large garden instead of the city centre. There are only a few dishes on the menu but they change every day.

So Tanya, I …

That is the end of section 2. You now have half a minute to check your answers.

[Pause the recording for 30 seconds.]

🎧 10   **LISTENING SECTION 3**

You will hear three students on a media studies course talking about a film they are planning to make. First you have some time to look at questions 21 to 26.

[Pause the recording for 30 seconds.]
Now listen carefully and answer questions 21 to 26.

Reza: Hi Mike.

Mike: Hi Reza, this is Helen.

Helen: Hello!

Mike: We're really pleased you've agreed to join us on this film project.

Helen: Yes, your experience is going to be so useful.

Reza: Well, I hope so. It's the technical side I know best – lighting, sound and stuff.

Mike: But you think the script is OK?

Reza: Yes, I think it's great! Um, have you decided where you're going to shoot?

Helen: Well, there's the water-mill scene at the end. And we've thought about some locations in town we can use. They're behind the shopping mall and on a couple of residential streets. And in an empty shop on campus. It means we don't have to worry about getting permission from a shopowner.

Mike: So **(21)** do you think we should go to all the locations with you?

Reza: It would be a good idea. We need to talk about the levels of background noise so we know they're all going to be reasonable places to film.

Mike: But the sounds of traffic will make it more natural.

Helen: I think Reza means things like aeroplanes, trains and so on that would mean we have to stop filming.

Reza: Exactly. And also I'll make notes for myself about what lighting I'm going to need. I think the university department has a good range of equipment, but I'll need to make a list for each location for my own reference. Anyway, once we've had a look round, **(22)** you can do the roadworks check.

Mike: What do you mean?

Reza: You need to find out about building work or roadworks. Because you could start filming one day and come back in the morning to find one of the roads has been dug up! The local council have to be informed about things like that so you can find out from them.

Mike: OK. Then I think we need to work from the script and put together a list of all the scenes and decide which ones we're going to film when. We need to **(23)** prepare the shooting schedule, day by day.

Reza: You're right. Then when you know how long filming is going to last, you can tell everyone when they're needed.

Helen: OK, so as soon as we can, we'll audition, and then when we contact people to offer them parts we can send the exact dates and **(24)** make really sure they are free. Because often the actors are all enthusiastic but then when you try to pin them down about whether they're really free at that time, you find they've got exams or something, or they're off to a festival just before and you have to rush about looking for replacements.

Mike: Then, we need people who can take over the main parts if one of our stars falls ill or something.

Reza: Yes, I agree. So offer the main parts to the people we really want, and then look at other volunteers who were OK.

Helen: **(25)** Yes. We can select the understudies once the main roles have been confirmed. So, once we've got that sorted and we've held all the rehearsals of the main scenes, we'll be ready to start filming.

Reza: Yes, that sounds good. Anything else?

Mike: Er, well, just housekeeping, really. We don't actually need costumes because actors will wear their own clothes. **(26)** My family has agreed to lend us some pieces of furniture which we need, so we'll go and fetch those the weekend before we start.

Helen: We'll provide food and drink during shooting so I'm going to borrow some cool-boxes.

Mike: And I've got a little van. Most of the locations are within walking distance of the halls of residence anyway. The only one further away is the water-mill.

Reza: Ah, yes, can you tell me about that?

Mike: Um, OK. Er, hang on a minute, I'll get my notes. There's a plan in them.

Before you hear the rest of the conversation, you have some time to look at questions 27 to 30.

[Pause the recording for 30 seconds.]
....

Now listen and answer questions 27 to 30.

Mike: Here's the mill. You see, basically you have a vertical water-wheel which was used to power the grinding stones.

Reza: Mm, it sounds really interesting. Will we film inside?

Helen: Yes. That's where the final scene between the girl and the man takes place. Our plan is to **(27)** fix one camera outside by the window next to the door, to film through the window, and then have another handheld camera inside the mill. That means we can get two views of the same scene. We were going to do something using a mirror, but we decided that would be too complicated.

Mike: Yes, by doing it that way, **(28)** <u>all we'll need is lights on the inside, next to the wall behind the wheel</u> which can shine across to the opposite wall.

Reza: Hmm. Will that give enough light?

Helen: I think so, because the scene is in the evening; it shouldn't be too bright. The actors will be carrying torches too.

Mike: And **(29)** <u>we'll have an old screen made of wood just inside the door,</u> because it's a new door and it'll look wrong. The lights won't shine directly on it so it'll be fine.

Reza: So you won't actually show the door open?

Mike: No. **(30)** <u>There's a huge box on the floor against the wall farthest from the wheel.</u> We'll see the girl approaching the mill on her bike. Then we see through the window and the man is inside looking at it, then the next shot is the girl, in the room with him, opening the box.

Reza: So it'll be a mysterious ending! Well, I think it's going to be a great project.

Mike: Good.

Helen: Thanks!

That is the end of section 3. You now have half a minute to check your answers.

[Pause the recording for 30 seconds.]

 LISTENING SECTION 4

You will hear part of a lecture about exotic pests given as the introduction to a course on ecology and environment. First you have some time to look at questions 31 to 40.

[Pause the recording for one minute.]

Now listen carefully and answer questions 31 to 40.

Lecturer: Good afternoon. I want this afternoon as an introduction to our ecology module to offer examples of exotic pests – non-native animals or plants which are, or may be, causing problems – which might prove a fruitful topic for seminar papers later in the term. People and products are criss-crossing the world as never before, and on these new global highways, plants and animals are travelling too.

Exotic plants and animals are turning up in Antarctica and on the most remote islands on Earth. For example, the Australian red-backed spider – it's made its way to countries fairly near home, such as New Zealand and Japan, as some of you may know – well, it's also been found on Tristan da Cunha, **(31)** <u>which is a remote island, thousands of miles from anywhere, way out in the middle of the Atlantic.</u>

Now, another famous animal invader in the other direction, so to speak, from England to Australia in the southern hemisphere, is the rabbit. This was in 1830 and it might seem less of a threat, but it became an extraordinarily destructive pest. The fact that rabbits increased so rapidly is perhaps more understandable when we remind ourselves that they had originally been introduced to England from continental Europe eight centuries earlier. **(32)** <u>This was because they were regarded as a luxury food source,</u> and in spite of having warm fur, they probably originated on the hot dry plains of Spain, which of course explains why they thrive in the climate of Australia.

A much less cuddly example of a pest introduced to Australia, this time from America, is fire ants. These are increasing and spreading very fast. **(33)** <u>Their huge nests can now be found in gardens in the city of Brisbane</u> and they are costing the Australian government a great deal of money in control measures. These were an accidental introduction, rather than a deliberate one, brought to Australia, probably in horticultural imports or in mud on second-hand machinery.

As a biologist and conservationist, I have become increasingly concerned about these matters. Exotic invasions are irreversible and deserve to be taken more seriously even when they aren't particularly damaging. For example, something that is not necessarily a major disaster compared to other ecological experiments: **(34)** <u>in 1975 an Australian species of earthworm</u> was deliberately introduced <u>to the northern hemisphere, in Scotland,</u> because they were bigger than the natives. **(35)** <u>The aim was that they would be more effective than native species, but in fact they don't do more for the soil condition</u> than the smaller locals which they displace. Although they don't do a lot of harm, as far as we know up to now, this will probably prove to have been a mistake.

A much more serious case, also in Scotland, as well as other countries, along with the latest victim, Iceland, is the New Zealand flatworm. This is a most unwelcome newcomer in these regions of **(36)** <u>north-west Europe.</u> Basically, this flatworm came into these countries by accident. It's now been realised that it was actually **(37)** <u>carried in the plant pots</u> containing exotic ornamental shrubs and so on, and as it eats local earthworms, and doesn't benefit the local ecology in any way, it is a real pest.

Next, there's a further instance, this time in the water and it's come from Japan. It's **(38)** <u>a delicious but very fast-spreading seaweed</u> and is one of many exotic species, large and small, in the seas covering the rocks around Australia. Unfortunately, it is replacing indigenous seaweeds and permanently altering the ecosystem. However, to look at the situation from a business point of view – it is now being harvested and exported, dried, back to Japan, its original home, where it's particularly popular. So sometimes we may find accidental benefits from apparently harmful arrivals.

Well, you could say that world ecology is now going the same way as popular culture. Global music and fashions, food and drinks are taking over from local ones in every land. And in ecosystems, we find vigorous exotic invaders overwhelming native species and natural habitats.

But can we find any examples of invaders which appear to be a problem and then find that in fact they may not be such a big issue after all? We might take as an example a native of Australia, the budgerigar, the most common pet parrot in the world, of course. Because there have been many escapes over the years, it is now to be found flying about in feral flocks where the climate suits it. So, these flocks of budgerigars have been getting very numerous **(39)** <u>in the south-east of the United States, particularly in residential areas.</u> People have been getting quite worried about this, but it has been observed that the size of the flocks has diminished somewhat recently. The fact that they are smaller is thought to be **(40)** <u>due to the fact that new competitors</u> for their habitat have arrived from other places.

That's the last example for now. What I'd like you to consider is this: Is the planet Earth moving towards a one-world ecosystem? How far would it be a wholly bad development?

That is the end of section 4. You now have half a minute to check your answers.

[Pause the recording for 30 seconds.]

LISTENING SECTION 1
Exam practice
Review

1 Two

2 Once

3 Ten

4 No, not necessarily

5 Yes

6 Specific information (e.g. dates, everyday objects, places, etc. and spelling)

7 Yes

8 Yes, you must spell your answers correctly.

9 At the end of the Listening test, after Section 4

Action plan reminder

Form completion

1 The instructions tell you

2 Yes

3 Whether you need to write a number, a date, etc., or what kind of words, e.g. a name, a place, a job, etc.

4 By writing too many words, by spelling incorrectly, by not writing exactly the words you hear, by leaving a gap empty

Questions 1–6

1 **edwinari / Edwinari / EDWINARI** (Remember not to confuse the pronunciation of the letters *e* and *i* or *a* and *r*!)

2 **New Zealander**
Distraction Clive makes a mistake when he asks 'And you're from Australia?' but Edwina corrects him, saying, 'I'm a New Zealander'. Clive mentions other countries when he apologises, 'Oh, I'm sorry. I bet it's really irritating being told you're an Australian. Like Canadians being asked what part of the States they're from'.

3 **play centre** (You need the name of a business or institution.)
Distraction The play centre was in Wellington, but 'of' after the word 'manager' tells you that you need the name of a business or institution, not a place.

4 **(a) professor** (You need the name of a job.)
Distraction Edwina describes her as a friend of her mother's and also as a former neighbour, but neither of these is her job; the place where she works (Institute of Education) is also incorrect for the same reason.

5 **first aid**: Edwina describes her first aid certificate as 'up-to-date', which matches 'current' on the form.
Distraction She also mentions her driving licence, but says it's not 'special'.

6 **sailing**
Distraction Clive says to Edwina 'you're a yachtswoman' but this is a person, not a qualification.

Action plan reminder

Table completion

1 The instructions tell you

2 The table heading and the column headings

3 By listening for the other words in that row

Questions 7–10

7 **sport** (You need a word that is the name of an activity or pastime.)
Distraction Although they mention the little boy's 'serious food allergy', knowing how to deal with that is not the special requirement [= 'what they mainly want'].

8 **twin/two**
Distraction 'five' is the boys' age, not how many there are!

9 **Scotland**
Distraction The 'city flat' and the 'island' don't tell you the location.

10 **cook** (You need a word that describes something you can do when camping.) The words 'They particularly wanted someone who would be prepared to [= be willing to]' tell you the answer is coming.

LISTENING SECTION 2
Exam practice
Review

1 One main speaker; another speaker may introduce the main speaker

2 Once

3 Two

4 Ten

5 No

6 No

7 Understanding specific information and selecting relevant information from what you hear

Questions 11–14

'A source of funding' could be an organisation, a business or a person that supplies money.

11 **D/E**

12 **E/D**
Distraction A: This was what was originally hoped for, not what actually happened: 'when the project was first discussed, we expected that a … central government grant would make up most of the rest'; C: 'when the project was first discussed, we expected that a multinational company would give us half our funding' – again, this was hoped for but not what eventually happened; B: 'local government decided they couldn't afford anything'.

'Pre-existing' means something which already exists.

You might find C–E at an airport.

13 B/C

14 C/B

Distraction A: The old [= pre-existing] football stadium was not on this site: 'the 1950s football stadium is on the other side of town and is shortly due to be pulled down and built over'; D and E: Although it was hoped these could be included, it was not actually possible: 'The other buildings, like the control tower, which would have made a great feature, and the aircraft hangars … were unfortunately not structurally sound enough [= too old and weak] to preserve'.

Questions 15–20

15 E

16 B

17 A

18 D

19 F

20 C

LISTENING SECTION 3
Exam practice
Review

1 The setting is always academic life – it might be a tutorial or a discussion between a tutor and some students or between students.

2 There are two to four speakers.

3 Once

4 Ten

5 No, not usually

6 Before you do the first task and there is a pause in the recording before you do the next task.

Action plan reminder

Multiple choice

1 Yes

2 No

3 Listen for words which mean the same as the questions.

4 Read the questions to give you an idea of what the recording is about.

Questions 21–25

Chloe is thinking of doing the course. It is a business studies course.

21 B: Ivan says: 'Is there something on the course that you're not sure about?' which tells you that you need to listen for the answer
Distraction A: Chloe says 'I'm used to dealing with figures and percentages [= maths]' so she's not concerned about it; C: Ivan says 'That will be really valuable experience' in response to Chloe's description of her present job and she agrees with him, so she doesn't think she lacks business experience.

22 C
Distraction A: Ivan says he was worried about his computer skills but then he says 'you only really need the basics', so those skills haven't improved; B: Ivan says about presentation skills 'I thought that would be hard, but we'd actually had such a lot of practice at school it was fine', so his presentation skills have stayed the same.

23 A: Chloe says: 'What really appeals to me ...'
Distraction B: Chloe says 'That's not so important for me' (but Ivan says it was for him); C: Chloe says she would like to use her foreign languages but that doesn't seem to be on offer.

24 C
Distraction A: Ivan says 'they really need to add more lecture rooms' not that he is 'pleased' that this is actually happening; B: Although Ivan says they've expanded the library, he goes on to say that they have taken some of the magazines and periodicals away so he thinks 'it was better as it was' (i.e. he is not pleased about the larger library).

25 A
Distraction B: Ivan says he 'read loads of prospectuses' but he doesn't suggest Chloe does this; C: Ivan says it's not worth visiting as 'it's holidays now and there's not much going on there'.

Questions 26–30

26 C
Distraction A: Ivan says 'it will be really useful'; B: Chloe says 'it doesn't look very demanding' but she doesn't say she definitely won't do it.

27 A
Distraction B: Ivan says 'I wasn't very impressed with that course'; C: Chloe says 'maybe I'd get a different tutor' but she will still definitely choose it.

28 A
Distraction B: Chloe says 'Although I don't want to be an accountant, ...' but she still thinks the course will be useful; C: Ivan says he isn't sure about being an accountant.

29 B: Chloe says 'I'd give that one a miss'.
Distraction A: Ivan says it's the most popular course and Chloe says her friend is really good at it.

30 C: Chloe says she will 'look at some of the other possibilities first' so she isn't sure.
Distraction A: Chloe says it 'sounds useful, but ...' (she isn't sure yet).

LISTENING SECTION 4
Exam practice
Review

1 One

2 A topic which is suitable for an academic lecture

3 Once

4 Ten

5 No

6 In Section 4 you only have time to read the questions at the beginning, not between the tasks.

Action plan reminder

Note completion

1 No, you should read the instructions which tell you the maximum number of words. You may need fewer than this.

2 Yes

3 What kind of word goes in each gap (e.g. a noun, adjective, etc.)

4 Yes, you mustn't change them.

5 Yes

Questions 31–35

When you hear the word 'almanacs' you should listen for the first answer.

31 **planets**
   Distraction The almanacs used the moon to make predictions but not its position.

32 **humidity**: 'the mid-fifteenth century' (1450), 'Nicholas Cusa' and 'a hygrometer' tell you the answer is coming.
   Distraction The sentence about sheep's wool explains how the hygrometer worked but 'weight', 'sheep's wool' and 'air conditions' don't make sense in the gap.

33 **water**
   Distraction Gabriel Fahrenheit invented the first mercury thermometer, not Galileo.

34 **(electric) telegraph**: 'from one part of the world to another' tells you the answer is coming.

35 **(weather) maps**: the date '1863' and 'France' tell you the answer is coming.
   Distraction 'weather forecasts' and 'observations' are mentioned but these weren't produced by the French every day.

Action plan reminder

Sentence completion

1 No, the instructions tell you the maximum number.

2 Yes

3 Yes

Questions 36–40

36 **airports**: 'Observation reports' and 'weather stations' tell you the answer is coming.
   Distraction 'a few are in urban centres' but most are at airports.

37 **dry air**
   Distraction 'moisture levels' are mentioned but these are shown by bright blue.

38 **cloud** [make out = distinguish]
   Distraction 'landscape' is wrong because although the meteorologists can see it, the speaker doesn't mention them distinguishing a 'particular' one.

39 **balloon** [equipment = instruments]
   Distraction 'box' is wrong because the instruments are inside a box (radiosonde) which is attached to a balloon.

40 **hurricanes** [the progress of = the movement of]
   Distraction Although the text says radar is also used by aircraft, it doesn't say for what purpose.

READING PASSAGE 1
Exam practice
Review

1 13

2 No

3 (about) 20 minutes

Action plan reminder

True/False/Not given

1 Factual information

2 Yes, they are in the same order.

3 Yes

4 No

5 Look at the title (and subtitle if there is one) and then read the text very quickly to get a general idea of what it is about.

6 Underline the important words.

Questions 1–7

The key words in each statement have been underlined.

1 **TRUE**: <u>Few people</u> recognise nowadays that human beings are designed to <u>function best in daylight</u>: 'This is a basic evolutionary fact, even though most of us don't think of ourselves [= few people recognise] as diurnal beings [= beings designed to function best in daylight] …'.

2 **TRUE**: <u>Most light pollution</u> is caused by the <u>direction of artificial lights</u> rather than their intensity: 'Light pollution is largely the result of bad lighting design, which allows artificial light to shine outward and upward into the sky [= direction] …' (there is no mention of the intensity of artificial lights being a problem).

3 **FALSE**: By <u>1800</u> the city of <u>London</u> had such a large population, it was already causing <u>light pollution</u>: The third paragraph says that in London in 1800 the nights were either moonlit or people used 'candles and lanterns', 'as they always had'.

4 **NOT GIVEN**: <u>The fishermen of the South Atlantic</u> are <u>unaware</u> of the <u>light pollution</u> they are causing: The fourth paragraph explains what the fishermen do and says that 'the glow from a single fishing fleet … can be seen from space' but it doesn't say if the fishermen are aware or unaware of this.

5 **NOT GIVEN**: <u>Shadows</u> from the planet <u>Venus</u> are <u>more difficult</u> to see at <u>certain times of year</u>: Although the fifth paragraph says that an 'unlit night' is required to see the shadows of Venus and that this is 'beyond memory almost', there is no mention of it being connected to 'certain times of year'.

6 **FALSE**: In some <u>Swiss valleys</u>, the total number of <u>bats declined</u> rapidly after the introduction of <u>streetlights</u>: The seventh paragraph is about bats in the Swiss valleys. It says one species of bat 'began to vanish' but the valleys 'were suddenly filled' with a different species of bat. The number of bats didn't therefore decline (but the species of bats changed).

7 TRUE: The <u>first attempts</u> to <u>limit</u> light pollution were carried out to <u>help</u> those <u>studying the stars</u>: The last paragraph mentions 'light pollution' affecting astronomers. 'In fact' links the next sentence to the astronomers and the text says 'some of the earliest civic efforts [= first attempts] to control [= limit] light pollution were made … to protect the view from Lowell Observatory [= to help those studying the stars – an observatory is where astronomers work].

Action plan reminder

Table completion

1 How many words to write

2 What kinds of words to look for (e.g. noun, verb, etc.)

3 Yes

4 No, you must use the same words as the text.

5 Yes

Questions 8–13

The gaps all need nouns or noun phrases except Question 8.

8 immature: 'immature birds suffer in much higher numbers than adults [= worst-affected].'

9 brightly lit buildings: The sixth paragraph says 'birds are apt to collide with [= bump into] brightly lit buildings [= they stand out at night]'.
Distraction 'searchlights', 'gas flares' and 'marine oil platforms' are wrong because the birds don't bump into these, they just fly round and round them.

10 predators: 'Other nocturnal mammals, like desert rodents and badgers, ... easier targets [= more at risk] for the predators ...'

11 nesting conditions: The eighth paragraph says 'Leaving prematurely [= early migration] may mean reaching a destination [= on arrival] too soon for nesting conditions to be right [= are not suitable]'.
Distraction 'destination' fits the meaning but it does not fit the gap grammatically.

12 dark beaches: The first three sentences of the ninth paragraph are about sea turtles. There is a lack of dark beaches. 'Nesting sea turtles, which seek out dark beaches, find fewer and fewer [= decreasing number] of them ...' Two sentences later the text says they 'suffer' because of this ('hatchling losses number in the hundreds of thousands every year').
Distraction 'artificial lighting' is wrong because this is what causes the problem whereas the answer has to be something the turtles need.

13 (major) highways: The second half of the ninth paragraph says 'Frogs and toads living on the side of [= near] major highways ... disturbing [= upset(ting)] nearly every aspect of their behavior [= routines], including their night-time breeding choruses.'

READING PASSAGE 2
Exam practice
Review

1 13 or 14

2 No

3 20 minutes

Questions 14–20

The key words in each heading have been underlined.

14 vii: <u>Academics</u> with an <u>unhelpful</u> attitude: The text describes 'the response of many of the senior researchers, who would say: "I'm doing my research for pure science, the industry can take it or leave it [= I don't care whether my research is made use of or ignored]"'.

15 i: A <u>comparison</u> between <u>similar buildings</u>: The text describes 'a study … that found inner-city Chicago apartment buildings surrounded by more vegetation suffered 52 per cent fewer crimes than apartment blocks with little or no greenery'. Other paragraphs mention different kinds of buildings, e.g. schools, hospitals, but they aren't compared.

16 x: The <u>expanding scope</u> of environmental psychology: The text says 'Environmental psychologists are … asked to contribute to the planning, design and management of many different environments, ranging from neighbourhoods, offices, schools, health, transport, traffic and leisure environments'.

17 ix: A <u>unique co-operative</u> scheme: The text says 'The collaborative [= co-operative] project currently stands as a one-off [= unique] experiment'.

18 iii: An <u>unusual job</u> for a psychologist: In the text, Barker, a recent graduate in psychology, says 'What I do is pretty rare to be honest' and goes on to describe that she feels 'very privileged to be able to use [her] degree in such a way'.

19 iv: A <u>type of building</u> benefiting from <u>prescribed guidelines</u>: The text says 'One area where the findings from environment–behaviour research have certainly influenced building is in hospital design. "The government has a checklist of criteria [= prescribed guidelines] that must be met in the design of new hospitals"'. It goes on to describe what the benefits are.

20 vi: A <u>failure</u> to use available information <u>in practical ways</u>: The text says 'Zeisel shares Chris Spencer's concerns that the lessons from environmental psychology research are not getting through. "There is certainly a gap between what we in social science know and the world of designers and architects," says Zeisel. He believes that most industries, from sports to film-making, have now recognised the importance of an evidence-based approach [i.e. the approach used by environmental psychologists]'.
Distraction ii: The <u>negative</u> reaction of local <u>residents</u>: There are references to the benefits to local residents in Paragraphs B and C and to research on local residents' needs in Paragraph D but none of the residents are described as being against something;
v: The <u>need</u> for <u>government</u> action: Government has taken action in producing criteria (Paragraph F). Taking action applies to

'senior researchers' in environmental psychology whom Spencer calls on to 'make a greater effort to communicate' (Paragraph A) and also the building trade which is not recognising that the research should be used in building projects (Paragraph G); viii: A refusal by architects to accept criticism: The text does not say that architects refuse to accept criticism, rather that architects and psychologists do not communicate enough: 'There is certainly a gap between what we in social science know and the world of designers and architects' (Paragraph G).

Questions 21–24

21/22 B/D (in any order)

B: Paragraph C refers to 'the rebuilding of one south London school as a striking example of how building design can affect human behaviour positively' and goes on to say 'Before its redesign, it was ranked as the worst school in the area – now it is recognised as one of the country's twenty most improved schools'. (The university students in Paragraph D are not said to have better results – the professor hopes they will have 'some understanding of the psychological issues involved in design');

D: Paragraph G says 'fewer medication errors [= mistakes in giving medicines] occur in private rooms' and 'a better balance between private and shared rooms in hospitals' as recommended by psychologist Zeisel, contributes to this.

Distraction A: Staff are mentioned in Paragraph E and the staff of companies, schools and hospitals are indirectly referred to in other paragraphs, but none of these specifically mentions 'better relationships between staff'; C: Improvements in working and living environments are mentioned in several paragraphs, but the text is concerned with psychological environments and does not focus on the issue of pollution; E: although Paragraph B refers to reduction of crime, the text says that there are fewer crimes committed, not that criminals are caught [= detected] more easily.

23/24 A/C (in any order)

A: Paragraph B refers to 'a study using police records [= information already collected by the police]' which related to 'inner-city Chicago apartment buildings'.

C: Paragraph E says 'the team carries out observational studies [= watching what people do] ... to identify exactly how occupants are using their building'.

Distraction B: Although the text discusses the planning and use of space in and around buildings, it does not mention measuring the space; D: Paragraph C describes psychologists' involvement in planning, but does not talk about analysing decisions later; Paragraph F mentions the government criteria, but again, this relates to the planning stage, not to later analysis; E: Patients are mentioned in Paragraphs G and F, but in neither case are patients' reactions to each other mentioned.

Questions 25–26

25 client group: Paragraph D says 'The psychology students [in England] encouraged the architecture students [in Scotland] to think about who their client group was [= the identity of the people who would use the buildings they were working on]'.

26 (basic) layout: 'patient outcomes' means the results of treatment. In Paragraph F Zeisel says 'If people get lost in hospitals, they get stressed, which lowers their immune system and means their medication works less well ... the truth is that the basic layout of a building is what helps people find their way around'.

READING PASSAGE 3
Exam practice
Review

1 Usually two or three

2 No

3 About 20 minutes

Action plan reminder

Multiple choice

1 The correct answer/option from A, B, C or D.

2 One

3 Yes

4 Read the text quickly

5 Yes

6 (Up to) a paragraph

7 No. In a multiple-choice task, you have to look for the writer's views or claims. These may be different from what you think you know about the subject.

Questions 27–30

27 D: The 'academic debate' refers back to the discussion between 'anthropologists' but the text goes on to say 'we have very little idea why' humans have adolescence and that studies 'could help us understand its purpose' (i.e. have a practical use today).

Distraction A and C: These both refer to information in the text but they don't answer the question; B: There is no mention of a 'misunderstanding' between anthropologists in the first paragraph.

28 A: The fourth paragraph says 'She thinks that *Homo erectus* had already developed ... adolescent spurt' and 'Turkana boy was just about to enter it'.

Distraction B: This is denied in the text: '... a rounded skull, and needs more growth to reach the adult shape'; C: His skeleton and teeth showed similar discrepancies to those from the 18th and 19th centuries (so they were compared with a 'more modern age'); D: He was slightly tall for his apparent age but the text doesn't compare him with others alive at the time – they might all have been this tall.

29 B: In the fifth paragraph Steven Leigh says 'many apes have growth spurts ... to coincide with the seasons when food is plentiful, they minimise the risk of being without adequate food supplies while growing'. He says that many apes have growth spurts in different parts of their bodies which mature at different times. He attributes this to the fact that they only grow at times when food is plentiful.

Distraction A: 'the whole [human] skeleton is involved' (different parts don't grow at different speeds); C: There is no mention of the difference between humans, only between humans and apes; D: He says that the growth spurts and the periods when food is plentiful are short. He doesn't suggest there are longer periods of growth when there is more food.

30 **D**: 'The rate at which teeth develop is closely related to how fast the brain grows and the age you mature'.
Distraction A: The text contradicts this: 'their growth is less related to … nutrition than is the growth of the skeleton'; B: The text suggests the opposite as 'their growth is less related to the environment and nutrition than is the growth of the skeleton' (they are good indicators of 'life history', not 'lifestyle'); C: The text suggests the opposite: 'Every nine days or so … how long the crown of a tooth took to form'.

Action plan reminder

Yes/No/Not given

1 The writer's opinions and ideas

2 If the idea given in each statement agrees with opinions/ideas in the text (Yes), or contradicts them (No), or if there is no information about that idea in the text (Not Given)

3 Look at the heading and illustration if there is one.

4 No, because they may not be important for understanding the main points of the text or answering the question or they may be explained in another part of the text.

5 Yes

6 Underline the important words.

Questions 31–36

The key words in each question have been underlined.

31 **YES**: It is difficult for anthropologists to do research on human fossils because they are so rare: The text says 'The human fossil record is extremely sparse [= rare], and the number of fossilised children minuscule [= very few].' In the next sentence 'Nevertheless' tells us this is a problem for anthropologists.

32 **NO**: Modern methods mean it is possible to predict the age of a skeleton with accuracy: The text says 'Even with a modern human, you can only make a rough estimate' of assessing how old someone is so there is no accuracy.

33 **NO**: Susan Anton's conclusion about the Turkana boy reinforces an established idea: 'If Anton is right, that theory contradicts [= the opposite of 'reinforces'] the orthodox [= established] idea linking late growth with development of a large brain.'

34 **YES**: Steven Leigh's ideas are likely to be met with disbelief by many anthropologists: 'many anthropologists will consider Leigh's theory a step too far [= don't feel they can believe it]'.

35 **NOT GIVEN**: Researchers in France and Spain developed a unique method of analysing teeth: Although the text mentions the 'findings' of the researchers in France and Spain and it describes the 'minute analysis of tooth growth' in the previous paragraph, there is no mention that the researchers in France and Spain developed a unique method.

36 **NOT GIVEN**: There has been too little research comparing the brains of *Homo erectus* and Neanderthals: Although the text mentions research into the teeth of Neanderthals and *Homo erectus*, there is no mention of research comparing their brains.

Action plan reminder

Matching sentence endings

1 Find the part of the text which matches the sentence beginnings.

2 No

3 Yes

4 No

Questions 37–40

37 **D**: The beginning of the second paragraph mentions the explanation for the delay of physical growth, held until recently, that the survival of young humans is dependent on others. 'Until recently, the dominant explanation was that physical growth is delayed by our need to grow large brains and to learn all the behaviour patterns associated with humanity … humans cannot easily fend for themselves … That way your parents and other members of the social group are motivated to continue looking after you.'
Distraction B: The fact that human beings walk on two legs ('upright locomotion') is mentioned later as a new theory; E: 'the cold, harsh environment' is mentioned later but is given as a possible reason for reaching adulthood quickly (i.e. the opposite of 'delayed growth').

38 **A**: 'When she tried to age the skeletons … she found … discrepancies [= inconsistencies] …'
Distraction G: She didn't discover much larger brains than previously; C: Although she examined 'dental age' there is no mention that she looked at the 'way' teeth grew.

39 **B**: 'According to his theory, adolescence evolved as an integral part of efficient upright locomotion …'
Distraction F: Although Steven Leigh links short growth spurts with an increased need for food, he doesn't say the existence of adolescence is connected to food; G: Although he thinks adolescence may be because of the need to 'accommodate more complex brains', there is no mention of the size of the brains or comparison of brain size with the past.

40 **E**: 'Ramirez-Rozzi thinks Neanderthals died young … because of the cold, harsh environment they had to endure in glacial Europe [= difficult climatic conditions].'
Distraction C: The paragraph talks about 'tooth growth' but the research doesn't connect their short lives with the way their teeth grew.

WRITING TASK 1
Training
Review

1 Data presented as a graph (bar or pie chart) or a diagram

2 Concisely and accurately

3 You should not use an informal style; you should write in a formal and academic style.

4 Yes, you should make sure you use a range of grammatical structures and try to be accurate.

5 About 20 minutes

6 At least 150

7 The most important or noticeable features, trends or points

8 Yes, when appropriate

9 Features of the data

Useful language: the introduction

1

Student's introduction	a: enough information?	b: accurate?
1	no: 'some information' gives no idea what kind of information we can learn from the table	no: '1928 till 2008' suggests that we can learn about *all* the years between (instead of just the three years given)
2	this is a better introduction than **1**; it could be improved by mentioning which three years it refers to	yes
3	no: there is no mention of the time period covered by the table	no: the reader gets the impression that the table only refers to the present time
4	this is a good introduction, except for one small error (see right →)	almost: but the table does not tell us 'how many students' came from overseas or within 30 miles – it tells us 'what percentage' (we would have to do a sum to find out how many!)
5	this is not a bad introduction, apart from one error (see right →)	no: the table does not tell us 'what area' the students come from

2 Sample answers

(Alternatives are possible)

1 In the table we can see ~~some~~ information about **the numbers of** students enrolled at Bristol University ~~from~~ **in** the year**s** 1928, ~~till~~ **1958 and** 2008.

2 The table shows the numbers of student enrolments at Bristol University, covering the number of students, the percentages of female and male, and where they came from, in three different years**, 1928, 1958 and 2008**.

3 This table shows the number of people who ~~are studying~~ **studied** at Bristol University **in 1928, 1958 and 2008** and the number of people of each gender as well. Also, it shows the distance that students ~~come~~ **came** from, divided into two categories: within 30 miles of Bristol and overseas.

4 The table illustrates some information about students at Bristol University. The table shows the percentages of male and female students and ~~how many students~~ **the percentages that** came from overseas or within 30 miles of Bristol in 1928, 1958 and 2008.

5 The table gives information about Bristol University student enrolments, the percentages of males and females and ~~what area~~ **whether** they came from **within 30 miles of the city or from abroad**, in the years 1928, 1958 and 2008.

3 1 <u>In the table we can see some information about</u> students enrolled at Bristol University from the year 1928 till 2008.

2 <u>The table shows</u> the numbers of student enrolments at Bristol University, <u>covering</u> the number of students, the percentages of female and male, and where they came from, in three different years.

3 <u>This table shows</u> the number of people who are studying at Bristol University and the number of people of each gender as well. Also, it shows the distance that students come from, <u>divided into two categories</u>: within 30 miles of Bristol and overseas.

4 <u>The table illustrates some information about</u> student enrolments at Bristol University. <u>The table shows the percentages of</u> male and female students and how many students came from overseas or within 30 miles of Bristol in 1928, 1958 and 2008.

5 <u>The table gives information about</u> Bristol University student enrolments, the percentages of males and females and what area they came from, in the years 1928, 1958 and 2008.

Useful language: drawing attention to important data

1 1 Also <u>noteworthy</u> is the low government expenditure on education.

2 <u>This graph shows</u> <u>a striking difference</u> between the younger age group and the older one.

3 <u>The most striking feature of the graph</u> is <u>the sudden increase</u> in the popularity of computer games.

4 <u>Another fact worth noticing</u> in the table <u>is</u> that females are <u>more numerous than</u> males.

5 <u>The most remarkable point</u> is that the number of males with a criminal record <u>increased dramatically.</u>

6 <u>It is noticeable that</u> expenditure on photography <u>remained stable</u> from 1992 to 2000.

2 Sample answers

(Tenses may vary. 'Table' may be used instead of 'graph'.)

1 Also noteworthy is the fall in graduate numbers.

2 This graph shows a striking similarity between teenagers in the USA and teenagers in South America.

3 The most striking feature of the graph is the sudden decline in the birth rate.

4 Another fact worth noticing in the graph is the high cost of fossil fuels.

5 The most remarkable point is that the growth rate increased suddenly.

6 It is noticeable that few schools have swimming pools.

Useful language: numbers and percentages

1 1 figure **2** percentages **3** size **4** amount **5** level
6 per cent **7** number **8** percentage **9** proportion
10 proportion **11** percentage **12** rate

2 Sample answers

1 The rate of unemployment rose steadily between 1979 and 1985.

2 The proportion of the population who own computers is still increasing.

3 The amount of energy consumed by industry doubled during the last decade of the twentieth century.

4 Since public transport prices were reduced, the number of cars on the roads has decreased.

5 The level of literacy fell after the last change of government.
6 The quantity of food wasted in affluent parts of the world continued to grow.
7 The share of global resources consumed by the poorest countries went down during that period.

Useful language: spelling

1 <u>Nowadays</u>, <u>knowledge</u> about the <u>environment</u> is <u>essential</u> and many <u>governments</u> understand the <u>benefits</u> of educating <u>children</u> to be aware of how they can contribute to this.

2 In my <u>experience</u>, <u>because</u> <u>society</u> is in some respects organised <u>differently</u> in other <u>countries</u>, <u>foreigners</u> find it relaxing to visit this part of the world.

3 It is my <u>opinion</u> that few people <u>believe</u> the information <u>which</u> is given in <u>advertisements</u>.

4 Teenagers <u>should</u> not be allowed to have <u>their</u> own cars <u>until</u> they are prepared to accept <u>responsibility</u> for the <u>effect</u> that bad driving can have on other road users.

Useful language: finishing your summary

a 3 (it is the 'percentages', not the 'numbers' of local and overseas students that varied)   b 2   c 1   d 4

Exam practice

Action plan reminder

1 • What the data is about
 • Select and report the main features, and make relevant comparisons

2 • It is about Bristol University student enrolments.
 • The three years (or dates) covered in the table
 • Total student numbers, percentages of males and females, what percentage came from within 30 miles of Bristol and what percentage came from overseas
 • New student numbers
 • Because it shows percentages of males and females
 • Because there is no row for students who come from within the UK but further than 30 miles from Bristol

Before you write

3 Include: ideas for an opening statement, the main piece of information and some items of information to compare or contrast

4 • The description of the table in the task
 • No, you should select the main features.
 • No. (However, if appropriate, you could comment briefly by using expressions such as 'it is (not) surprising to see that ...'.)

After you write

5 Check that you have read the data accurately; check your spelling; check that you have included the main points or trends.

Sample notes

1 opening statement	info about student numbers and percentages of male/female, foreign – Bristol University, years 1928, etc.
2 main information	growth, proportion local and overseas, male and female

3 compare/contrast	percentage of females over the 3 years percentage of local students big change – in percentage of local and overseas students

It is important not to spend too much time on this task because Task 2 requires more time.
You will lose marks if you write less than 150 words.
The increase was greater between 1958 and 2008.
The percentage of female enrolments was lowest in 1958.
The percentage of overseas students rose most markedly between 1958 and 2008.

Model answer

Please note that this is only one possible interpretation of the task. Other approaches are equally valid.

> In the table we can see information about the numbers of students enrolling at Bristol University in the three years, 1928, 1958 and 2008. It compares the percentages of females and males, and also students from abroad and those from within 30 miles of the city.
>
> The most noticeable changes concern the overall growth of student numbers, from 218 in 1928 to 6,377 in 2008, and the proportions of local students, who constituted 50% of the total in 1928, but only 1–2% in 2008.
>
> It is surprising to note that the percentage of female enrolments did not rise steadily, but dropped between 1928 and 1958. However, at the same time, the percentage of the student population who came from abroad remained almost unchanged between 1928 and 1958, being 5% and 6% respectively, but rose markedly after that, so that by 2008 foreign students represented 28% of the total.

WRITING TASK 2
Training
Review

1 A formal discussion essay

2 expressing ideas; evaluating ideas; appropriate style; grammar; spelling; paragraphing; you are NOT tested on your general or academic knowledge or the 'correctness' of your ideas – you can express any opinion provided you support it with examples

3 At least 250

4 By giving examples from your own knowledge or experience

5 You should briefly re-state your opinion.

Useful language: conditionals

1 1 had   would do
 2 was   could be
 3 may be regarded   analyse
 4 spend   have

2 1 b   2 a   3 d   4 c

3 1 have/should have
 2 would not/wouldn't give
 3 did not/didn't earn

4 had been (referring to their financial situation at the time in the past when they wanted healthcare) / were (referring to their financial situation at any time up to now)

5 would have dealt / would be dealing (if the disaster has happened recently and people are dealing with it now)

6 were brought up / are brought up

7 would have been (speaker feels certain) / might have been (speaker is less certain)

Useful language: referring to people

1 customers (of a particular company); 'consumers' are people who buy goods or services in general

2 competitors (in a race or in business); 'contestants' take part in a contest of talent or skill

3 visitors (to a place or person); 'passengers' ride on a vehicle

4 member (of a closed group); a 'participant' is someone who takes part in an activity

5 patients (of medical practitioners); 'clients' pay a professional (e.g. an architect) for a service

6 Individuals (people); 'humans' are people as opposed to other animals

Sample answers

1 Consumers need an organisation to defend their rights, especially when suppliers control the market.

2 Many young people dream of appearing as a contestant in a television game show.

3 It is the duty of a transport company to make the journey as pleasant as possible for their passengers.

4 A language student who is an active participant in class discussions will find it useful practice for exams.

5 The relationship between lawyers and clients can be a very delicate matter.

6 It is humans who are the greatest threat to other species on the planet.

Useful language: positive and negative comments

1 1 b   **2** a   **3** d   **4** e   **5** c

2 Sample answers

1 The first disadvantage of working for a large company is the impersonal atmosphere.

2 The main benefit of access to the Internet is fast access to information.

3 The negative aspect of living in a village is that everyone knows your business.

4 One of the advantages of cheap public transport is reduced traffic congestion.

5 Another negative result of studying abroad is having fewer useful contacts back home.

6 A major drawback of large families is the lack of privacy.

Exam practice

Action plan reminder

1 • ALL of it. Any part of the instructions may change slightly.
  • 40 minutes, including planning and checking
  • Relevant examples from your own knowledge or experience
  • The important parts of the task
  • No, you can agree or disagree, provided you support what you say.
  • Yes, you should use your own words.

Before you write

2 *See sample notes below.*

After you write

3 • Yes
  • No, this is a waste of time. It is better to spend time planning your essay and checking it carefully. If you write clearly and cross out any mistakes neatly, that is fine.
  • overall structure; paragraphing; clearly linked ideas; clear handwriting; formal or neutral style; subject–verb agreement; spelling; capital letters at the beginning of sentences; verb tenses; your own habitual errors

It does not matter whether your information is up-to-date; humour is out of place in this kind of formal essay; quotations are not appropriate.

Sample notes

1	introduction	shopping used to be a chore – now a leisure activity
		not sure if it's a good thing
2	discussion	Para 1 in the past – many small shops, not much choice, not much money/credit
		Para 2 recent years – supermarkets, shopping malls – comfortable –cafés. Etc.
3	my opinion	life has changed – busy parents – I've seen all together shopping – good? other things e.g. sport wd be better
		young people – shopping mall, clean safe place but influence of ads + easy credit – debt – not so healthy
4	conclusion	good for business, but not so good for people?

Model answer

Please note that this is only one possible interpretation of the task. Other approaches are equally valid.

Going shopping used to be a chore, but recently it has become a leisure activity or a pleasant outing. To my mind, it is debatable whether this can be regarded as a wholly positive development.

For earlier generations, buying food or consumer products involved visiting several shops, each with the same limited range on offer. Customers had less money and credit was not widely available. By contrast, shoppers nowadays can find almost anything in the supermarket or shopping mall. The comfortable environment, the variety of goods and attractions such as cafés and cinemas make spending money enjoyable.

Nowadays, with many parents working full-time, families have little time together. In my experience, it is normal to see families in the local shopping mall at weekends. Undoubtedly, one of the benefits of this is that they are together as a family. Nevertheless, this is not ideal, especially if it leaves no time for other activities, such as sport.

Another negative result of this change in attitudes is the effect it has on young people all over the world, who spend time in shopping malls. The reasons for this are the influence of advertising and the availability of credit cards. On the one hand, they are with friends in a safe environment, but on the other, it can tempt them to buy things they do not really need and may cause them to get into debt. Moreover, it would be better for their health if they met friends to go swimming.

In conclusion I would like to suggest that although shopping now is less tedious, this is not necessarily a positive trend. It may be good for the retailers, but not for consumers if it replaces other, healthier activities.

SPEAKING PART 1
Training

Review

1 ID or passport

2 Personal experiences and interests

3 No, you will be asked questions on several different topics but they will all be about your own life and interests.

4 No, you get a mark for the three parts together.

Useful language: work and studying

1 I went to Canada ~~for studying~~ **to study** engineering. (The 'to' + infinitive is used to talk about a purpose or reason for doing something; we can also say 'in order to study'.)

2 I am ~~learning~~ **studying** history at university. (We 'study' a subject on an educational course or by using academic methods but we 'learn' a skill (e.g. learn to drive, learn to cook, etc.).

3 I would like **to** study overseas. ('would like' is always followed by 'to'.)

4 I have been study**ing** English for ~~half a year~~ **six months**. (Verbs in continuous tenses always use the *-ing* form. When talking about part of a year we say two/three/six months; we do say, however, 'in the first/second half of the year'.)

5 I have classes ~~at~~ **in** the daytime and I work in the evening. ('at' is used before times (e.g. at 6 pm, at midnight) but not before most periods of time (e.g. in the morning, in the spring [**NB** at night]).)

6 I have a part-time ~~work~~ **job** (or ~~a~~ part-time work) in a restaurant. ('work' is an uncountable noun so we don't say 'a work'.)

7 I am hoping to get a good ~~employment~~ **job** when I graduate. ('employment' is uncountable so we can't say 'an employment' and we don't use 'employment' to talk about a specific job; we can say 'I'm looking for (full-time) employment' but when speaking we are more likely to say 'I'm looking for work / a job'.)

8 I finish ~~my~~ work at five o'clock. (We don't say 'my work' – see 6.)

9 There are lots of foreign ~~pupils~~ **students** at my university. ('students' is used for both schools and universities, 'pupils' is only used for schools.)

10 I want to ~~gain~~ **earn** a lot of money. (We always 'earn' money.)

Useful language: tenses

1 1 What <u>is</u> your job?

  2 How long <u>have you been working</u> there?

  3 What <u>do you enjoy</u> about your job?

  4 What job <u>did you want</u> to do when you <u>were</u> a child?

  5 Do you think you <u>will do</u> a different job one day?

2 1 Questions 1 and 3 ask about now. The present simple is used and you should use that in your answer.

  2 Question 4 asks about the past. You should use the past simple or 'used to' in your answer.

  3 Question 5 asks about the future. You could begin your answer with 'I hope to …', 'I'm planning to …', 'I might …' or you could say 'I'm not sure' or 'I haven't decided'.

  4 Question 2 asks about a length of time. The present perfect continuous tense is used. In your answer you will probably also use the past simple to talk about when you started your job (e.g. 'For two years – I went there straight from school').

SPEAKING PART 2

Training

Review

1 A card with a task on it and a piece of paper and a pencil

2 A minute

3 On the paper, not the card

4 Two minutes

SPEAKING PART 3

Training

Review

1 No, they will be connected to the topic in Part 2.

2 No, they will be about more abstract ideas.

Useful language: starting sentences with *-ing*

1 **2** Learning by doing
   3 Doing some kind of paid work
   4 Being loved is
   5 Being faced with
   6 Owning a car

2 **Sample answers**
   1 very popular with people of all age groups.
   2 make children think it is acceptable to behave in an aggressive way.
   3 is something that the media feel they have a right to do.
   4 is a useful way of learning everyday expressions.

Useful language: making general statements

Sample answers

1 For some people it's really important that they are dressed in the latest fashions but I don't think most people care that much about it.

2 In general, when people go on holiday they are interested in relaxing and enjoying themselves and because of that they may not really learn much about the local culture.

3 It's widely acknowledged that recycling is a good way of protecting the environment but in fact it makes a very small impact on climate change.

4 Most people recognise that computers and other technology are taking the place of books and I agree that books are becoming less and less important.

TEST 2 TRANSCRIPT

 12 LISTENING SECTION 1

You will hear a man who runs a recruitment agency talking to a young woman looking for a job. First you have some time to look at questions 1 to 6.

[Pause the recording for 30 seconds.]

You will see that there is an example that has been done for you. On this occasion only, the conversation relating to this will be played first.

Clive: Hello, Edwina, is it? Have a seat.

Edwina: Yes, Edwina. Thanks. I'm looking for a job as a nanny. I like working with children. I talked to you yesterday?

Clive: Oh, yes. Well, we covered most of the ground on the phone yesterday. I've got a form I need to complete for my records. So, **(Example)** you're Edwina Riley, and how should we contact you?

The woman's name is Edwina Riley, so 'Riley' has been written in the space. Now we shall begin. You should answer the questions as you listen, because you will not hear the recording a second time. Listen carefully and answer questions 1 to 6.

[repeat]

Edwina: By email. I check it regularly.

Clive: What's the address?

Edwina: **(1)** It's Edwina like my name then R–I, the first two letters of my surname, at worldnet dot com.

Clive: E–D–W–I–N–A–R–I at worldnet dot com?

Edwina: Yes.

Clive: Good. And you're from Australia?

Edwina: **(2)** Actually, I'm a New Zealander.

Clive: Oh, I'm sorry. I bet it's really irritating being told you're an Australian. Like Canadians being asked what part of the States they're from.

Edwina: I'm used to it. It happens to us all the time.

Clive: And now, you said on the phone that you could bring me some references? One from someone who's known you in a professional capacity and one personal one?

Edwina: Ah, yeah. Here's one from **(3)** John Keen, who was the manager at the play centre in Wellington where I worked for three years after I left school. It's got all his contact details on.

Clive: Thank you. So this was your last employer?

Edwina: Yes, apart from a bit of waitressing recently, but that was just temporary. I'm sure John will answer any questions if you contact him.

Clive: We do run checks, yes. And a personal reference?

Edwina: Ah, you can contact the friend of my mother's I'm staying with here in London: **(4)** Eileen Dorsini. She's a professor. She's known me all my life because she used to be our neighbour back home when she was a primary school teacher there. Now she's working here at the Institute of Education.

Clive: Oh good!

Edwina: I've got her contact details here for you.

Clive: Thanks. I think I have some jobs to suit you. Oh, do you have any practical qualifications, by the way? Life-saving, music, anything?

Edwina: Um, **(5)** I've got an up-to-date first aid certificate. I did a course when I was working.

Clive: That's good. First aid. Anything else?

Edwina: Well, I've got a driving licence, as I told you on the phone. But that's not special, you said, almost everyone needs that really. **(6)** I've got a sailing qualification, it's a certificate of competence.

Clive: So you're a yachtswoman?

Edwina: I love sailing.

Clive: Well, I'll note you have a certificate. Hmm.

Before you hear the rest of the conversation, you have some time to look at questions 7 to 10.

[Pause the recording for 30 seconds.]

....

Now listen and answer questions 7 to 10.

Clive: Now, as I mentioned yesterday, there are three families and the job description is much the same for all of them, as I explained. There are a few other things you need to know. Anyway, the first family's here in London.

Edwina: Yes, I did make a few notes. London, er, that's the Bentons? With two children?

Clive: Yes. That's right, a girl of three and her brother who's eight. The little boy has a quite serious food allergy. Did you learn about things like that on your course?

Edwina: Oh, well, I know what to do if someone has an allergic reaction.

Clive: Good, but **(7)** what they mainly want is someone with an interest in sport, as that's the kind of family they are.

Edwina: Oh that's OK. I'll enjoy that.

Clive: Good. Now the next people are in the country, near Oxford.

Edwina: Oh yeah, the Grangers?

Clive: So, **(8)** they have twin boys of five, who are a bit of a handful, I suspect, but it's a lovely place, quite a grand house, and the family is extremely welcoming. They keep horses. Do you ride?

Edwina: I did when I was younger. I like animals generally.

Clive: Well, 'animal-lover' was their special request, so you'd be fine there. The last family …

Edwina: Yes?

Clive: I don't think I told you **(9)** they live in Scotland.

Edwina: Really? What's their name?

Clive: Campbell.

Edwina: Oh, yes. And they have four girls under ten?

Clive: That's it. They have a lovely city flat, and they own a small island.

Edwina: Wow!

Clive: Actually, you might get on with them very well. **(10)** They particularly wanted someone who would be prepared to cook when they go camping on the island.

Edwina: Camping would really suit me and I'm used to taking my turn doing the food. But it is a long way from London.

Clive: Mm. Yeah, well, you can think about it. Um, then as soon as I've checked your references, we can arrange for you to talk to all of the families.

Edwina: Right. Thanks very much!

Clive: Thank you! I'll email you as soon as I can.

That is the end of section 1. You now have half a minute to check your answers.

[Pause the recording for 30 seconds.]

 LISTENING SECTION 2

You will hear a woman talking to a group of people who are looking round a sports and leisure centre. First you have some time to look at questions 11 to 14.

[Pause the recording for 30 seconds.]

Now listen and answer questions 11 to 14.

Guide: Ladies and gentlemen, I'm very pleased to be able to welcome you to 'Cityscope', our lovely modern sports and leisure facility. I've brought you up to the rooftop café on top of the stadium so that you can enjoy the view while I explain briefly what we have here and point out to you the major features of the site. Then we'll go round and have a look at ground level.

We're extremely proud of this new facility. You see, when the project was first discussed, we expected that a multinational company would give us half our funding and the central government grant would make up most of the rest, with a smaller contribution from local business. Well, we'd got quite far into the planning stage when the multinational pulled out and both central and local government decided they couldn't afford anything, so we ended up with a beautiful project, a small amount of sponsorship promised by local organisations and nothing else.

We thought we'd never build it, but at the last moment, **(11/12)** we had an amazing donation of several million pounds from a national transport company, and that got us going again and **(11/12)** we managed to get all the rest from local fundraising. There's hardly a street in the city that hasn't made its contribution one way or another, so there's a true sense of local ownership here.

So, this is what we got. We wanted a new stadium because the 1950s football stadium is on the other side of town and is shortly due to be pulled down and built over. This site was the old airport with some playing fields on one side of it and a few buildings from the 1930s when the airfield first opened. So we were able to plan a new stadium with plenty of room for all the things people wanted. **(13/14)** The playing fields have been upgraded and refenced so they are now a set of top-quality outdoor pitches for amateur football, hockey and so on. We have both sports and other entertainments here. We want to encourage all kinds of people onto the site and hope some of them may come to use the cinema or the café and end up trying the fitness centre. These are all grouped together: **(13/14)** the café is in the original 1930s passenger hall and the architects have managed to retain some of the elegant style of the building. The other buildings, like the control tower, which would have made a great feature, and the aircraft hangars which we had hoped might house the fitness centre, were unfortunately not structurally sound enough to preserve. So everything else is newly built, opened in 2010.

Before you hear the rest of the talk, you have some time to look at questions 15 to 20.

[Pause the recording for 30 seconds.]

....

Now listen and answer questions 15 to 20.

Right, now if you'd like to gather a little closer to the window I'll point out the various buildings. We're at the highest point of the stadium here in the rooftop café, on the opposite side to the main entrance doors. **(15)** On our left, you can see two buildings just beyond the end of the stadium. The closest one is the business centre, used for meetings and conferences, and so on, which provides a good source of revenue for the upkeep of the sports facilities; and next to the business centre the bigger building is the hotel which is rented from us by an independent company. As you see, they are served by the perimeter road which runs round three-quarters of the site. Now, coming round to the front of the building, **(16)** immediately in front of the entrance, that circular open space at the end of the road is the transport hub. From here, there are buses and a monorail link to the free car park, about ten minutes from here, but you can't see that. There's also a large secure cycle park. Oh, and disabled parking, of course. People find it's very convenient and it keeps the site virtually car-free.
OK. Now if you look as far as you can over to the right, beyond the buildings, you can see our outdoor pitches, which I mentioned earlier. Between the pitches and the entrance is a little kind of pedestrian plaza … are you with me? OK, **(17)** with the cinema in the building furthest away from us, next to the pitches, then there's the ten-pin bowling between the cinema and the road.

(18) Near the far end of the perimeter road and between the mini-roundabout and the pitches – there's our fitness centre, with all kinds of equipment, and a small pool, and changing rooms for teams using the pitches. Then, **(19)** joined on to the stadium, next to the entrance, is a range of small shops which all specialise in sports equipment, clothes, shoes. They sell toys and so on as well, all that sort of thing. They seem to be doing well! As you see, the service road goes right round, but we keep the traffic and the pedestrians well apart, so it's all very relaxed round the plaza, popular with families. And **(20)** just in front of the bowling is our lovely restaurant. You can see it from here – it's that building on the plaza between us and the bowling. It's open all day and in the evenings. There's quite a queue there at weekends, I'm pleased to say.
So, now you've got the layout, we can go and have a closer look at everything.

That is the end of section 2. You now have half a minute to check your answers.

[Pause the recording for 30 seconds.]

 LISTENING SECTION 3

You will hear two people called Chloe and Ivan talking about a business studies course. First you have some time to look at questions 21 to 25.

[Pause the recording for 30 seconds.]

Now listen carefully and answer questions 21 to 25.

Chloe: Oh, hi Ivan.

Ivan: Oh, hi Chloe.

Chloe: I'm glad I bumped into you because I've been looking at this prospectus about courses at the university. I'm thinking of doing a business studies degree. Isn't that what you're doing?

Ivan: Yes, I'm about to start my third year. I think you'd enjoy it. Is there something on the course that you're not sure about?

Chloe: Well, you know I've been working for a publisher for the last four years as a production assistant ...

Ivan: That will be really valuable experience because a lot of people go to university straight from school and don't have that kind of background.

Chloe: Yeah, I know and I'm used to dealing with figures and percentages and things, but **(21)** it's been a while since I've sat down and put my ideas into an essay. I was never that good at it and I'm not sure I can do it now.

Ivan: But you did OK at school, so I'm sure you'll soon get into it again. I was worried about different things when I started, like if I'd be able to use all the computer programs, but you only really need the basics. You have to do a lot of presentations and I thought that would be hard, but we'd actually had such a lot of practice at school it was fine.

Chloe: But did you find writing essays easy?

Ivan: It was OK but **(22)** I was hopeless at getting them in by the deadline and I was always late for lectures, so I had to work hard at that and I tend to be early now.

Chloe: It's good that you've sorted yourself out before you go and get a job or you might not have it very long! I think the course looks really interesting.

Ivan: It is and it also gave me the chance to spend six months working in a local business last year.

Chloe: That's not so important for me unless I could go abroad to use my foreign languages but that doesn't seem to be on offer, which is a shame. **(23)** What really appeals to me, though, is the idea of being assessed throughout the year. I think that's a much more productive way of learning instead of everything being decided in an exam at the end.

Ivan: It's good for people like you who are hard-working all year round. You'll be spending all your time in the library. They've just expanded it too.

Chloe: That's good.

Ivan: Well, yes and no. They've made the study area bigger but it means they've taken some of the magazines and periodicals away, so I think it was better as it was. The university's expanding all the time and **(24)** there are lots of new courses coming next year.

Chloe: Well, that's great news, isn't it? It means the college will have a better reputation as more people will hear about it, so that's good for us.

Ivan: Mm, I agree but they really need to add more lecture rooms as we often have lectures in tiny rooms.

Chloe: Well, you obviously think overall it's a good place to do a degree. I should probably go and have a look round.

Ivan: Well, it's holidays now and there's not much going on there.

Chloe: Oh, so it's probably not worth going in now.

Ivan: But **(25)** you could email my tutor – I know he'd be happy to answer any questions. I can give you his email address. I looked at quite a lot of other universities and read loads of prospectuses but I thought this one was the best.

Before you hear the rest of the conversation, you have some time to look at questions 26 to 30.

[Pause the recording for 30 seconds.]

....

Now listen and answer questions 26 to 30.

Chloe: I was a bit unsure about all the different subjects you can choose on this course.

Ivan: Well, I can tell you a bit about them. There are some subjects you have to do and some that you can choose. The most interesting course I've done is **(26)** public relations.

Chloe: From what I've read it doesn't look very demanding – some of it is really just common sense.

Ivan: But it will be really useful if you want to go into marketing or advertising.

Chloe: That's true, but I need to find out a bit more about it first before I decide – if it will really help me. It's difficult to tell from the prospectus.

Ivan: But you are interested in marketing?

Chloe: Oh, yes.

Ivan: Well, you can choose a **(27)** marketing course. I wasn't very impressed with that course actually. The tutor didn't make it very interesting.

Chloe: Mm, it's good to put on your CV that you've done a marketing course, though, so that would be a definite for me and maybe I'd get a different tutor. What other courses did you choose?

Ivan: I'm doing **(28)** taxation as I was thinking of training to be an accountant but I'm not sure now.

Chloe: Oh, that will be a good option for me because I enjoy working with figures. Although I don't want to be an accountant, it'll be good to have an understanding of taxation, especially if I ever run my own business.

Ivan: Then there's the most popular course, which is **(29)** human resources and a lot of people seem to get jobs in that field.

Chloe: My friend works in human resources and she's really good at it, but I don't think I've got the right personality so I'd give that one a miss. I'm more interested in how businesses actually work – the structure.

Ivan: That's a compulsory course – the structure of business – but you might find **(30)** information systems helpful.

Chloe: Is that kind of computer programs?

Ivan: Some of it is, but also databases, project management, and other things.

Chloe: Oh, sounds useful, but I'll have to look at some of the other possibilities first. You know, Ivan, this course sounds as though it would suit me. I'm going to apply.

Ivan: Great! If there's anything else you want to ask me, you've got my number.

Chloe: Thanks!

That is the end of section 3. You now have half a minute to check your answers.

[Pause the recording for 30 seconds.]

You will hear a talk by a meteorologist about weather forecasting. First you have some time to look at questions 31 to 40.

[Pause the recording for one minute.]

Now listen carefully and answer questions 31 to 40.

I work for the National Weather Service and as part of your course on weather patterns, I've been asked to talk to you about how we predict the weather. We're so used to switching on our TVs and getting an up-to-date weather forecast at any time of day or night that we probably forget that this level of sophistication has only been achieved in the last few decades and weather forecasting is actually an ancient art. So I want to start by looking back into history.

The earliest weather forecasts appeared in the 1500s in almanacs, which were lists of information produced every year. **(31)** Their predictions relied heavily on making links between the weather and where the planets were in the sky on certain days. In addition, predictions were often based on information like if the fourth night after a new moon was clear, good weather was expected to follow.

But once basic weather instruments were invented, things slowly started to change. **(32)** In the mid-fifteenth century, a man called Nicholas Cusa, a German mathematician, designed a hygrometer which told people how much humidity there was in the air. To do this, Cusa put some sheep's wool on a set of scales and then monitored the change in the wool's weight according to the air conditions.

A piece of equipment we all know and use is the thermometer. **(33)** Changes in temperature couldn't really be measured until the Italian Galileo Galilei invented his thermometer in 1593. It wasn't like a modern-day thermometer because it had water inside it instead of mercury. In fact, it wasn't until 1714 that Gabriel Fahrenheit invented the first mercury thermometer. In 1643 another Italian called Evangelista Torricelli invented the first barometer which measured atmospheric pressure. This was another big step forward in more accurate weather predicting.

As time went on, during the seventeenth, eighteenth and nineteenth centuries, all these meteorological instruments were improved and developed and people in different countries began to record measurements relating to their local weather. However, **(34)** in those days it was very difficult to send records from one part of the world to another so it wasn't possible for them to share their information until the electric telegraph became more widespread. This meant that weather observations could be sent on a regular basis to and from different countries. By the 1860s, therefore, weather forecasts were becoming more common and accurate because they were based on observations taken at the same time over a wide area. **(35)** In 1863, France started publishing weather maps each day. This hadn't been done before, and other nations soon followed. So that was the start of national weather forecasting and I'll now tell you how we at the National Weather Centre get the information we need to produce a forecast.

....

Even today, one of the most important methods we use is observations which tell us what the weather is doing right now. Observation reports are sent automatically from equipment at a number of weather stations in different parts of the country. **(36)** They are nearly all based at airports although a few are in urban centres. The equipment senses temperature, humidity, pressure and wind speed direction.

Meteorologists also rely really heavily on satellites which send images to our computer screens. What we see on our screens is bright colours. **(37)** Orange represents dry air and bright blue shows moisture levels in the atmosphere. The satellites are located 22,000 miles above the surface of the Earth and it's amazing that despite that distance **(38)** it's possible for us to make out an individual cloud and follow it as it moves across the landscape.

In addition to collecting data from the ground, we need to know what's happening in the upper levels of the atmosphere. So a couple of times a day from many sites across the country, we send radiosondes into the air. **(39)** A radiosonde is a box containing a package of equipment and it hangs from a balloon which is filled with gas. Data is transmitted back to the weather station.

Finally, radar. **(40)** This was first used over 150 years ago and still is. New advances are being made all the time and it is one method for detecting and monitoring the progress of hurricanes. Crucial information is shown by different colours representing speed and direction. Radar is also used by aircraft, of course.

All this information from different sources is put into computer models which are like massive computer programs. Sometimes they all give us the same story and sometimes we have to use our own experience to decide which is showing the most accurate forecast which we then pass on to you.

So I hope next time you watch the weather forecast, you'll think about how we meteorologists spend our time. And maybe I've persuaded some of you to study meteorology in more depth.

That is the end of section 4. You now have half a minute to check your answers.

[Pause the recording for 30 seconds.]

Test 3   Key

LISTENING SECTION 1

Questions 1–10

1 youth

2 comedy
Distraction The woman has appeared in musicals but the drama club hasn't tried doing one yet. She also mentions 'a historical play' but the man doesn't mention the club performing these.

3 12th March / March 12th / 12 March / March 12
Distraction There are auditions on two dates in March but the next ones are on the 12th.

4 publicity / design / lights (in any order) [We're very short of people / we haven't got enough people = help is needed.]

5 community
Distraction Performances take place in The Manor Theatre.

6 sports centre [on the other side of the road = opposite]
Distraction The car park is just before the hotel but not opposite it.

7 180
Distraction It costs £15 per month.

8 costumes / costume hire
Distraction Photocopying and posters are included.

9 Sawdicott

10 07955 240063

LISTENING SECTION 2

Questions 11–20

11 C

12 B
Distraction 'benefits such as shortening the length of stay in hospital'

13 C
Distraction 'The organisation's been around since 1986, and it gradually expanded during the 1990s.'

14 C
Distraction 'There are of course some similar charities in other parts of the country, in London and so on.'

15 B
Distraction 'This is a former village school … It was modernised and refurbished by the present owners last year.'

16 B

17 B

18 C

19 B

20 A

LISTENING SECTION 3

Questions 21–30

21 C

22 A

23 I

24 F
Distraction They counted the cars but didn't find out about other aspects such as journey times.

25 G

26 E
Distraction Employment and leisure are mentioned as reasons for people coming to the city but they didn't ask questions about these.

27 B
Distraction Stefan will check the statistics but Lauren will draw the graphs and maps.

28 C
Distraction Lauren says maybe one of them should choose the photographs but she changes her mind when the tutor disagrees with her.

29 A
Distraction Stefan rejects the tutor's suggestion that they might write the report together. Stefan says he will use Lauren's notes but he will write it.

30 C
Distraction Lauren thinks Stefan should do the presentation on his own but the tutor wants them both to do it.

LISTENING SECTION 4

Questions 31–40

31 land
Distraction '<u>not</u> on the geographical location of where they lived'

32 industries / trades
Distraction 'minerals' does not relate directly to 'farmers'; 'owners of great estates' is too many words.

33 glass
Distraction brewing, silk-weaving, ribbon-making, knitting – but these are not linked with 'French settlers'.

34 salt

35 villages

36 local

37 fuel

38 waterproof

39 wastage / waste

40 mixture / mix / combination

READING PASSAGE 1

Questions 1–13

The answers to questions 1–6 are in Paragraphs 2–5.

1 mirrors
Distraction The answer cannot be 'sheets of steel' as these are the 'metal panels', nor can it be 'fibre-optic cables' as they don't reflect 'natural' (i.e. 'polar' light).

2 93.3 metres
Distraction The other figures refer to the entrance building, the vaults and the distance between the entrance and the rooms on the right.

3 office: [seeds are processed = make an inventory of the samples]

4 (electrical) current: [the electrical current is reduced = transform the incoming electrical current down]

5 an airlock: 'the two keyed doors separated by an airlock'

6 moisture: [lack of moisture = the minimal moisture level; cold = low temperature; the seeds are conserved = ensure low metabolic activity]

7 TRUE: The seventh paragraph says 'If any more are unearthed … they can be added, too …'.

8 FALSE: The eighth paragraph says the temperature 'will be kept constant' [= all the seeds are kept at the same level of refrigeration].

9 FALSE: The ninth paragraph says 'the cold Arctic air … without human intervention' [= not monitored by staff].

10 NOT GIVEN: The ninth paragraph says that '… during warmer periods, refrigeration equipment will engage' but there is no mention of a back-up refrigeration system.

11 NOT GIVEN: The ninth paragraph says it is hard not to feel respect for the 2,300 or so people who live here but it doesn't say they work at the vault.

12 TRUE: The last paragraph says it is 'sealed inside a watertight package which will never be tampered with while it is in the vault' [= it remains unopened].

13 TRUE: The last paragraph says 'those who receive them are expected to germinate them and generate new samples, to be returned to the vault'.

READING PASSAGE 2

Questions 14–26

The answers to questions 14–16 are in Paragraph A.

14 presentation: 'their presentation varies wildly [= it is their presentation which makes them differ from each other]'

15 (daily) routine: 'The daily routine can be put to one side and they liberate the user … [= offer people an escape from their daily routine].'

16 cultures: 'provide an opportunity to delve into distant cultures [= give the user the chance to inform themselves about other cultures]'

17 E: 'Cookbooks thus became a symbol … the revolutions in America and France [= periods of unrest].'

18 D: 'Recipes were distorted [= altered] through reproduction.'

19 F: 'Two centuries earlier, an understanding of rural ways had been so widespread that … The growing urban middle class needed details, and Beeton provided them in full.'

20 D: 'The invention of printing … the reverse was true.'

21 C: 'But then, they were not written for careful study … Such cooks would have been capable … from the vaguest of instructions.'

22 D: Paragraph H says 'a collection of recipes … a book of chemistry experiments … her book is reassuringly authoritative … no unnecessary spices'.

23 A: Paragraph B says 'the author had been obscure on purpose'.

24 E: Paragraph I says 'David's books were not so much cooking manuals … wish to eat'.

25 B: Paragraph F says 'If Beeton's recipes were not wholly new, though, the way in which she presented them certainly was. She explains …'.

26 C: Paragraph G says 'many of whom still consider it the definitive reference book'.

READING PASSAGE 3

Questions 27–40

27 YES: The first paragraph says 'This lack of awareness has become … very big business indeed'; 'this way of thinking … can be found almost nowhere … mainstream media'.

28 NO: The second paragraph says 'The ensuing debate … same old squabbling between partisan factions … nonsense is talked …'.

29 NOT GIVEN: The fourth paragraph says 'Greenfield's prose is full of mixed metaphors and self-contradictions' but there is no mention of whether her writing has changed.

30 NOT GIVEN: Although the seventh paragraph says books have a different role: '… the unique ability of books to engage and expand the human imagination', there is no suggestion that video games will assume the role of some books.

31 YES: The seventh paragraph says 'Games in which friends and relations gather round a console … growing in popularity. The agenda is increasingly being set by the concerns of mainstream consumers …'.

32 NO: The eighth paragraph says 'No matter how deeply … inappropriate response to technology of any kind'.

33 **C:** The third paragraph says 'there is potentially a profound shift in the way children's minds work'; 'video games … a worldview … less empathetic, more risk-taking and less contemplative'.
Distraction A: The text doesn't suggest that the games give children an adult view of the world; B: The text says Greenfield is articulating widely held fears but these are not children's fears; D: The text suggests children do learn from them but maybe the wrong things.

34 **A:** The fourth paragraph says 'So how do our lawmakers regulate something that is too fluid to be fully comprehended or controlled?'
Distraction B: Although the text says 'A generational divide has opened', it doesn't say this with reference to the lawmakers; C: Although radio and TV are mentioned, it is with regard to 'generational divide', not 'lawmakers'; D: There is no suggestion lawmakers have decided it is too late.

35 **B:** The fifth paragraph says 'Computer games teach and people don't even notice they're being taught.'
Distraction A: Although he mentions 'addictiveness', there is no suggestion of people trying to become less addicted; C: Although he talks about 'a set of challenges', he does not say anything about people competing with each other; D: The writer suggests the possibility of learning being narrow but Martin does not.

36 **B:** The sixth paragraph says 'Games, he points out, generate satisfaction … not by their robotic predictability'.
Distraction A: He thinks they do offer educational benefits: 'more intellectual engagement ... satisfaction via the complexity of their virtual worlds'; C: He thinks that 'the complexity of the problems children encounter within games exceeds that … they might find at school'; D: He thinks games can be compared to scientific procedures: 'Testing the nature and limits of the laws … scientific methods'.

37 **C:** The whole text examines people's attitudes towards video games and whether they are appropriate in today's world. It makes the point that we have to look forward not back.
Distraction A: There is a discussion about whether video games affect people's behaviour and other forms of entertainment but not about their effect on other forms of technology; B: Young people are discussed but their opinions are not given; D: There is a discussion of how the role of video games has developed and changed but not of the principles behind the development.

38 **B:** The ninth paragraph says 'the dire predictions many traditionalists have made ... cannot be upheld … But literacy standards have failed to decline'.

39 **A:** The ninth paragraph says 'a recent $1.5m study funded by the US government – suggests that even pre-teens are not in the habit of blurring game worlds and real worlds'.

40 **C:** The last paragraph says 'Times change: accept it; embrace it.'

WRITING TASK 1
Model answer

Please note that this is only one possible interpretation of the task. Other approaches are equally valid.

The graph shows the overall numbers of tourist arrivals in five parts of the world between 1990 and 2005. In 1990 over 70 million tourists visited North America, more than twice as many as the next most popular destination shown, Central and Eastern Europe. However, between 2000 and 2005 there was a decrease of approximately 1,500,000 in the numbers going to North America whereas there was an increase of nearly 20 million tourists visiting Central and Eastern Europe. The result was that in 2005 the number of tourists arriving in North America and Central and Eastern Europe was almost equal at around 90 million each. The number of tourists visiting South-East Asia rose steadily over the whole period but by 2005 the total was still under 50 million. The regions with the fewest tourist arrivals were South America and Sub-Saharan Africa. The number of tourists going there was similar between 1990 and 1995 but after that there was a greater increase in tourists going to Sub-Saharan Africa than to South America.

WRITING TASK 2
Model answer

Please note that this is only one possible interpretation of the task. Other approaches are equally valid.

Everybody knows that you need money to survive, but it is often said that money does not bring happiness. Although the ideal situation may be to have an enjoyable job that also provides a good salary, that is not always possible. It is important to remember that some people might not have a choice of jobs because they did not have the chance of a good education or because they have a large family to support.

Some people spend large sums of money without thinking about it. However, they could manage with less money and have a better life by taking a job they enjoy or by working fewer hours. I have observed that in families who go on expensive holidays and always have a new car, it is often the father who works such long hours that his children rarely see him. In my opinion that is not an attractive lifestyle and it would be better if he found a less well-paid job that enabled him to spend more time at home.

On the other hand, life is easier for those who have plenty of money as they can do what they want and do not have to think constantly about whether they can afford something or not. In addition, earning a good salary makes it easier to be healthier because you can eat good food and join a gym.

To sum up, I think it is more important to have a job you enjoy if you can afford it. In my view, most people need less money than they think because they waste a lot on buying things they do not need.

TEST 3   TRANSCRIPT

 16 LISTENING SECTION 1

You will hear a number of different recordings and you will have to answer questions on what you hear. There will be time for you to read the instructions and questions and you will have a chance to check your work. All the recordings will be played once only. The test is in four sections. At the end of the test you will be given ten minutes to transfer your answers to an answer sheet. Now turn to section 1.

Section 1. You will hear a woman talking to a man about joining a drama club. First you have some time to look at questions 1 to 6.

[Pause the recording for 30 seconds.]

You will see that there is an example that has been done for you. On this occasion only, the conversation relating to this will be played first.

Man: Hello. Robert Gladwell speaking.

Woman: Oh hi. My name's Chloe Martin. I was given your name and phone number by Ben Winters. I work with him and he said you're a member of Midbury Drama Club.

Man: Yes, I am.

Woman: Well, I've just moved to the area and I'm keen to join a drama club.

Man: Great! Yes, I can give you some information. We're one of the oldest drama clubs in the area as (**Example**) the club started in 1957. We now have about 60 members. Our youngest member is ten and our oldest member is 78.

The year the drama club started was 1957, so '1957' has been written in the space. Now we shall begin. You should answer the questions as you listen because you will not hear the recording a second time. Listen carefully and answer questions 1 to 6.

[repeat]

Woman: I think I saw a picture in the newspaper the other day of some of your members being presented with a prize.

Man: Yes, (**1**) the youth section did very well in a competition and won £100 which will help with their next production. Anyway, tell me a bit more about yourself.

Woman: Well, I've done a bit of acting. I was in a couple of musicals when I was at university and a historical play more recently.

Man: (**2**) Mm … we mainly do comedy plays. We get good audiences for that kind of thing. We haven't attempted a musical yet, but we might do one soon.

Woman: Oh! When do you usually meet?

Man: On Tuesdays.

Woman: Presumably I'll need to do an audition?

Man: Yes, there were a few auditions last Tuesday and we'll be doing more at our next meeting which is in two weeks' time, (**3**) that's on Tuesday the 12th of March. There'll be another opportunity two weeks after that which will be on the 26th of March.

Woman: Oh, well I can come to your next meeting. And if I don't get an acting part in a play, I'd be happy to help with something else. (**4**) I've designed publicity before.

Man: Great! We're very short of people who can do that, so that would be really good. There are a lot of people who like making scenery so we get plenty of help with that, but we haven't got enough people to do the lights at the moment so if you think you can do that or you have any friends who would like to, do bring them along. We can show you what to do if you haven't got any experience.

Woman: Mm … I'll have to think about it. So do you meet in the theatre?

Man: We do our performances in The Manor Theatre but we only hire that for the nights of the actual performances. (**5**) We meet to rehearse every Tuesday evening in the community hall. We rent a room there.

Woman: Oh, I'm not sure where that is. I'll be coming by car because I don't live in the town centre.

Man: It's in Ashburton Road. As you're coming towards the centre down Regent Street, you need to turn left at the crossroads.

Woman: Oh, I know, there's a big car park down there, just before you get to a hotel. (**6**) It's on the other side of the road from the sports centre.

Man: That's it. That's the closest place to leave your car and you don't have to pay in the evening to park there. We meet at 7.30 and we usually finish by 9.30 or 10.

Woman: OK!

Before you hear the rest of the conversation, you have some time to look at questions 7 to 10.

[Pause the recording for 30 seconds.]

....

Now listen and answer questions 7 to 10.

Man: I haven't mentioned that we have to make a charge. (**7**) Everyone pays a subscription of £180 to be a member for a year. You can pay for the whole year at once or you can pay £15 every month. It works out the same. There are reductions for retired people and under-18s but I don't think you come into either category?

Woman: No. I'm 26!

Man: Oh! That fee covers all the costs like photocopying of scripts and producing the posters but (**8**) it excludes the costumes for the performances. We ask people to pay for the hire of those themselves. It does mean they look after them properly as they know they won't get their deposit back otherwise.

Woman: Mm … can I come along to the next meeting then?

Man: Of course. We'd love to see you. And if you want to know more about how we run the auditions or the next play we're doing, why don't you give our secretary a ring? She'll be really pleased to help you.

Woman: What's her name?

Man: It's Sarah Sawdicott. (**9**) That's S–A–W–D–I–C–O double T.

Woman: Got that. And her phone number?

Man: I've only got a mobile number for her. Um … just a minute … let me find it. Ah! (**10**) It's 07955 240063.

Woman: Great. Thanks for your help.

That is the end of section 1. You now have half a minute to check your answers.

[Pause the recording for 30 seconds.]

Now turn to section 2.

🎧 17 LISTENING SECTION 2

You will hear a radio programme in which a presenter called Jasmine tells her colleague Fergus about a charity. First you have some time to look at questions 11 to 15.

[Pause the recording for 30 seconds.]

Now listen carefully and answer questions 11 to 15.

Fergus: And now here's Jasmine, who's come to tell us about this week's charity.

Jasmine: Hi Fergus. This week I'm going to talk about *Forward thinking* and their plans for the Colville Centre.

So, in recent years people have realised how useful the arts can be within healthcare. **(11)** The idea behind *Forward thinking* is to use the arts to promote wellbeing. The charity develops projects for people with special needs and health problems, and also delivers training to healthcare professionals in using the arts, as well as supplying them with information and advice. *Forward thinking* doesn't just run art and craft classes to distract people who are ill, or recovering from illness, but arranges longer-term projects and courses, as it's been shown that the arts can bring all sorts of positive changes in patients, including **(12)** benefits such as shortening the length of stay in hospital and reducing the amounts of medicine they need.

Fergus: I see.

Jasmine: *Forward thinking* has experience of working with a broad range of people from young adults with learning difficulties to older people in homes or daycare centres, and people with physical disabilities.

The organisation's been around since 1986, and it gradually expanded during the 1990s. Then, in the new millennium, it was decided to find a memorable name, **(13)** so it's been operating as *Forward thinking* for several years, er, in fact since 2005.

It's quite a locally based charity, mainly for people in **(14)** the southern part of this region, which includes all rural and urban communities outside the city of Clifton, which has its own organisation. There are of course some similar charities in other parts of the country, in London and so on.

Fergus: Mm. And what's the present fundraising in aid of?

Jasmine: Yeah. Well, the charity needs funding in order to buy the Colville Centre. This is a former village school, which was built in 1868. It was modernised and refurbished by the present owners last year, so **(15)** it's ideal for art classes and for small social events, performances, seminars and so on. *Forward thinking* is fund-raising to purchase the building so they can use it to continue running classes and so on for the general public and eventually also for some of the people they help.

Before you hear the rest of the talk, you have some time to look at questions 16 to 20.

[Pause the recording for 30 seconds.]

....

Now listen and answer questions 16 to 20.

Fergus: Right, so can you give us a few ideas about what classes people might do there? Is it all art classes?

Jasmine: Um, well, there are some very good art classes, but there are lots of other things going on as well. So, for example, there's 'Learn Salsa!' with Nina Balina's team. They say that salsa is an easy dance to learn. It's also an excellent form of exercise, according to Nina, and **(16)** that class is for both men and women, of course. It's ideal for beginners and what they call 'refreshers'. That's £100 for ten sessions.

Then another class is called 'Smooth Movers'. It's with Kevin Bennett and **(17)** it's for you if you don't have the same energy levels as you used to when you were a teenager. It's a gentle exercise class, geared to the needs of whoever is in the group in a particular session. And Kevin is qualified to teach classes to people getting over injuries and so on, and balance training. That's £60 for ten sessions.

Then there's a day called 'Art of the Forest', with Jamie Graham, where you discover Upper Wood, a short walk from the Colville Centre, and learn how to design in 3-D with natural materials. It's an unusual and exciting way to be creative.

Jamie is an artist, with a background also as a country park ranger. **(18)** For this day, youngsters must be accompanied by a parent or guardian and the costs are: adults £40, under-14s £10, but it's best value at £80 for a family of four.

The next one is 'The Money Maze', and this is **(19)** a series of talks by Peter O'Reilly, an Independent Financial Adviser. He gives advice on family finances, things like everything parents need to know about managing the costs of bringing up children, sending them to university, and actually, also, about care for elderly relatives. It's £10 per talk, which will all go to support *Forward thinking*.

And as a final example of what's on offer, there's 'Make a Play'. **(20)** That's for 8–14s and this activity is such a hit that it usually sells out within days of being announced. Basically what you do is write, rehearse and perform a play in just two days and it doesn't require any previous experience. I gather there's lots of fun and silliness along the way and the best bit perhaps is that there's a performance for family and friends at the end. It's just £50 for two days.

Fergus: Pretty good range of activities, I think. And all raising money for a good cause.

Jasmine: Yes! And the all-important contact details are: colville@forwardthinking.org.uk or write to me ...

That is the end of section 2. You now have half a minute to check your answers.

[Pause the recording for 30 seconds.]

Now turn to section 3.

🎧 18 LISTENING SECTION 3

You will hear two students talking to their tutor about a Geography trip. First you have some time to look at questions 21 to 26.

[Pause the recording for 30 seconds.]

Now listen carefully and answer questions 21 to 26.

Tutor: Now, Stefan and Lauren. You worked together on the assignment for your Urban Geography course, didn't you? I know you made a plan of what you were going to do before you went on the field trip. Did you stick to it?

Stefan: More or less!

Tutor: OK. So where did you start?

Stefan: Well, first of all we selected one area of the city to work in – we decided on the centre – and we looked in detail at how it has been developed by doing a survey.

Lauren: Yeah … **(21)** We did that by walking round and dividing the area into different categories such as residential, commercial and industrial so we could record land use. We're going to find some maps from 50 years ago and from 100 years ago so we can look at what has changed.

Tutor: Good! So that gives you a foundation. Then what did you do?

Stefan: Um, I was interested in looking at how polluted the city was.

Lauren: I thought that was too general a topic and would be difficult to check. But Stefan persuaded me and actually it was quite interesting because before we started, we assumed that a lot of the pollution problems would be caused by industry.

Stefan: In fact, most of the industrial development has been on the outskirts and most pollution is caused by the traffic which passes through the city centre every day. **(22)** There are five major road junctions around the edge of the city so we set up equipment to check the air quality on each of those three times on one day.

Lauren: In the morning and evening, which is when most journeys are made in and out of the city, and at 2.30 in the afternoon.

Stefan: **(23)** On the same day, we went to the two *busiest* junctions in the morning and evening to calculate the traffic flow into the city.

Tutor: Right.

Stefan: We'll be able to produce some graphs from the figures we collected.

Lauren: Yeah.

Tutor: Presumably you then looked at where all these cars ended up?

Lauren: I thought we should look at why people were coming into the city – um, whether it was for employment or education or leisure activities but Stefan thought that would be too difficult.

Stefan: Because most people were in cars it would be hard to ask them. **(24)** So we decided to spend an afternoon examining the parking facilities available instead. We established the capacity of each car park and we spent an afternoon counting cars in and out so we have an idea of how long people spend in the city centre.

Tutor: So do you have evidence that most journeys are made by car within the city centre?

Stefan: We checked local government statistics to see if that was true but they were inconclusive.

Lauren: Everything is quite close together in the city centre and there are wide pavements so you would expect people to walk from one place to another.

Stefan: So we chose a number of locations and **(25)** we noted how many pedestrians passed a particular spot.

Tutor: Um, how did you choose where to do that?

Stefan: Oh, we stood at two places in the business district, one in the shopping area and the other was in an area where there are more tourists.

Tutor: Right.

Lauren: I thought it was really important to talk to people so we carried out a survey on how people usually travelled into the city. **(26)** We asked them about their usual means of transport.

Stefan: We found out that it varied according to why people were travelling – if they were employed in the city they wanted to get there quickly but if they were coming in for their leisure time they didn't mind using the bus.

Lauren: That's all we had time for while we were there.

Before you hear the rest of the conversation, you have some time to look at questions 27 to 30.

[Pause the recording for 30 seconds.]

....

Now listen and answer questions 27 to 30.

Tutor: OK. So shall we talk about what you're going to do next and how you're going to divide the tasks up? How are you going to present the data you've got?

Stefan: Well, some of the information can be presented as graphs or maps.

Lauren: **(27)** I'm quite good at the software.

Stefan: You'd better do that then, Lauren. I'll help you check all the statistics before you start.

Lauren: OK.

Tutor: Um, it's good to present as much as you can visually. Is there anything else you can use as visuals?

Stefan: Mm … we've got a lot of photographs which we can go through.

Tutor: Aha.

Lauren: Er, we both took them so some will be duplicated. It's going to take ages to go through them all. Maybe one of us should just choose some.

Tutor: **(28)** It's better if you collaborate. That way you'll end up with the best of what you've got.

Lauren: That's fine, we'll do that.

Tutor: And, er, when the graphs and maps are done, **(29)** you'll need to write a report, an analysis of the data. Will you do that together?

Stefan: I think that should be my responsibility if we're going to share the work out evenly. I can use some of Lauren's notes as well as my own.

Tutor: OK. And finally, you'll be presenting your project to the rest of the group in a couple of weeks' time.

Lauren: We thought it'd be better for Stefan to do that as he's got more experience at that kind of thing.

Tutor: **(30)** I would prefer to have input from both of you as I have to do an assessment.

Stefan: We'll take turns then. We'll divide it into sections and talk about a few things each.

Tutor: Good. You'll find it easier, Lauren, than doing a presentation on your own. Well, if you need to ask me any more questions while you're working on this, email me. I look forward to seeing what you produce.

Lauren and Stefan: Thanks!

That is the end of section 3. You now have half a minute to check your answers.

[Pause the recording for 30 seconds.]

Now turn to section 4.

🎧 19 **LISTENING SECTION 4**

You will hear a lecturer giving the beginning of a talk on the history of British pottery. First you have some time to look at questions 31 to 40.

[Pause the recording for one minute.]

Now listen carefully and answer questions 31 to 40.

Lecturer: Thank you for coming to this series of talks. Before I talk in detail about the experiments and innovations of the British ceramicists, I'd like to give you a summary of the social and manufacturing background in which they lived and worked. So, we're talking about England, or more specifically, the region known as 'The Midlands', and we need to go back, mainly to the eighteenth century and, briefly, even earlier, to put it in a global context.

Now, at that period **(31)** the majority of the population, whatever their station in life, as you might say, were dependent for their living, in one way or another, not on the geographical location of where they lived, but on the physical characteristics of the actual land they lived on. This is true, whether we're talking about the aristocracy, the owners of great estates, who incidentally had no snobbery about the concept of making money from all the reserves of coal, or timber, or stone on their rolling acres, or the farmers making a fat living from the rich soils. And besides these groups, and the less affluent ones, **(32)** the deposits of iron ore and lead, the limestone and flint and the brown and yellow clays also sustained the numerous industries in the area.

It's important to recognise that it was already an industrial region, and had been so for centuries. There were many Midland trades, some of them indigenous, some of them not. For example, **(33)** there were immigrants from France who came as early as the late sixteenth century and they were producers of glass. A century later, there is plenty of evidence that the variety of trades was enormous: there was brewing in Burton-on-Trent; silk-weaving and ribbon-making near Coventry; framework knitting around Nottingham. And of course, **(34)** in Cheshire men dug the salt, as we still do nowadays even, which in that era was sent downriver to the estuary of the Mersey.

Now, among these well-established trades, one of the oldest of the local crafts was pottery. As you will probably be aware, ceramics has always been a mix of science, design and skill, and a good potter is in a sense an experimental chemist, trying out new mixes and glazes, and needing to be alert to the impact of changes of temperature on different types of clay. For two hundred years, up to the time we are concerned with, **(35)** potters had been making butterpots and pitchers and patterned plates, using the clay which was plentiful in the area where they lived – in a handful of North Staffordshire villages dotted along the low hills.

Now I want to explain a little about the industrial processes which had preceded the great breakthrough in Germany in 1708. That's when the formula for porcelain was discovered, a secret that had been held in China for a thousand years. In the Midlands, in England, as elsewhere, there had basically been two kinds of pottery. The first was known, is still known, as 'earthenware'.

Now this was a bit rough and ready, but it was deservedly popular for several reasons. To start with, it was relatively cheap, so it could be used by most households. This was because **(36)** it could be made from local clay without any complicated processing or added materials. **(37)** From the potter's point of view there was another reason for its cheapness. This was that it could be fired in simple ovens, or kilns, and at relatively low temperatures, so he didn't have to spend so much money on fuel to achieve the necessary heat. On the other hand, after one firing in the kiln, the problem with earthenware was that it remained porous so had limited usefulness. So for most purposes **(38)** it had to go back in the kiln for a second firing before it became waterproof.

And another thing was that it was extremely breakable – I mean, before it had even been sold. I suppose the potter wouldn't have minded so much if people just had to keep coming back for more every time they broke a jug or whatever! – but it was very inconvenient because it meant there was a lot of **(39)** wastage in the course of the manufacturing process.

Anyway, for all these reasons, if people could afford it, and that would be all but the very poor, they would buy **(40)** stoneware, a much tougher product.

Now, for this, the potter used a slightly more expensive raw material, which was made by combining clay and flint and this mixture was fired at a far higher heat, with the result that the ingredients vitrified, that is to say, in effect the whole thing became glassy and because of this it was non-porous, and naturally, this was regarded as a great advance.

Well, that's the situation in the eighteenth century. Are there any questions at this stage? OK. So, now we can go on to look at the age of innovation.

That is the end of section 4. You now have half a minute to check your answers.

[Pause the recording for 30 seconds.]

That is the end of the listening test. In the IELTS test you would now have 10 minutes to transfer your answers to the Listening Answer sheet.

LISTENING SECTION 1

Questions 1–10

1 Oskar

2 52C
Distraction 5: This is his neighbour's address, for delivery

3 Avenue

4 cash
Distraction 'will you be paying by debit card or credit card? … Well, er, I don't have any cards yet. I'll have some shortly …'

5 city

6 Living
Distraction '664? That's, um, not "Home Office"?'

7 collect

8 green

9 lock

10 3rd October / 3 October / October 3
Distraction 'today's the 29th of September'; 'I'll drop in tomorrow morning to pay'

LISTENING SECTION 2

Questions 11–20

11/12 A/D (in any order).
Distraction B: not 'unusual' because these are 'events you would expect a museum to have'; C: again, not unusual because 'sheep, cows and hens … are much the same as those you see on modern farms'; E: not 'unusual' because 'All the buildings are filled with furniture, machinery and objects. You may be able to see these in other museums …'.

13/14 C/E (in any order).
Distraction A: You can buy sweets, not bread: '… you can watch a demonstration of someone making bread, … old-fashioned sweets for sale'; B: Although 'you can watch horses being exercised in the old stables', there is no suggestion that visitors can ride them; D: You can buy stationery: 'There's a stationer's shop which sells … all available for purchase by visitors' but the posters are part of a demonstration and there is no mention of them being for sale: 'Upstairs in the same building, a printer demonstrates the production of posters …'.

15 E: After the crossroads the exhibition centre is the larger of two buildings on either side of the path.
Distraction D is the smaller of the two so it cannot be the correct answer.

16 A

17 C: The path crosses the railway line to get to the farmhouse. You can get to all the other buildings without crossing the railway line.

18 H
Distraction G cannot be the correct answer because the coal mine is just in front of the entrance.

19 F
Distraction I, D and G cannot be the correct answer because from the crossroads you don't have to walk through the woods to get to them.

20 B

LISTENING SECTION 3

Questions 21–30

21 A

22 H

23 B

24 G

25 D

26 E

27 B
Distraction A: 'store room' is a cupboard for objects, not a shop; C: she mentions people she didn't know: 'I mistook some important visitor for a colleague, because I didn't know who anyone was' but there is no mention of being asked to meet 'visitors'.

28 A
Distraction B: Cressida didn't see this as 'fortunate': 'Unfortunately it meant I spent the next three days stuck in the editing suite'; C: Cressida went with the reporter who did the interview: '… when the senior reporter needed someone to go out with him when he went to interview a junior minister, I got to go along' but this was so she could do the 'technical side', there is no suggestion she did any interviewing.

29 B
Distraction A: There is no mention of the business side of things; C: She doesn't say she needs to improve her teamwork, in fact she is pleased with it: '… I feel much more confident … I did actually make a contribution'.

30 C: The rest of Cressida's speech explains that the disagreement was about the actions of the presenter, which she found to be unethical.
Distraction A: This contradicts the statement: 'this wasn't some public relations expert'; B: The end of the same sentence also contradicts the statement: 'this wasn't … or government professional spokesperson'.

LISTENING SECTION 4

Questions 31–40

31 violin

32 blues

33 steel / metal
Distraction not 'traditional gut' which is what other guitars used

34 Frying Pan / frying pan

35 magnets

36 plastic
Distraction It is compared to guitars made of wood.

37 solid
Distraction 'All previous guitars had been hollow …'

38 mass production

39 Precision / precision

40 gold

READING PASSAGE 1

Questions 1–13

(The table is arranged in a logical way, but the information is not in exactly the same order as it is given in the passage.)

1 identical: The first paragraph says 'The students' performance ends up looking just like a monkey's. It's practically [= almost] identical'.

2 balls of paper: The sixth paragraph says '… showed it two groups of balls of paper … changed the quantities' (although the text mentions 'siblings' and 'brothers', the experiment did not use other chicks).

3 female: The last paragraph says 'researchers in America found that female coots appear to calculate' (the text also mentions 'an intruder', but it was the 'counting' behaviour/behavior of the coots that the researchers were interested in).

4 fruit flies: The second paragraph says 'tempted salamanders with two sets of fruit flies held in clear tubes'.

5 mosquitofish: The third paragraph says 'studies of mosquitofish, which instinctively join the biggest shoal'.

6 surface area: The fourth paragraph says 'The team arranged these shapes so that they had the same overall [= total] surface area and luminance [= brightness] …'.

7 sugar water: The fifth paragraph says 'two chambers – one which contained sugar water, which they like, while the other was empty. … The bees quickly learned … the correct chamber'.

(Questions 8–13 come in the same order as the information in the passage.)

8 TRUE: The first paragraph says 'rhesus monkeys and university students … had to decide which set contained more objects. … monkeys, like humans, make more errors when two sets of objects are close in number'; primates are defined in the second paragraph: 'Humans and monkeys are mammals, in the animal family known as primates.'

9 FALSE: The fifth paragraph says 'the number of shapes [= how many shapes, not the actual shape of individual numerals]'.

10 NOT GIVEN: Although the sixth paragraph says 'If chicks spend their first few days surrounded by certain objects', this is a general statement, not how long the experiment lasted; 'three- and four-day-old chicks' tells us the age of the chicks, but it does not say that the experiment took place on two days; we do not know whether it was repeated on more than one day.

11 TRUE: The sixth paragraph says that these were almost newborn 'three- and four-day-old chicks' and that they 'scuttled [= ran] to the larger quantity at a rate well above chance. They were doing some very simple arithmetic, claim the researchers'.

12 NOT GIVEN: Although the last paragraph says 'Animals on the prowl … decide which tree has the most fruit, or which patch of flowers will contain the most nectar' and that this would be an 'obvious advantage[s] of numeracy', we are not told whether any researchers have carried out experiments involving the animals searching for these foods.

13 TRUE: The last paragraph says 'female coots appear to calculate … and add any in the nest laid by an intruder [= another bird]'.

READING PASSAGE 2

Questions 14–26

14 vi: 'The facts, however, do not justify our unease.'

15 i: '… a squall [= storm] of conflicting initiatives … It's a squall that dies down and then blows harder from one month to the next.'

16 v: '… there's nothing quite like plastic.'

17 iii: '… there is one law of plastic that … prevails over [= is more important than] all others …: a little goes a long way … And in the packaging equation, weight is the main issue …'

18 vii: 'To target plastic on its own is to evade the complexity of the issues.'

19 C: Paragraph E says '… explains that in fact they found apples in fours on a tray covered by plastic film needed 27 per cent less packaging in transportation than those sold loose [= not wrapped before they are sold]'.

20 A: Paragraph B says 'It is being left to the individual conscience'.

21 B: Paragraph C says '… in the UK, waste in supply chains [= the way goods get from producer to consumer] is about 3 per cent'.

22 D: Paragraph E says 'the hunger [= desire] to do something quickly is diverting effort away from more complicated questions'.

23 A: Paragraph E says 'Plastic as a lightweight food wrapper is now built in as the logical thing … It only makes sense if you have a structure [i.e. social structure, society] such as exists now.'

24 industrial (Paragraph A)

25 indestructible (Paragraph A)

26 seasons (Paragraph A)

READING PASSAGE 3
Questions 27–40

27 **A**: The first paragraph says 'intelligence involves the capacity … to adapt to one's environment'.
Distraction B: There is no suggestion in the text that we change behaviour according to what other people do; C: The word 'environment' is used in this text in a more abstract way, i.e. 'surroundings'; D: Although the text states that the 'capacity … to learn from experience' is one feature of intelligence and we can suppose that coping with 'unexpected setbacks' would be one outcome of learning from experience, which is one feature of intelligence, this is not stated anywhere in the text.

28 **B**: The second paragraph says 'The former group ['psychometricians' in the previous paragraph] has examined the issue by determining how children's abilities on a wide range of tasks intercorrelate, or go together.'
Distraction A: Although there is a wide range of 'tasks', there is no suggestion that any of them are 'cooperative'. However, psychometricians are interested in how the individual tasks 'intercorrelate, or go together'; C: The text only states that psychometricians have used statistics in their research, not that they use mathematical models to predict results; D: 'Common sense' [= good practical, logical abilities] is not the same as 'general intelligence' [overall intellectual ability].

29 **D**: The third paragraph says 'studies of age-related changes … For instance, … Horn and Cattell … fluid abilities peak in early adult life, whereas crystallised abilities increase up to advanced old age'.
Distraction A: Horn and Cattell didn't argue with each other. Instead they 'argued for' something [= they put forward the idea]; B: It is true that 'Their research concerned both linguistic and mathematical abilities' (tests of 'mental manipulation of abstract symbols' and 'comprehension and information') but this is not why Horn and Cattell are mentioned; C: Their research was about certain special skills, but not general intelligence.

30 **B**: The fifth paragraph says 'the focus should be on the thinking processes involved rather than on levels of cognitive achievement'.
Distraction A: In fact the text tells us the opposite: 'a second element concerns the notion that development proceeds … in a set order'; C: The text does not tell us what materials he used, only that his work was 'backed up by observations'; D: The text does not describe exactly the range of either ages or intelligence.

31 **NO**: The first paragraph says 'quite difficult to define [= what is meant by] in unambiguous terms and unexpectedly controversial [= people disagree about it]'.

32 **YES**: The second paragraph says 'general measures of intelligence tend to have considerable powers …. Nevertheless, it is plain that it is not at all uncommon for individuals to be very good at some sorts of task and yet quite poor at some others'.

33 **NO**: The third paragraph says the test suggests the opposite of the statement: 'Crystallised abilities' which are 'assessed by tests of comprehension … increase up to advanced old age', whereas 'Fluid abilities … that require mental manipulation of abstract symbols' 'by contrast … peak in early adult life'.

34 **YES**: The fourth paragraph says 'These findings seemed to suggest a substantial lack of continuity [= a big difference] between infancy and middle childhood. However, it is important to realise that the apparent discontinuity [= what appears to be a difference] will vary according to which of the cognitive skills were assessed in infancy.'

35 **NOT GIVEN**: In the fifth paragraph we are told Piaget was influential regarding both ('immense body of research' and 'subsequent thinking') but there is no mention that either one of these things had a bigger impact than the other.

36 **NO**: The last paragraph says 'his view that the child is an active agent of learning … has stood the test of time [= it is still respected]', even if the previous paragraph states that 'most of his concepts have had to be … radically revised, or rejected'.

The summary outlines the ideas in the fourth paragraph.

37 **C**: verbal: 'verbal abilities are more important later on'.

38 **A**: adult: 'It has been found that tests of coping with novelty do predict later intelligence' (the text does not deal with 'academic ability' in particular).
Note: 'academic ability' is the natural collocation, not 'academic intelligence'

39 **E**: inquisitive: 'their interest in and curiosity about the environment'.

40 **I**: unfamiliar: 'the extent to which this is applied to new situations'.

WRITING TASK 1
Model answer

Please note that this is only one possible interpretation of the task. Other approaches are equally valid.

> The graph compares the percentage of their income which people in the UK and USA spend on petrol. From the data, we can see two clear differences.
>
> Firstly, the difference between the poorest 10% and the richest 10% is greater in the UK than in the USA. In the former, the poorest spend less than 0.5% of their income on petrol, suggesting that they do not use cars very much, and the richest spend around 3%. By contrast, in the US, the poorest spend around 4–5% while the richest spend between 2 and 3%. This suggests that virtually everyone in the USA uses a car sometimes. Secondly, in the USA it is also noticeable that the percentage of income spent by the poor can be twice that spent by the rich. However, in the UK, the percentage spent rises quite steeply for the poorer members of the population but then remains almost constant apart from the very richest, where it falls again. In both countries people on middle incomes spend about the same percentage. Overall, the percentage of income spent on fuel generally gets higher in the UK, the more you earn, whereas it decreases in the US.

WRITING TASK 2

Model answer

Please note that this is only one possible interpretation of the task. Other approaches are equally valid.

Using the Internet has become a normal part of everyday life for many people. They use it to book airline tickets, or to access news about world events, or to follow the fortunes of their favourite football club. Millions of people across the world belong to social networking groups where they keep in touch with their friends and, if they live away from them, their family. In my opinion these are all good ways to use the Internet.

When it comes to finding out information there are some very good sites where it is possible to check, for example, someone's biographical details or statistics about global warming. However, information from the Internet should be used with caution, because although there are many reliable sites, such as academic journals and well-known newspapers, there are also unreliable ones, so it is important to check where information originates from before using it.

Some students use websites which offer ready-made assignments. This is not a good idea, even if you ignore the fact that it is cheating, because such websites may contain factual errors or biased views. In a recent case, a student found herself in serious trouble when she submitted an essay from one of these sites only to discover that it was about Austria, not Australia, but had an error in the title.

Nevertheless, it is nowadays possible for people all over the world to study or do business on an equal footing, in a way that was unimaginable only a few years ago. On the whole I believe that the Internet is an excellent way both to communicate and to find information, as long as it is used intelligently.

TEST 4 TRANSCRIPT

 **LISTENING SECTION 1**

You will hear a number of different recordings and you will have to answer questions on what you hear. There will be time for you to read the instructions and questions and you will have a chance to check your work. All the recordings will be played once only. The test is in four sections. At the end of the test you will be given ten minutes to transfer your answers to an answer sheet. Now turn to section 1.

Section 1. You will hear a woman who works in a furniture store taking a telephone order from a man. First you have some time to look at questions 1 to 5.

[Pause the recording for 30 seconds.]

You will see that there is an example that has been done for you. On this occasion only, the conversation relating to this will be played first.

Sally: Good afternoon. Megequip. This is Sally speaking. How may I help you?

Oskar: Oh hello. Um, I'd like to order some items from your catalogue.

Sally: Yes. Are you an existing customer?

Oskar: Er, no. I've only just moved here from South Africa. But I picked up your winter catalogue in the city centre yesterday.

Sally: Fine. The winter catalogue is our current one. As you're a new customer, I need to take a few details from you.

The customer is using the winter catalogue, so 'winter' has been written in the space. Now we shall begin. You should answer the questions as you listen because you will not hear the recording a second time. Listen carefully and answer questions 1 to 5.

[repeat]

Oskar: Sure.

Sally: Your name is?

Oskar: Oskar Greening. That's **(1)** <u>Oskar with a 'K'.</u>

Sally: <u>O–S–K–A–R?</u>

Oskar: <u>Yes.</u>

Sally: Greening. And your address?

Oskar: Um, York Terrace.

Sally: Here in the city?

Oskar: Yes.

Sally: What number?

Oskar: It's a flat. **(2)** <u>Number 52C.</u>

Sally: <u>C.</u> Got that. And would that be the same address for delivery?

Oskar: Um, no, actually, I'm out all day. But my neighbour can take delivery at number 5 York **(3)** <u>Avenue.</u> It's just round the corner.

Sally: OK, fine, number 5, I've got that. And will you be paying by debit card or credit card?

Oskar: Well, er, I don't have any cards yet. I'll have some shortly, but I want these things this week if possible. **(4)** <u>Could I come to the store and pay cash in advance?</u>

Sally: Well, I guess so. I'll make a note. I'm afraid that payment method doesn't entitle you to a discount.

Oskar: No, I didn't expect one for that. But what about my address? It says on the cover of the catalogue –

Sally: Oh yes, you're right. Of course **(5)** <u>York Terrace is within the city so you get free delivery and 5% discount</u> on your order.

Oskar: Oh, good.

Before you hear the rest of the conversation, you have some time to look at questions 6 to 10.

[Pause the recording for 30 seconds.]

....

Now listen and answer questions 6 to 10.

Sally: So what would you like to order? You have our current catalogue, you say?

Oskar: Yes. I need three things for the room where I study – my office, I guess. Um, the most urgent is a desk lamp. Is your catalogue, number 664 in stock?

Sally: 664? That's, um, not 'Home Office'? **(6)** <u>It's in the 'Living' section of the catalogue?</u>

Oskar: It is. I want a small one that clips onto the edge of the desk.

Sally: Yes, no problem. In which colour?

Oskar: I'd like the greyish-coloured one, please.

Sally: Oh you mean the shade we call 'slate'. Yes, it's a nice colour.

Oskar: And, um, I wondered, could I get that when I come in to pay rather than waiting for delivery? I really need to be able to read at night and the lights in this flat are useless.

Sally: Yes, I'm sure that'll be OK. **(7)** <u>I'll note down that's – 'customer will collect'.</u> What else did you want?

Oskar: Well, I need a chair which gives good support when I'm using my computer. I saw one in your 'Home Office' section and I think it would suit me. It's on page 45, item number, oh, um, 129.

Sally: Um, yes?

Oskar: And it's fully adjustable, isn't it?

Sally: Let me see. Height, yes, back, yes, I'm not sure about the arms though.

Oskar: Oh, that could be a problem … I'm very tall.

Sally: What about 131 on the same page? That has adjustable arms, seat, everything!

Oskar: **(8)** <u>But can I get that in the same colour, I mean the green, like the one it shows?</u>

Sally: <u>Oh, they all come in the full range of colours.</u>

Oskar: <u>OK, so I'll go for 131 in green then.</u>

Sally: Mm … I think you'll like that. My brother's very tall and he uses one. We can make sure there's one on the delivery van to you early next week.

Oskar: Oh good, thanks. And so, lastly, I need a filing cabinet for my documents. A little filing cabinet. With two drawers?

Sally: OK. Two drawers. Do you want the ordinary one or the lockable one? It's an extra twenty pounds.

Oskar: Sorry, what's that?

Sally: **(9)** You can have it with a lock, which is more secure.

Oskar: Oh, yes, please.

Sally: OK … so that's number 153.

Oskar: It doesn't by any chance come in slate, does it?

Sally: Well, it's similar. But the commercial office furniture doesn't come in so many shades.

Oskar: So it's grey?

Sally: That's right.

Oskar: Fine, that'll do.

Sally: Now, about delivery. The two items will probably come at different times as we have the chair in stock here so our van will bring it, as I said. **(10)** The filing cabinet will be coming direct from London, so – today's the 29th of September, say, not more than four days, that'll be delivered on or before the 3rd of October. You'll have them both within four days.

Oskar: That's fine. I'll drop in tomorrow morning to pay and get the lamp. Um, thanks for all your help.

Sally: Thank you for your order. Let me know if we can do anything else for you.

Oskar: Thank you. I will. Bye.

Sally: Bye.

That is the end of section 1. You now have half a minute to check your answers.

[Pause the recording for 30 seconds.]

Now turn to section 2.

 21 LISTENING SECTION 2

You will hear a man taking a group of tourists around a museum site. First you have some time to look at questions 11 to 14.

[Pause the recording for 30 seconds.]

Now listen carefully and answer questions 11 to 14.

Guide: Welcome to Brampton Museum. I'm going to tell you a little bit about the museum first and then show you round. As you can see, Brampton is an open-air museum. The first open-air museums were established in Scandinavia towards the end of the 19th century, and the concept soon spread throughout Europe and North America and there are several in Britain, all of which tell the history of a particular part of the country.

Brampton focuses on life during the 19th century. The site was chosen because there were already some historic 19th-century buildings here and **(11/12)** others have been dismantled in different parts of the region, and rebuilt on the site. This hadn't been attempted before in these parts so we're very proud of what we have here. All the buildings are filled with furniture, machinery and objects. You may be able to see these in other museums but not in their original settings. **(11/12)** What also sets Brampton apart from other museums is that the story of the exhibits is told not by labels but by costumed staff like myself. I look after sheep, cows and hens, which are much the same as those you see on modern farms,

but I use traditional methods to care for them. You will also be able to see a blacksmith and a printer, as well as other craftspeople. If you talk to them, you'll be able to find out what life was really like 150 years ago. Our programme of activities during the year has guided walks, an agricultural fair and all the other events you would expect a museum to have, but remember: here you experience them in the real surroundings.

The site is divided into different areas. The main building contains our High Street which is a street of 19th-century shops, offices and some homes. There's a stationer's shop which sells a range of specially selected cards, prints and copies of Victorian stationery, all available for purchase by visitors. Upstairs in the same building, a printer demonstrates the production of posters, business cards and advertising material. Across the street from the stationer's is a clothes shop and there's a baker's where you can watch a demonstration of someone making bread, cakes and pastries. We also have a sweet shop which has old-fashioned sweets for sale. **(13/14)** Vintage trams travel along from one end of the street to the other, carrying visitors on their journey into the past. We will also be visiting the farm and taking a ride on a steam train. Of course the main form of transport in those days was the horse and you can watch horses being exercised in the old stables. This part of Britain was famous for coal-mining and on the site we have part of a mine which opened in 1860 and was worked for over a hundred years, before closing in 1963. **(13/14)** Visitors can put on a hard hat and take a guided tour underground to see how coal was worked and to experience the working conditions in the early 1900s.

Before you hear the rest of the talk, you have some time to look at questions 15 to 20.

[Pause the recording for 30 seconds.]

....

Now listen and answer questions 15 to 20.

Now if you'd like to look at your map, we'll begin our tour. The site is a bit like a circle with the railway going round the edge. You can see where we are now by the entrance and we're going to start by walking to the High Street. **(15)** We'll go to the crossroads in the middle of the map and go straight on, making our way between two buildings on either side of the path. The larger one is an exhibition centre but it's not open today, unfortunately. The other building is offices. **(16)** The path leads directly to the High Street building which is at the opposite side of the site to the entrance. Here you're free to wander around and take a ride up and down on a tram. **(17)** We'll then take the path which follows the railway line and crosses it to the farm. If you wish, you can have tea in the farmhouse and there'll be time to look at the animals and the machinery. **(18)** Then, we cross the railway line again and visit our special attraction which is the coal mine. It's just in front of us here at the entrance. **(19)** We'll return to the crossroads and walk through a small wooded area to the Manor House. This is one of the original buildings on the site and belonged to a wealthy farmer. You can look round the house and gardens and talk to our guides who can tell you what it was like to live there. **(20)** We will then follow a path which goes past the pond and will take us to the Railway Station, which is situated between the path and the railway line. Finally we'll take the steam train back around the site, passing alongside the High Street and the Coal Mine back to the entrance. So if you'd like to follow me …

That is the end of section 2. You now have half a minute to check your answers.

[Pause the recording for 30 seconds.]

Now turn to section 3.

22

LISTENING SECTION 3

You will hear a conversation between Cressida, a student of journalism, and her tutor, Dr Erskine, about a work placement that she has recently done. First you have some time to look at questions 21 to 26.

[Pause the recording for 30 seconds.]

Now listen carefully and answer questions 21 to 26.

Dr Erskine: Well, Cressida, that was an interesting presentation you gave yesterday on your placement at the TV news centre.

Cressida: Thank you, Dr Erskine, I did work hard on it.

Dr Erskine: Yes and **(21)** you did entertain the class, they enjoyed your humour, but you informed them too. But I felt there was a bit of a back story – you know, something you weren't telling us? So how was it really?

Cressida: Yeah, well, I learnt a lot, as I said. But I think some of the lessons weren't ones I wanted to share with the whole group. I mean, **(22)** my expectations about what it would be like were too high. I'd been fantasising a bit about what I'd be doing. I mean, it all worked out OK in the end … but I got off to a bad start.

Dr Erskine: Yes, I heard something similar from **(23)** the producer – um, Ainsley Webb – who assessed your performance. He was quite negative about some of the things you did, and your initial attitude, I'm afraid. Would you like to give me your version?

Cressida: I didn't prepare properly is the main thing. On my first morning, I hadn't checked my commuting route properly, and I didn't notice that it says the buses don't start till six. I had to run all the way to the studio, but I was still late, and I looked a mess.

Dr Erskine: Well, **(24)** better at this stage of your career than later. To be honest, I made the same kind of mistakes when I was your age. But anyway, as I say, I think the presentation yesterday went extremely well, and I will bear that in mind when I grade your work experience overall.

Cressida: Thank you for being so understanding.

Dr Erskine: Right. Now, have you completed your diary of what you did there? **(25)** Professor Jenkins hasn't received it, he says.

Cressida: Um, yes, I have finished it, but I wanted to just tidy it up a bit. Some of it was written in a bit of a hurry. I'll email it to him this afternoon.

Dr Erskine: OK. But I'm afraid he says this will have to be the last time you submit late. Journalism is all about deadlines and if you can't manage them on your course he can't give you a diploma saying you're competent, can he?

Cressida: Oh. Yes. I'll do it straight after this. I didn't realise.

Dr Erskine: Well, he can be a bit abrupt if he's kept waiting. It's the one thing he really doesn't like. I'm sure everything is going to be fine. You're getting very good grades on your work, so, as long as you remember that.

Cressida: Yes.

Dr Erskine: Now, did you manage OK generally, do you think?

Cressida: Yeah, OK, I think. Well, it took a while to get to grips with all the equipment. Some of it was quite old, not as fast as what we have here in college and at first I kept thinking it was my fault – I wasn't pressing the right buttons, or something. The thing was, none of **(26)** the TV centre staff asked me if I wanted instructions.

If I asked them how to do some particular operation, they were perfectly civil and would show me, and even say thank you for what I did do, but I felt awkward to keep asking.

Before you hear the rest of the conversation, you have some time to look at questions 27 to 30.

[Pause the recording for 30 seconds.]

Now listen and answer questions 27 to 30.

Dr Erskine: Now, um, well, let's just review where you are, your write-up, and what you're going to include going forward to next term. First of all, did you eventually feel you were given enough to do?

Cressida: The first couple of days were manic, the production team was short of staff and **(27)** I was rushing all over the building taking messages to various people and fetching things. Of course, I didn't know my way around, so I kept ending up in some store room or somewhere instead of the studio I was meant to be in. Or I mistook some important visitor for a colleague, because I didn't know who anyone was. Then after that, things sort-of calmed down, so sometimes I was hanging about until someone decided to give me a chore. **(28)** But I had a piece of luck at the end of the week because they got a new bit of equipment which was the same as we have in the editing suite here and I knew how to use it, which none of them did. So that gave me a bit of status. Unfortunately it meant I spent the next three days stuck in the editing suite. But by the end, I'd shown I wasn't just a silly student, so then, when the senior reporter needed someone to go out with him when he went to interview a junior minister, I got to go along because he knew I could handle the technical side.

Dr Erskine: Well, that's good.

Cressida: Yes. Well, I know **(29)** I need to learn from my mistakes. I mean, basically I need to think more about forward planning, but on the other hand I feel much more confident now; I did survive, I didn't ruin anything, I did actually make a contribution, according to the producer. **(30)** One thing I want to take forward to my final assignment, though, is some reflections on ethics.

Dr Erskine: Yes?

Cressida: I had a bit of an argument with one of the senior presenters. He was editing part of an interview and he just changed something someone said. When I questioned him he just snubbed me. And I mean, this wasn't some public relations expert or government professional spokesperson, it was, like, a member of the public, but he said 'Oh they never remember what they said anyway'.

Dr Erskine: Mm … you want to develop this into part of your final assignment? It would be a very positive line. I can give you some references.

Cressida: Oh, thanks, that would be great.

That is the end of section 3. You now have half a minute to check your answers.

[Pause the recording for 30 seconds.]

Now turn to section 4.

You will hear a lecturer talking about the history of the electric guitar. First you have some time to look at questions 31 to 40.

[Pause the recording for one minute.]

Now listen carefully and answer questions 31 to 40.

Lecturer: During today's lecture in this series about the history of popular music, I'm going to look at the different stages the electric guitar went through before we ended up with the instrument we know so well today.

The driving force behind the invention of the electric guitar was simply the search for a louder sound. In the late 1890s Orville Gibson, founder of the Gibson Mandolin-Guitar Manufacturing Company, **(31)** <u>designed a guitar with an arched or curved top, as is found on a violin.</u> This made it both stronger and louder than earlier designs but it was still hard to hear amongst other louder instruments.

During the 1920s with the beginnings of big-band music, commercial radio and the rise of the recording industry, the need to increase the volume of the guitar became even more important. Around 1925 John Dopyera came up with a solution. He designed a guitar, known as 'The National Guitar', with a metal body which had metal resonating cones built into the top. **(32)** <u>It produced a brash tone which became popular with guitarists who played blues</u> but was unsuitable for many other types of music.

Another way of increasing the volume was thought of in the 1930s. The C. F. Martin Company became known for its 'Dreadnought', **(33)** <u>a large flat-top acoustic guitar that used steel strings instead of the traditional gut ones.</u> It was widely imitated by other makers.

These mechanical fixes helped, but only up to a point. So guitarists began to look at the possibilities offered by the new field of electronic amplification. What guitar players needed was a way to separate the guitar's sound and boost it in isolation from the rest of a band or the surroundings.

Guitar makers and players began experimenting with electrical pickups which are the main means of amplification used today. The first successful one was invented in 1931 by George Beauchamp. **(34)** <u>He introduced to the market a guitar known as 'The Frying Pan'</u> because the playing area consisted of a small round disk. The guitar was hollow and was made of aluminum and steel. **(35)** <u>He amplified the sound by using a pair of horseshoe-shaped magnets.</u> It was the first commercially successful electric guitar.

So by the mid-1930s, an entirely new kind of sound was born. Yet along with its benefits, the new technology brought problems. The traditional hollow body of a guitar caused distortion and feedback when combined with electromagnetic pickups. Musicians and manufacturers realised that a new kind of guitar should be designed from scratch with amplification in mind.

In 1935 Adolph Rickenbacker produced a guitar which took his name – 'The Rickenbacker Electro Spanish'. **(36)** <u>It was the first guitar produced in plastic,</u> which, because of its weight, vibrated less readily than wood. It eliminated the problems of earlier versions which were plagued by acoustic feedback. 'The Electro Spanish' had its own problems, however, because it was very heavy, smaller than other guitars of the period, and was quite awkward to play. Developments continued and in 1941 Les Paul made a guitar which he called 'The Log', and true to its name, **(37)** <u>it was totally solid.</u> All previous guitars had been hollow or partly hollow. It looked slightly strange but the next step had been made towards the modern electric guitar.

The first guitar successfully produced in large numbers was made in 1950 by Leo Fender. His Spanish-style electric guitar, known as a 'Fender Broadcaster', had a bolt-on neck, and was initially criticised by competitors as being very simple and lacking in craftsmanship. Yet it was immediately successful and **(38)** <u>was particularly suited to mass production,</u> spurring other guitar companies to follow Fender's lead.

In 1951 Leo Fender revolutionised the music world yet again when he produced an electric bass guitar. This was the first commercially successful bass model to be played like a guitar. It was easier for players to hit an exact note: **(39)** <u>that's why it was called 'The Precision'.</u> Although there had already been electric standup basses, this was much more portable. It is now standard in the line-up of any rock band and some historians suggest that entire genres of music, such as reggae and funk, could not exist without it.

In 1952 the Gibson company became Fender's first major competitor when Ted McCarty created 'The Gibson Les Paul' guitar. It was distinctive because **(40)** <u>it was coloured gold.</u> The reason for this was to disguise the fact that it was made from two different kinds of wood. In 1954 Leo Fender responded to this successful instrument by introducing 'The Fender Stratocaster'. It is easily identified by its double cutaway design and three pickups. This model may be the most influential electric guitar ever produced. The modern guitar as we know it was here to stay.

That is the end of section 4. You now have half a minute to check your answers.

[Pause the recording for 30 seconds.]

That is the end of the listening test. In the IELTS test you would now have 10 minutes to transfer your answers to the Listening Answer sheet.

LISTENING SECTION 1

Questions 1–10

1 743002
Distraction 1800 705 639 is the car hire phone number.

2 international
Distraction He is arriving at the domestic terminal.

3 (0)6.45 (a.m.) / 6.15 (p.m.) / 18.15
Distraction 'ten past six' is when his plane lands.

4 thirty / 30
Distraction $50 is the amount saved; $60 is the daily hire cost.

5 Echo

6 credit card
Distraction He has to show his driving licence when he collects the car.

7 seven / 7 days / one / 1 week / a week
Distraction He says he'll only use the car on some of the days, but he'll keep it for the whole week.

8 1,000 / a / one / 1 thousand

9 (his/the) luggage

10 pavement

LISTENING SECTION 2

Questions 11–20

11 A
Distraction B: Although the conference organiser is part of 'the team which sets up … events for all our centres', the speaker goes on to say that 'This would mean being based full-time in our London office'.

12 C
Distraction B: Being a chef is described as 'a popular career choice in many parts of the world' but there is no mention of willingness to travel abroad as an essential requirement for the catering job.

13 B
Distraction A: Foreign languages are not mentioned as essential, in spite of the need to travel abroad.

14 C

15 A
Distraction C: Although a degree is mentioned, it is not essential and, in fact, the text says having lived and worked abroad is preferable to a qualification.

16 F
Distraction A: This is what the candidate prepares and sends in, a summary of his/her education, qualifications and career so far.

17 A
Distraction E: Evidence of qualifications is not required till later, after the initial interview.

18 G
Distraction E: This is not required until after the interview.

19 E
Distraction B: International Finest Group contact referees after the interview: 'we contact your referees'; C: This was necessary before registering interest at the beginning of the recruitment process.

20 D
Distraction G: The 'initial interview … will take place by telephone', but the candidate will go to the seminar in person.

LISTENING SECTION 3

Questions 21–30

21/22 B/D (in any order)
Distraction A: The tutor asks: 'So there'd be public access?' but this is not discussed as a problem; C: Although the student mentions time with regard to saving money: 'they would save that much in approximately five years', no time scale is discussed with regard to construction.

23/24 A/E (in any order)
Distraction B: Although 'drainage issues' are mentioned, both student and tutor agree that they 'have been well understood for quite a long time' (i.e. they are not 'recent'); C: The student talks about tank designs but not as a 'recent development' ('fairly conventional storage tanks, the kind that have been in use for decades'); D: They agree on the need 'to use lightweight materials' but these do not need to be modern. The tutor suggests 'You can even use quite traditional ones such as wood' and the student comments that these 'look good' and aren't 'too heavy'.

25 F

26 H

27 C

28 D

29 B

30 A

LISTENING SECTION 4

Questions 31–40

31 beach erosion

32 (fixed) camera

33 storm

34 continent

35 geology (must be spelt correctly)

36 rounded / round

37 spoon
Distraction 'tool' is too general.

38 permanent marker

39 (layers of) newspaper
Distraction '(complicated) apparatus' is what you don't need.

40 (identification) label

READING PASSAGE 1
Questions 1–13

1 FALSE: The first paragraph says 'The Philadelphia Zoo … embodied ideas about how to build a zoo that stayed consistent [= remained the same] for decades' so its ideas remained fashionable.

2 TRUE: The first paragraph says 'The zoos came into existence … during the transition of the United States from a rural and agricultural nation to an industrial one' [= a trend for people to live in urban areas].

3 NOT GIVEN: In the second paragraph we are told that natural history studies changed ('grew into separate areas') but not how they compared in popularity with other scientific subjects.

4 TRUE: The third paragraph says zoos became 'emblems of civic pride on a level of importance with art museums …'.

5 NOT GIVEN: The fifth paragraph says there was 'stagnation' and even 'neglect' amongst zoos in the 1940s, 1950s and 1960s and that 'new zoos continued to be set up' but it doesn't say the older zoos had to move.

6 TRUE: The sixth paragraph says 'Many zoos that had been supported entirely by municipal budgets [= local government money] began recruiting private financial support and charging admission fees'.

7 FALSE: The seventh paragraph says that historians have paid little attention to zoos, and there is no mention of disagreement.

8 reptiles: Paragraph four says 'as many different mammal and bird species as possible, along with **a few** reptiles'.

9 monkeys: Paragraph four says 'dozens of zoos built special islands for their large populations of monkeys'.
Distraction 'rhinoceros' is also mentioned but is described as a 'rarity'.

10 habitat(s): Paragraph five says 'according to their continent of origin [= where they came from] and designing exhibits showing animals of particular habitats'.

11 behavior / behaviour: Paragraph five says 'a few zoos arranged some displays according to animal behavior'.

12 vets: Paragraph six says 'zoos began hiring full-time vets' [hiring = employing, especially in US English].
Distraction The text says 'More projects were undertaken by research scientists' but they are not described as being employed by the zoos.

13 conservation: Paragraph six says 'increasingly, conservation moved to the forefront of zoo agendas [= to the top of zoos' lists of plans]'.

READING PASSAGE 2
Questions 14–26

14 E: 'they are a "cop-out" [= avoiding doing something that is expected of you which you think is too difficult] that allow us to continue living the way we do, rather than reducing carbon emissions.'

15 B: 'Geoengineering has been shown to work, at least on a small, localised scale, for decades. May Day parades in Moscow … to disperse clouds.'

16 E: 'there's the daunting prospect of upkeep and repair of any scheme [= maintenance problems] as well as the consequences of a technical failure.'

17 F: 'The main reason why geoengineering is countenanced by the mainstream scientific community is that most researchers have little faith in the ability of politicians to agree [= lack of confidence in governments].'

18 A: 'while a few countries are making major strides in this regard, the majority are having great difficulty even stemming the rate of increase, let alone reversing it [= more success in some parts of the world than others].'

19 birch trees: Paragraph D says 'their white bark would increase the amount of reflected sunlight' so they discourage the melting of ice and snow.
Distraction: Evergreen pines also discourage the melting of ice and snow but not because of their colour.

20 (Russian) rivers: Paragraph D says 'diverting Russian rivers to increase cold-water flow to ice-forming areas'.

21 pumps: Paragraph C says 'Using pumps to carry water from below the sea ice, the spray would come out as snow or ice particles, producing thicker sea ice'.

22 cables: Paragraph C says 'the sort of cables used in suspension bridges could potentially be used to divert [= prevent the ice from travelling in one direction], rather than halt [= stop], the southward movement of ice'.

23 volcanic explosions: Paragraph B says 'The idea is modelled on historical volcanic explosions'.

24 C: Paragraph E says 'I would consider geoengineering as a strategy to employ only while we manage the conversion to a non-fossil-fuel economy [= a short-term solution]'.

25 D: Paragraph E says 'You may bring global temperatures back … the tropics will be cooler than before industrialisation'.

26 A: Paragraph F says 'But human-induced climate change has brought humanity to a position … despite the potential drawbacks'.
Distraction B: In paragraph C Kallio mentions a project which is less likely to succeed than others, but Rasch, Lunt and Sommerkorn don't compare projects; E: In paragraph E Lunt says that projects may go further than they expected [= overshoot] but he doesn't say they don't know what they're aiming at.

READING PASSAGE 3

Questions 27–40

27 **B**: The first paragraph says 'this is set to challenge the widely held view [= may revolutionise accepted ideas] that the Americas were first colonised … at around 10,000 BC, only moving down into Central and South America in the millennia thereafter'.
Distraction C: Although the Bering Straits are mentioned, it is the timescale that is the focus of this sentence, not the places or people; A and D: there is no mention of either the 'primitive people' or the 'variety of cultures' in the text.

28 **A**: The second paragraph says 'painted using the natural undulating contours [= curved shapes] of the rock surface, so evoking [= reminding the viewer of] the contours of the surrounding landscape'.

29 **D**: The fourth paragraph says 'the artists … tended not to draw over old motifs (as often occurs with rock-art) …'.
Distraction A: Although the text refers to 'a wide range of subject-matter' ('the diversity of imagery and the narrative the paintings create'), it suggests these were made by 'different artists … at different times'; B: Although the text says 'the paintings create' a 'narrative', it does not suggest there is anything 'unusual' about this; C: The text mentions different 'styles' but with regard to them being drawn on top of one another, not in 'one' painting.

30 **NO**: 'Most of the art so far discovered from the ongoing [= not yet complete] excavations comes from the archaeologically-important National Park of the Serra da Capivara in the state of Piauí'.

31 **YES**: 'In ancient times, this inaccessibility must have heightened the importance of the sites, and indeed of the people who painted on the rocks.'

32 **NOT GIVEN**: Although the text describes drawings of animals: 'The artists depicted the animals … as though trying to escape from hunting parties', there is no mention of the animals being sacred.

33 **NO**: 'Due to the favourable climatic conditions, the imagery on many panels is in a remarkable state of preservation' [= there is little damage]; any damage is because of the 'chemical and mineral qualities' of the rock rather than the weather.

34 **YES**: 'this form of natural erosion and subsequent deposition has assisted archaeologists in dating several major rock-art sites'.

35 **NOT GIVEN**: 'Along with the painted fragments, crude stone tools were found.' (It doesn't say what they were used for.)

36 **NO**: 'Several North American researchers have gone further and suggested that the rock-art from this site dates from no earlier than about 3,730 years ago …'

37 **C**: 'the non-existence of plant and animal remains'

38 **E**: 'these conclusions are not without controversy … the hearths may in fact be a natural phenomenon, the result of seasonal brushwood fires'

39 **A**: 'where these artists originate from is also still very much open to speculation … some palaeo-anthropologists are now suggesting that modern humans may have migrated from Africa … while others suggest a more improbable colonisation coming from the Pacific Ocean'

40 **B**: 'Despite the compelling evidence from South America, it stands alone [= it is not supported]: the earliest secure human evidence yet found in the state of Oregon in North America only dates to 12,300 years BC.'

WRITING TASK 1

Model answer

Please note that this is only one possible interpretation of the task. Other approaches are equally valid.

This diagram shows that there are a number of processes involved in the commercial production of frozen fish pies. The main ingredients consist of fresh salmon, peas and sauce, with sliced potatoes, and they are prepared separately. The potatoes, which may have been delivered up to a month in advance, are cleaned, peeled and cut into slices. The slices are boiled and then chilled before being stored until needed. The preparation of the fish is more labour intensive than the preparation of the potatoes. Within twelve hours of being delivered to the factory, the fresh fish is cooked by being steamed with lemon juice and salt. Then the skin and bones are removed by hand and disposed of, before a visual inspection takes place.

After this, the pies are assembled in microwaveable containers. Peas and sauce, which have also been prepared, are added to the fish and then the pie is covered with a layer of cooked potato slices. The pies are then wrapped and frozen. At this point they are ready for dispatch, or they may be stored at the factory before being dispatched.

WRITING TASK 2

Model answer

Please note that this is only one possible interpretation of the task. Other approaches are equally valid.

In some parts of the world, parents encourage their children to begin studying while they are still toddlers, using a variety of books and computer games which teach them to count or to learn their letters. The parents choose a first school for their four-year-old which focuses on academic ability in order that, by the time they enter the next school, the children are well ahead of their age group, with high marks in important subjects such as maths and language, or are equipped to take competitive entrance examinations for other schools if that is relevant.

In other countries, children are at home or playschool until they are around seven years old. They do not even begin to study reading until then, but they listen to and tell stories, they paint and draw, they make models and build tree houses, they swim and play ball games, they keep fish and grow plants in the playschool garden.

In my opinion, the question is not which method produces the most able students, because all over the world, the majority of those who reach university do so at around the same age, wherever they are educated. A brilliant scientist from one country may be working in a laboratory alongside an equally brilliant scientist from another country and the educational start of each career may have been in complete contrast. Therefore, it is clear that the two approaches can both produce able academics, all other things being equal. Nevertheless, it is probable that one method is preferable to the other.

It seems to me that spending early childhood struggling to acquire academic skills in a competitive atmosphere is not the best way to produce a balanced personality. Learning through play and developing social skills equips a child for adult life in essential ways that the competitive parents neglect. If the child has academic ability, this will manifest itself as the child develops and does not need to be forced at an early age.

TEST 5   TRANSCRIPT

 **24** LISTENING SECTION 1

You will hear a number of different recordings and you will have to answer questions on what you hear. There will be time for you to read the instructions and questions and you will have a chance to check your work. All the recordings will be played once only. The test is in four sections. At the end of the test you will be given ten minutes to transfer your answers to an answer sheet. Now turn to section 1.

Section 1. You will hear a man talking to a woman about hiring a car. First you have some time to look at questions 1 to 5.

[Pause the recording for 30 seconds.]

You will see that there is an example that has been done for you. On this occasion only, the conversation relating to this will be played first.

Woman: Hello, how can I help you?

Man: Hi. I'm Carlton Mackay, and you booked me some flights recently, to Australia – and some internal ones?

Woman: Oh, yes, Mr Mackay, I remember you now, of course.

Man: Well, I find I'm going to need car hire while I'm in Sydney after all. I think you said you could recommend a good-value company?

Woman: Yes, that's right. Costwise Cars. They're very good and don't charge lots of extras. **(Example)** They have three offices in the Sydney area, including one office right at the airport.

The number of offices in Sydney is 3, so '3' has been written in the space. Now we shall begin. You should answer the questions as you listen because you will not hear the recording a second time. Listen carefully and answer questions 1 to 5.

[repeat]

Man: So, I'll just book it online?

Woman: Yes, you can book online but you should have their phone number too, just in case.

Man: Mm, of course.

Woman: That's 1800 705 639. It's on the website. And you can get a discount if you quote **(1)** your booking reference from us.

Man: Oh, what's that?

Woman: I mean the one you got from me when we booked your flights. I have it here – 743002.

Man: Oh, thanks. I guess I've got it at home, but I'll write it down again in case. A discount is good. So where exactly is the office? I'll be coming to the domestic terminal from Melbourne.

Woman: (2) It's immediately outside the international terminal.

Man: OK. And, another thing I want to check is, will they be open when I arrive? Or is it just office hours?

Woman: (3) Mm … they open at quarter to seven and close at 6.15 in the evening. So, let's see, you're due to land at ten past six. By the time you've collected your bags and so on, which will take a little while, they won't be open, but if you arrange it in advance, **(4)** they can wait for you. You do have to pay an extra $30 for that, though.

Man: OK. Well, I'm staying near the airport the first night, so I could go back in the morning and save a day's hire?

Woman: Yes, that'd be better. That'd save you about $50.

Man: Do you know what kind of cars they have?

Woman: Quite a variety, I think. Er, the best value should be under $60 a day with luck. **(5)** That would be the 'Echo', I guess.

Man: Sorry?

Woman: E–C–H–O, like when your voice bounces back?

Before you hear the rest of the conversation, you have some time to look at questions 6 to 10.

[Pause the recording for 30 seconds.]

....

Now listen and answer questions 6 to 10.

Man: I suppose I have to book online before I leave?

Woman: Mm, that's the best way. Er, they won't deduct any charges until you finish with the car, but **(6)** they do need your credit card number when you book and of course they'll want to see your driving licence when you collect. How long will you need it?

Man: (7) I'm in Sydney for seven days. I'll only actually need to use it on three or four of those days, I hope, but I'll keep it for the whole week. I guess it's going to be a few hundred dollars. Can you suggest anything I can do to keep the cost down?

Woman: (8) Oh, you get quite a big discount if you do less than 1,000 kilometres in the week.

Man: Oh, that's good. I don't suppose I will be driving that far, actually.

Woman: But, oh, yes, the other thing I should mention is the insurance. It's included in the price.

Man: Oh, that is good value then.

Woman: Yes, but what you must remember is that it doesn't cover anything except the car, so you must be careful not to leave anything at all in it when you park **(9)** because your luggage isn't insured, even if it's out of sight, locked in the boot.

Man: Yeah, well, I think my travel policy will cover that actually.

Woman: Good!

Man: OK. And can I return the car outside office hours? My flight home is very early in the morning. Can I put the keys through the door, or something?

Woman: (10) There's a secure box just outside the office on the pavement. You just drop the keys in there.

Man: Oh, good.

Woman: And one other thing: you should remember to buy petrol before you leave it. If you don't drop the car back with a full tank you get charged to fill it. I recommend you go to a supermarket before you go out to the airport.

Man: Thanks for the tip!

Woman: Not at all. Do call in again if there's anything else I can help with.

Man: I will. Many thanks.

That is the end of section 1. You now have half a minute to check your answers.

[Pause the recording for 30 seconds.]

Now turn to section 2.

 LISTENING SECTION 2

You will hear a speaker from the hotel industry addressing a group of young people about careers with her firm. First you have some time to look at questions 11 to 15.

[Pause the recording for 30 seconds.]

Now listen carefully and answer questions 11 to 15.

Speaker: Good morning. It's a great pleasure to be here in London and to see so many people interested in working in hotels. We in the International Finest Group of hotels are very proud of our business and we are always on the lookout for quality recruits in every department.

Now, I'm going to outline some of the areas of work where we are currently recruiting and the essential skills or qualifications for them, then I'll run through our recruitment procedure. OK?

At the moment we're looking for a number of people for administrative posts in different parts of the world and also some roles which involve a lot of travelling.

One of our main business streams is hosting special events for other businesses. If you have good communication and organisational skills **(11)** with a good level of fluency in at least one European and one non-European language, I'd suggest you think about becoming part of the team which sets up these events for all our centres. This would mean being based full-time in our London office. The work ranges from setting up small meetings a few days ahead to organising international conferences two years in advance, so there's plenty of variety. Some of the conferences we run have as many as a thousand delegates, so it's quite challenging.

Then there are some posts available for professionals in the catering field. Chefs we can find; it seems this is a popular career choice in many parts of the world as in the UK these days, in spite of the exacting standards, but **(12)** people to manage catering departments need more than a love of producing quality food. We're after really energetic and totally efficient young managers, who already have the relevant business qualifications – no training on the job here – and they must share the team's determination to make everything run smoothly at any time of the day or night.

Or, if you are the type of person who enjoys a challenge, what about becoming one of our relief housekeepers? You'll be a good people person, well organised, and supremely flexible. As well as covering UK holidays, maternity and paternity leave, **(13)** there will be times when you have to fill a key post when someone's sick, which could be anywhere in our European, Middle Eastern or Far Eastern hotels, so you must be prepared to hop on a plane at five minutes' notice.

The International Finest brand name attracts visitors from all over the world and on all kinds of business and leisure trips. Our swimming pools and gyms need to be run by people with the highest standards of customer service. You don't have to be a great athlete, but smart appearance and a pleasant manner are necessary. **(14)** A diploma in sports science would be the minimum requirement here.

Lastly, I'd just like to mention that the main London office has another vacancy. Most bookings come online, especially from the Far East for people coming to Europe. **(15)** If you have fluency and some keyboard skills in, for example, Spanish, or any Far Eastern languages, either having taken a degree, or preferably from having lived and worked overseas, you might be just the person we're looking for to deal with email bookings and queries in the office here. A flexible attitude to working hours is also important as you may have to come in outside normal office hours.

Before you hear the rest of the talk, you have some time to look at questions 16 to 20.

[Pause the recording for 30 seconds.]

....

Now listen and answer questions 16 to 20.

So that's an overview of the kind of jobs, now how to get them! First of all, provided you have a UK work permit, you can go online and register an interest in working for us. By return, you'll receive a unique applicant's code, which is your personal identification number and which we'll use in all communications. **(16)** Along with that you get access to the Human Resources website, where you should make sure you understand the legal terms and conditions which apply to all our employees. That's also where you can then download **(17)** the application form – fill it in and send it back along with your CV. You'll know within 48 hours whether you're being considered as you get an automated response. Sorry if it's a bit impersonal, but at least it's quick. Hopefully, if we like the sound of you, there will be in that automated response **(18)** a list of times for an initial interview which will take place by telephone during the following week. You confirm by email which of the time slots will suit you. Provided the interview is satisfactory, at that point we'll ask for **(19)** any evidence of qualifications required, which might be your degree or diploma certificate or so on, which you have to send certified copies of, and we contact your referees. The last thing you have to do is you come along and have a look round the International Finest Group head office, get to know some of our team in Human Resources face to face, and **(20)** participate in a one-day recruitment seminar, which involves a number of group and individual activities along with other potential employees.

Then, with luck, we'll offer you a job! So, I hope you like the sound of joining our organisation.

That is the end of section 2. You now have half a minute to check your answers.

[Pause the recording for 30 seconds.]

Now turn to section 3.

 LISTENING SECTION 3

You will hear a student of landscape architecture discussing a project with his tutor. First you have some time to look at questions 21 to 24.

[Pause the recording for 30 seconds.]

Now listen carefully and answer questions 21 to 24.

Tutor: So, let's hear what you're doing for your next project.

Student: I've decided to design a roof garden for a supermarket. I've been looking at some on the web and I think that a garden on top of a building is the up-and-coming thing.

Tutor: OK. So you've done a bit of reading already? What benefits would there be for the client? **(21/22)** Why do you think a supermarket chain would be willing to meet the expense of construction? You do realise that would be the first thing they raise.

Student: Yes, I know. But I'd explain that in spite of the initially high expense, they would save that much in approximately five years. Well, I'd have to do sums, I mean calculate specifically …

Tutor: Yes, how would the saving come about?

Student: Mainly through lower heating and aircon bills. The extra insulation offered by having a layer of living plants in the soil would make a huge difference.

Tutor: OK. **(21/22)** But they might feel the expense of maintenance would be an issue. After all, supermarkets don't normally employ gardeners.

Student: What I thought was, if they made it a community garden, rather than a simple low-maintenance green roof …

Tutor: So there'd be public access?

Student: Oh, yes! Then there'd be a sense of ownership in the local community and people could take responsibility for it, instead of the supermarket paying a commercial company, and it'd really boost their public relations.

Tutor: That's a good point. And have you been looking into how roof gardens are built nowadays?

Student: I'm still exploring that, but if I take advantage of the latest technologies for roof gardens, it shouldn't be too difficult. But in any case, you have to use lightweight materials.

Tutor: But that's a matter of making the right choices. You can even use quite traditional ones such as wood for the planting areas.

Student: Yes, that's what I thought. It'll look good and it isn't too heavy.

Tutor: But for the basic construction, the issue you have to address first is the material used between the building and the garden.

Student: **(23/24)** You mean the barrier fabric, which ensures there's no chance of rainwater leaking down into the building?

Tutor: Yes, nowadays that is very good, and quite easily sourced.

Student: Then on the other hand, there's the business of water within the roof garden itself.

Tutor: You mean drainage? That's an important feature of the construction in any roof design.

Student: Yes, but I think most drainage issues have been well understood for quite a long time.

Tutor: OK, but another thing is with plants in an exposed situation, **(23/24)** you usually need to find ways to optimise rainfall.

Student: Yes, because rainwater is best for the garden, if you can store it for when it's needed. What I've been looking at are some buildings which use fairly conventional storage tanks, the kind that have been in use for decades, but have them linked to modern automatic watering systems.

Tutor: Sounds complicated!

Student: It's less so in practice than it sounds, I think. I've been researching them and actually the latest ones definitely work very well and they can be electronically regulated to suit the local microclimate.

Tutor: Mmm, that sounds interesting. You seem to have been doing some thorough research! Make sure you reference all your sources when you write it up.

Student: Yes, sure. Um, there's one more aspect I'd just like to run past you, if there's time? I want to include a light feature in the design.

Tutor: Of course.

Student: I've got a sketch here.

Tutor: Let's have a look then.

Before you hear the rest of the conversation, you have some time to look at questions 25 to 30.

[Pause the recording for 30 seconds.]

....

Now listen and answer questions 25 to 30.

Student: Well, I was really impressed by something I saw on a roof in Cornwall and I'd like to design something similar. Um, you have an area of planting, and I'm thinking of installing this lighting in an area filled with low-growing evergreen shrubs.

Tutor: Mmm. You'd have to have lights and things well away from anywhere children might be. But I can see this could be very effective, if a bit complicated. How would it work? On this drawing, this is a section view? **(25)** You have this low wall on the right?

Student: Yes, that's it. This is just one element and these areas would be repeated all round the planted area. I think this will probably be a wooden wall, using reclaimed timbers, with an angled ceramic top surface.

Tutor: Perhaps even ridge tiles like they use on roofs?

Student: Oh, yes, that'd be just the sort of thing. And that'd make it weatherproof. Um, and then **(26)** the heavy duty electric wiring comes up through the floor just outside the planted area and into the wall. Then it's brought through to a projector low in the side of the wall, and that sends a beam of light along the fibre optic cable.

Tutor: So there's no electricity in the actual lights. **(27)** The fibre optic goes across the surface of the soil in the planting area.

Student: Yes, that's the beauty of it. The shrubs will soon grow to cover it up, of course, and then the cable goes **(28)** past a wooden post which is between the shrubs, and can be a support for them as they grow bigger, and then runs up into each element of the installation.

Tutor: So **(29)** the light beam is carried up to the top of each element and illuminates a kind of conical glass cap? I see! Is that the bit which would glow in the dark?

Student: Yes.

Tutor: And what's the cap supported on? Is it a wall?

Student: No, **(30)** it's a slender acrylic rod, er, like the stem of a flower or mushroom, which the cable runs up inside of.

Tutor: Well, I'll be interested to see the final drawings.

Student: Thank you! I'm looking forward to putting it all together.

That is the end of section 3. You now have half a minute to check your answers.

[Pause the recording for 30 seconds.]

Now turn to section 4.

You will hear a geography student giving a presentation about sand to fellow students. First you have some time to look at questions 31 to 40.

[Pause the recording for one minute.]

Now listen carefully and answer questions 31 to 40.

Student: First, I would like to tell you how the Argus computerised photography system has helped marine researchers. Then I shall talk a bit about sand collecting.

Well, Argus is the system Doctor Rob Holman developed when he was working at a research pier on the coast of North Carolina, about 20 years ago.

This pier stretches out over the water, and it's the longest research pier in the world, with an observation tower on the end of it. The researchers there make precise measurements of how the sand moves about under the waves. **(31)** This research is critical to the study of beach erosion in places where the coastline is being worn away.

The Argus system helps to solve the difficulties encountered by these researchers. **(32)** The system correlates the data from under the water with what Dr Holman gets from his fixed camera, which is mounted above the water on the pier and uses time-lapse photography.

Some of Doctor Holman's results have changed the way people understand how sand moves. To quote S. Jeffress Williams, a coastal geologist with the United States Geological Survey, the system is 'a critical piece of new technology' and '**(33)** The Argus system allows us to quantify and document visually the changes to the coast on a variety of different time frames. A lot of these take place when there is a storm or at other times when it is difficult to have people out on the beach making observations and taking measurements.'

Up to now Argus installations have been installed in places in Oregon, California, Hawaii, England, the Netherlands, Australia, New Zealand, Spain, Italy and Brazil, as well as in North Carolina.

Now I'd like to introduce Dr Holman's sand collection. He started collecting sand in the 1980s, and he still collects it now, even though he has around a thousand samples. They come from his travels and from geologists and amateurs all over the world – and **(34)** the collection includes sand from each continent, including Antarctica.

People send him sand in envelopes, plastic bags, paper towels and all sorts! Each is stored in a glass jar, which Dr Holman labels by latitude and longitude of its origin, as well as he can work them out – sometimes the information is a bit sketchy!

Anyway, **(35)** it's mainly geology students at the university who study his collection, and they can learn a lot from it.

For instance, one set of tubes displays sand from the East Coast of the US. So you can see that the sand gets lighter and finer from north to south. By the time a grain of sand eventually washes up on a beach in Florida **(36)** at the southern end of that journey, it has been battered by waves for a long time so the grains are fine and rounded because most of the time sand is not stationary on the beach.

OK, so if you'd like to collect sand and maybe even send some to Dr Holman, how should you go about it? Well, the list of equipment is very short and easy to find, but you should keep a supply when you're travelling, as you never know when you'll come across an interesting sand sample.

(37) One really handy thing for digging sand, especially if it's hard or frozen, is a spoon. It's perfect for that. If you're travelling by air it'll have to be plastic, but metal is preferable, as plastic tends to break. You need something to put the samples in that is damp-proof and easy to carry. You can just use plastic bags, **(38)** but you need to record the location and date on the bag, so you must also have a permanent marker with you, because you can never assume you will remember where you gathered a sample from later on and you don't want it to rub off before you get home.

And that's about all you need in the field to collect sand. When you get home, your samples should be logged in a notebook or computer. You need to note the location and be really specific as to exactly whereabouts on the beach you gathered your sample – low tide mark, under cliff area, etc.

Then, you store your sample. You want to keep everything in good condition and avoid contamination. So first you make absolutely sure that each sample is perfectly dry. You don't need any complicated apparatus for this, **(39)** you can just air it out on layers of newspaper, which is suitably absorbent. Most people find that's the best way.

Then, lastly, but this is really important, before there can be any chance of confusing this latest sample with another, you put it in a clean small bag or a jar, and **(40)** you must stick an identification label on straight away. Some people put one inside as well in case the outer label falls off, but that's up to you.

Well, that's about all you need to know to get started as a sand collector.

Any questions?

That is the end of section 4. You now have half a minute to check your answers.

[Pause the recording for 30 seconds.]

That is the end of the listening test. In the IELTS test you would now have 10 minutes to transfer your answers to the Listening Answer sheet.

LISTENING SECTION 1

Questions 1–10

1 41

Distraction It's under $30 for a bed in a dormitory and $50 for a double room without membership; membership costs $35.

2 museums

Distraction Membership also offers discount on skydiving, white-water rafting, bicycle and car hire but these don't fit the gap 'entry to ...'.

3 hour

Distraction 15 minutes costs $1 not $3.

4 Elliscoat

5 ferry

6 summer

Distraction The hostel isn't busy in winter.

7 1887

Distraction It was turned into a hostel in 1985.

8 scooter(s)

Distraction The man says 'it would be quicker than cycling' but there's no mention of cycle hire.

9 entertainment

10 kitchen

Distraction 'There's no café …'

LISTENING SECTION 2

Questions 11–20

11 B

12 H

Distraction Computers are beside the reference books on the next floor.

13 C

Distraction 'newspapers' are in the café, not to the left of it; 'fiction' and other books are mentioned, but only to explain that 'You are not allowed to take [them] into the café'.

14 E

Distraction B: Although the guide also mentions 'fiction', it does not say these books are opposite the café; G: 'reference books' and F: 'photocopiers' are also mentioned, but these are on other floors ('next floor' and 'basement').

15 A

Distraction B and E: 'authors of both fiction and non-fiction' are mentioned, but there is no suggestion that these types of books are housed here; H: the 'study area' is mentioned, but this is where the talks are advertised, not held.

16 A

Distraction B: You only pay for a lost membership card ('any lost cards are charged at £5'); C: A passport or identity card is only necessary when you first register ('There's no need to show a passport again').

17 C

Distraction A: 'five days' is the length of time books are held after you've been contacted; B: If the book is in 'another library', you can usually have it 'within a week' but 'it can take a few weeks' if someone else has borrowed it.

18 C

Distraction A: Reference books can only be borrowed for 'one day'; B: CD-ROMs can be borrowed for the same period as books ('fourteen days').

19 B

Distraction A: The library closes earlier than it used to on Wednesdays, not later; C: The library is going to be open on Sunday mornings but this is a 'new development'.

20 B

Distraction A: You can get change for the lockers on the first floor; C: You 'are not allowed' to take large bags to the exhibition area on the third floor.

LISTENING SECTION 3

Questions 21–30

21 C

Distraction A: Lee says that he 'remembered Chapman' but there is no suggestion he was Lee's childhood hero; B: Although Johnny Appleseed came from one of Anita's childhood 'American story books', they chose the introduction of the apple into the US because they thought it would make 'a good case study', not because they necessarily wanted to talk about the US.

22 B

Distraction A: The tutor mentions the data on their laptop but this is to say where they **should have** recorded their source information; C: The tutor mentions 'data', but there is no mention of a 'database'.

23 A

Distraction B: Although the tutor mentions 'native species', this refers to trees, not people; C: It is Lee, not the tutor, who talks about 'traditional American apples' being either introduced or bred by 'Europeans' (and not necessarily in Europe).

24 C

Distraction A: 'grafting techniques' were what particularly interested Lee, not the audience; B: The apple trees in Kazakhstan were 'wild', not 'cultivated'.

25 A

Distraction B and C: Anita says 'I felt we could do both [produce a paper and put it on the website]. And we could do a poster …' but Lee and the tutor do not agree with her and she accepts their opinion.

26 A

27 B

28 C

29 B

30 A

LISTENING SECTION 4

Questions 31–40

31 cans

Distraction Although 'drink' is mentioned several times, only the can, not the drink was changed.

32 lime

33 tasteless

Distraction 'minty': This is the flavour that the gum had to start with and which disappeared after a few minutes.

34 returns

35 warm

Distraction 'chilled'/'cooled': The drink tastes less sweet if chilled or cooled.

36 soundproof(ed)

37 fresher

38 texture / thickness

Distraction 'flavour'/'strength': In this context, these words mean 'taste' so the answer makes no sense.

39 liquids

40 strawberry

Distraction sugar (but this has the opposite effect: 'When the sweetness was taken away … they could hardly taste anything').

READING PASSAGE 1

Questions 1–13

Questions 1–4 refer to paragraphs one and two

Note: The answers must be actual words from the passage (not synonyms).

1 tropical

2 (a) (twig) snake

3 (a / the) forest (of Magombera) / Magombera (forest)

4 (the) nose

5 TRUE: Paragraph two suggests only two other creatures can do this: 'The most remarkable feature of chameleons … rivalled only by cuttlefish and octopi in the animal kingdom'.

6 FALSE: Paragraph three says 'They show an extraordinary range of colours, from nearly black to bright blues, oranges, pinks and greens, even several at once'.

7 FALSE: Paragraph three says 'each species has a characteristic set of cells … which determines the range of colours and patterns they can show … placing a chameleon on a Smartie box generally results in a stressed, confused, dark grey or mottled chameleon'.

8 FALSE: Paragraph four says both are important: 'When two male dwarf chameleons encounter each other … They puff out their throats and present themselves side-on with their bodies flattened to appear as large as possible and to show off their colours'.

9 NOT GIVEN: Paragraph four tells us that the struggle takes place on a branch. There is no information about where the defeated animal goes afterwards.

10 TRUE: Paragraph five says 'Females also have aggressive displays used to repel male attempts at courtship … Most of the time, females … aggressively reject males by displaying a contrasting light and dark colour pattern, with their mouths open and moving their bodies rapidly from side to side'.

11 TRUE: Paragraph six says 'Many people assume [= the popular explanation] that colour change evolved to enable chameleons to match a greater variety of backgrounds in their environment. If this was the case, then the ability of chameleons to change colour should be associated with the range of background colours in the chameleon's habitat, but there is no evidence for such a pattern [= this idea cannot be supported]'.

12 NOT GIVEN: In paragraph six there is a comparison between grasslands and forest habitats concerning different species of chameleons' range of colours but there is no mention of how many predators there are in different habitats.

13 FALSE: Paragraph seven says 'recent scientific advances have made it possible to obtain such measurements in the field [= in their habitat, not elsewhere]'.

READING PASSAGE 2

Questions 14–26

14 F: The whole paragraph explains this idea.

15 D: 'facing many possibilities leaves us stressed out [= causes tension]'

16 C: 'working hard toward a goal, and making progress to the point of expecting a goal to be realized, … activates [= produces] positive feelings'

17 A: 'Self-appointed [= they themselves claim to be] experts'

18 B: '… people are remarkably adaptable.'

19 B: 'activities that are … attention-absorbing, and thus less likely to bore us'

20/21 B/D (in any order): In Paragraph A 'Eric Wilson fumes that the obsession with happiness amounts to a "craven disregard" [= ignoring in a cowardly manner] for the melancholic perspective [= unhappy view] that has given rise to [= produced] the greatest works of art. "The happy man," he writes, "is a hollow [= empty, i.e. not creative or thoughtful] man."'; In Paragraph C 'Russ Harris, the author of *The Happiness Trap*, calls popular conceptions of happiness dangerous because they set people up [= prepare people] for a "struggle against reality" … "If you're going to live a rich and meaningful life," Harris says, "you're going to feel a full range of emotions."'
Distraction A: Seligman argues for the need to study happy as well as unhappy feelings; C: Lyubomirsky is concerned with the way people seem to need constant change to be happy; E: Schwartz is concerned with the fact that too much choice causes unhappiness.

22/23 C/D (in any order): C: Paragraph E says 'Besides, not everyone can put on a happy face. Barbara Held, a professor of psychology at Bowdoin College, rails against [= complains about] "the tyranny [= something having too much power] of the positive attitude ... it makes them feel like a failure on top of already feeling bad"'; D: Paragraph A says 'This happiness movement [= the idea that we should be happy all the time] has provoked a great deal of opposition among psychologists who observe that the preoccupation with happiness has come at the cost of sadness, an important feeling that people have tried to banish from their emotional repertoire'.

Distraction A: The fact that wealth may not increase happiness is discussed in Paragraph B, but earned wealth is not compared to inherited wealth; B: This is not identified as a mistaken belief. In Paragraph B, it is discussed as a cause of unhappiness; E: Although Allan Horwitz of Rutgers laments [= says he is disappointed] that 'young people who are naturally weepy [= tearful, unhappy] after breakups [= the end of a romantic relationship] are often urged to medicate themselves', there is no discussion of whether extreme emotions in general are normal.

24 moods [optimal = best] (Paragraph A)

25 milestone [= something which shows us how far we have travelled] (Paragraph B)

26 pessimistic: a 'naturally pessimistic architect, for example' (Paragraph E)

READING PASSAGE 3

Questions 27–40

27 C: The first paragraph says 'It is amazing that human ... visit our nearest celestial neighbor before ... explore the Midocean Ridge'.
Distraction A: The writer mentions robots on Mars, but does not say that it is surprising; B: The writer says this is ironic, not that it is surprising; D: The writer mentions sending spacecraft both beyond and within our solar system but he does not discuss the exploration of either our solar system or others beyond it.

28 A: The second paragraph says 'understates the oceans' importance. If you consider instead three-dimensional volumes [= the depth as well as the surface area] ... less than 1% of the total'.
Distraction B: The word 'estimate' refers to the size of the upper sunlit layer of the ocean; C: The submarine landscape is not mentioned in relation to the proportion of the earth covered by the oceans; D: 71% is the suggested proportion of the earth covered by the water in the oceans, but does not take into account whether or not life is possible in all of it.

29 C: The third paragraph says 'they could swim to the bell to breathe air trapped underneath it rather than return all the way to the surface'.
Distraction A: The bell stayed in one place and was not attached to an individual; B: Piped air, 'supplied through hoses', was a later development; D: This was 'later', using 'other devices'.

30 A: The fourth paragraph says 'Science then was largely incidental [= accidental, by chance] – something that happened along the way'.
Distraction B: The people who made the discoveries are described as 'not well known' but it is not suggested they were not scientists (Beebe was a biologist); C: Although the people who made the discoveries are described as 'not well known', there is no suggestion that their ideas were rejected; D: Although the developments are compared to developments in aviation, the text does not say that ideas were borrowed from that (or any other) field.

31 NO: The first paragraph says 'vast volcanoes continue to create new submarine landscapes'.

32 YES: In the second paragraph, the writer quotes the estimate '2 or 3%' and uses it in his argument.

33 YES: The fifth paragraph says 'It was not until the 1970s that ... reach the Midocean Ridge and begin making major contributions to a wide range of scientific questions. A burst [= sudden explosion] of discoveries followed in short order [= quickly]'.

34 NOT GIVEN: In the fifth paragraph, the writer emphasises the continuing importance of deep sea exploration: 'biologists may now be seeing ... No one even knew that these communities existed before explorers began diving to the bottom in submersibles' and mentions 20th-century explorers in the final paragraph. However, he does not suggest that numbers have increased this century.

35 NOT GIVEN: Although Paragraphs six, seven and eight mention several dangers to deep sea vehicles 'vegetation [= plant life]' is not one of them.

36 YES: Paragraph seven says 'submersibles rarely have much insulation'.

37 E: [sturdy = strongly built]
Distraction G: 'energetic' means 'lively', not strong; I: 'heavy' also does not necessarily mean 'strong'.

38 D: [hollow = not solid]
Distraction I: how 'heavy' the creatures are is not relevant to their ability to withstand pressure; G/H: these aspects of the creatures are also not relevant and not mentioned.

39 B
Distraction A: this does not make sense – the craft is a space where people can breathe; F: does not mean the same as 'air' [atmosphere = layer of air which surrounds the earth].

40 H: 'violent' is the only word which collocates with 'explosion' to give the correct meaning.

WRITING TASK 1

Model answer

Please note that this is only one possible interpretation of the task. Other approaches are equally valid.

These charts give information about the rainfall and temperatures for the cities of Brasilia and Recife, with additional data about hours of sunshine and days with thunder.

Although temperatures in Brasilia can be quite extreme, from just above freezing to 37°C, the average daily temperatures in Recife are not so variable. In Brasilia the range can be as great as 15 degrees, but in Recife average daily temperatures generally vary from 22°C to 31°C throughout the year.

The most noticeable contrast is in the rainfall. Brasilia is wettest from September to May, with only two or three wet days in June, July and August. During the wet months, there is thunder on approximately half the days. By contrast, Recife has at least ten wet days, even in its driest season, which lasts from October to January. From April to August there is rain on over twenty days per month. However, thunder is less common there, with a maximum of three thundery days in April.

WRITING TASK 2

Model answer

Please note that this is only one possible interpretation of the task. Other approaches are equally valid.

The number of vegetarians in a community may depend on various factors, for example the traditions of the country, the wealth of the country, the religion or the age group. Therefore, the reasons why people choose to exclude meat and fish from their diet may also vary.

Some people become vegetarians because they believe that this will benefit their health. Undoubtedly, eating too much meat, especially too much red meat, is not to be recommended. Moreover, the fact that there are healthy populations in some parts of the world where no one eats meat proves that it is not, as some people claim, an essential part of the human diet. However, it is important to ensure that enough protein, for example, is included in the diet from other sources. Where vegetarianism is not a tradition, this may require some careful planning.

In my experience, it is quite common for people to become vegetarians because they feel that it is selfish to eat meat or because meat production increases global warming. They may also feel that if no one ate meat, there would be no food shortages, because meat production uses up food resources. This idealistic point of view is very attractive, but it is hard to judge whether it is in fact correct.

In some families, if a teenager decides to become a vegetarian, they may do so partly out of a spirit of rebellion, because this behaviour can be interpreted as a criticism of their parents' way of life. However, provided that they continue to eat healthily, the parents should not raise objections, in my opinion. Vegetarianism is a valid choice in life. Moreover, research shows that vegetarians tend to be healthier in many ways than meat-eaters.

Personally, I think that being a vegetarian is a good idea in principle as there are proven health benefits and probably social benefits as well. However, it does not suit everybody, and I doubt whether it will ever be a universal choice.

TEST 6   TRANSCRIPT

 28 LISTENING SECTION 1

You will hear a number of different recordings and you will have to answer questions on what you hear. There will be time for you to read the instructions and questions and you will have a chance to check your work. All the recordings will be played once only. The test is in four sections. At the end of the test you will be given ten minutes to transfer your answers to an answer sheet. Now turn to section 1.

Section 1. You will hear a woman talking to a man who works in a tourist information office. First you have some time to look at questions 1 to 6.

[Pause the recording for 30 seconds.]

You will see that there is an example that has been done for you. On this occasion only, the conversation relating to this will be played first.

Man: Good morning. Can I help you?

Woman: I hope so! I have a friend in Spain and her two daughters are coming to the city to study for a month. So I thought the Tourist Information Centre was the best place to ask about hostels. Can you recommend any?

Man: Of course. Ah, I usually suggest one of the Hostelling International places. HI West End is a big hostel in a residential area, but it's only ten minutes from downtown (***Example***) if you take a bus. It's really popular.

The journey time is by bus, so 'bus' has been written in the space. Now we shall begin. You should answer the questions as you listen because you will not hear the recording a second time. Listen carefully and answer questions 1 to 6.

[repeat]

Woman: OK. Sounds good! I need to know how much it costs. The girls want a double room to themselves. They don't want to share with other people.

Man: That makes it more expensive. The price is under $30 for a bed in a dormitory but they'll be paying $50 a night. **(1)** But if they become members of Hostelling International, the price comes down to $41 a night. Membership costs $35.

Woman: Right.

Man: And membership offers them benefits too on all kinds of activities.

Woman: Ah, what kind of things?

Man: Oh, er, skydiving and white-water rafting. Things like that.

Woman: Mm, I don't think they're interested in that kind of thing. **(2)** If they become members, will they get cheaper entrance tickets to museums?

Man: Oh, yes and also discounts on bicycle and car hire.

Woman: OK. It's probably worth it. Is the hostel very noisy? They're coming here to do some studying.

Man: Ah, I think it is quite noisy as it's a really big hostel. And if they want to use the Internet this hostel still makes a charge unfortunately. It's $1 for 15 minutes and **(3)** $3 for an hour.

Woman: Mm … it might not be ideal for them. What else can you recommend? Is there anything in a quiet area?

Man: There's Elliscoat Hostel.

Woman: Mm, how do you spell that?

Man: **(4)** E–L–L–I–S–C–O–A–T.

Woman: I've never heard that name before. And where is that?

Man: It's on the beach looking over the bay. Here, look on the map. It's quiet but not far from Dragon Island – there's plenty going on there in the evening.

Woman: Oh, that's a nice area. And if they want to go to Dragon Island **(5)** it only takes a couple of minutes to walk down to the ferry. So how much is a room there?

Man: It's in such a nice spot that the rooms are a bit more expensive. They're $62.

Woman: Does that include any meals?

Man: Unfortunately not. It is possible to buy meals in the hostel at a reasonable price but because it isn't very busy in the winter, **(6)** they only cook in summer.

Before you hear the rest of the conversation, you have some time to look at questions 7 to 10.

[Pause the recording for 30 seconds.]

....

Now listen and answer questions 7 to 10.

Woman: Oh, I think I know the place you mean. It's an old building, isn't it?

Man: Yes, it's well known as it's one of the oldest in the city. **(7)** There's been a hotel there since 1887 when it was first built. It was turned into a hostel in 1985 and they've invested a lot of money restoring it inside.

Woman: Mm, they'd like that but I'm just looking on the map at where their college is – it's right in the centre. It is a bit far for them from there.

Man: **(8)** The hostel actually has scooters for hire at a very good price. So they could do that. Er, it would be quicker than cycling or walking to the centre.

Woman: Mm, it is a bit expensive ... But it sounds like the best one so far unless there's something a bit cheaper?

Man: OK. Er, well, what about the Backpackers Hostel? That's not so expensive. It's in a side street **(9)** in the entertainment district. They wouldn't need to go far to find everything they want – they could walk everywhere. And it's very reasonable. Only $45 and another $5 if they want to have breakfast.

Woman: Mm, but what about other meals?

Man: There's no café but on each floor in this hostel **(10)** there's a kitchen for residents to cook in. I'm not sure how well equipped they are but it should be fine for basic meals.

Woman: Well, that's really very helpful. I'll pass all this information on now.

Man: Do ask your friends to ring me if they need to know anything else.

Woman: I will. Thank you.

That is the end of section 1. You now have half a minute to check your answers.

[Pause the recording for 30 seconds.]

Now turn to section 2.

 LISTENING SECTION 2

You will hear an audio guide to a public library. First you have some time to look at questions 11 to 15.

[Pause the recording for 30 seconds.]

Now listen carefully and answer questions 11 to 15.

Welcome to the Selmore Public Library which has just been reopened after major refurbishment. This tour will introduce you to the building and its services. At any time you can stop the tour. We enter by the café and our tour begins at the issue desk.

If you stand between the information desk and the issue desk and look at the opposite wall, you will see shelves of books in the left-hand corner. **(11)** This is where you will find a large number of novels and short stories. They are arranged alphabetically. If you're looking for something in particular and it's not on the shelf you can reserve it. The next area, directly opposite the issue desk, **(12)** is a section where people can study. The library provides computers for users free of charge on the next floor beside the reference books but this area is for people to use their own laptops. You should ask for the internet passcode at the information desk.

In the right-hand corner of this floor there is a café. A selection of daily newspapers is always available there **(13)** but you can also take magazines into the café to read while you have a drink. You will find these on the racks to the left of the café and there is a large selection. They are for reference only and cannot be borrowed but you are welcome to photocopy any articles of interest. We ask you to return them when you have finished. You are not allowed to take fiction or any other books from the shelves into the café.

Next to the café is the exit door leading to the stairs and escalator to the other floors. The largest collection of books in the library is fiction **(14)** and the next largest is non-fiction which is in the corner of this floor opposite the café. These can all be borrowed as opposed to the reference books on the next floor, most of which cannot be taken out of the library – but they can be photocopied. There are several photocopiers available for this purpose downstairs in the basement. To one side of the issue desk is a door leading onto a gallery. This was added to the library as a public space where talks are given once a week on a Saturday by visiting authors of both fiction and non-fiction. **(15)** It also houses the biography section. There are notices advertising the talks in the study area.

Any books that you want to borrow should be taken to the issue desk. Before we leave this floor I will give you some information about using the library. There are also helpful notices by the information desk.

Before you hear the rest of the talk, you have some time to look at questions 16 to 20.

[Pause the recording for 30 seconds.]

....

Now listen and answer questions 16 to 20.

To join the library and take books out, you need a membership card. Take your passport or identity card, as well as proof of your home address, to the information desk and you will be issued with a card. **(16)** After a period of two years, all readers are required to go to the desk with a document that has their name and current address on it so the library can keep up-to-date records of where people are living. There's no need to show a passport again and there is no charge for this but any lost cards are charged at £5.

If you can't find the book you want on the shelves, you can reserve it. If it's in another library in the city, we can usually get it for you within a week. If someone else has borrowed it, it can take a few weeks. **(17)** Either way, we notify you by phone or email when the item is available to be picked up. We will hold it for you for five days.

Books can be borrowed for fourteen days and can be renewed for a further two weeks. Children's books also have a two-week borrowing period. The same system exists for CD-ROMs and CDs but **(18)** DVDs, both children's and adults', can only be borrowed for up to seven days. It isn't possible to renew them. Some reference books can be borrowed but normally only for one day, so 24 hours.

The library opening hours have been changed slightly. Instead of opening late on Wednesday evenings till 8pm, we will be closing at 6, as on other weekdays, **(19)** but we will close at 7 instead of 5.30 on Saturdays and – a new development – we are going to open on Sunday mornings from next month – 9 to 1. We are closed on public holidays and notices are posted in the library about these.

Before you go upstairs, please note that if you are going to the exhibition area on the third floor, large bags are not allowed. **(20)** There are lockers beside the reference area on the second floor where you can deposit them. If you need change, you can get that from the information desk on the first floor.

Now press 'pause' and proceed to the second floor. When you reach the top of the stairs press 'play'.

That is the end of section 2. You now have half a minute to check your answers.

[Pause the recording for 30 seconds.]

Now turn to section 3.

 LISTENING SECTION 3

You will hear a university tutor talking to two students about a presentation they have made in a recent botany seminar. First you have some time to look at questions 21 to 25.

[Pause the recording for 30 seconds.]

Now listen carefully and answer questions 21 to 25.

Tutor: Well, Anita and Lee. That was an interesting presentation you made about John Chapman. There are a few points I'd like to run through before you write it up. One thing which you didn't explain was why you decided to do a presentation on this man who spread apple varieties across the US?

Anita: Well, ages ago, we were chatting about stuff we'd read as children, and I told Lee the Johnny Appleseed story – I had these American story books when I was small. Then **(21)** when we were looking into the area of domesticated species of plants for our presentation, we realised that the introduction of the apple with the settlers in the US would be a good case study …

Lee: And I remembered Chapman, so we looked up the real guy behind the legend.

Tutor: Right. I think that would have made a good intro.

Anita: I thought it was too personal.

Tutor: Just a couple of minutes would have drawn your listeners in. Anyway. Now a more serious point. You didn't mention the sources of some of your information.

Lee: We used some books and journal articles and did an internet search and found some good sites.

Anita: (22) We've put them on the back of the handout we gave everyone at the end.

Tutor: Ah, let me see. Oh, here it is. *Johnny Appleseed: Man and Myth*, 1967. Well, the thing is, you really have to make this explicit when you talk. And anything you show, data you project from your laptop, etc., you must have the source on it.

Anita: Right, OK.

Tutor: At least you have got it all documented. I was a bit concerned about that.

Anita: Sorry.

Tutor: Anyway. Now, the content of your talk. **(23)** What your listeners wanted to understand was whether there were apples in the US before the Europeans started to live there. You told us the early settlers had brought young apple trees but that few of them had thrived because the climate was harsh, but what about native species? I don't think you were very clear about species already there.

Lee: Um, according to what I've read, there were some crab apples, but that was all. Everything that people now think of as traditional American apples, were species that the Europeans either introduced or bred by chance.

Anita: Because they tended to sow seeds rather than use grafting.

Tutor: Yes, quite. But **(24)** what to me was fascinating – and I saw most members of your audience start to take notes – was when you discussed how the apple genes spread via the Silk Route into Europe from the wild apple woods of Kazakhstan.

Lee: Yes, well, I'd like to have said more about the development of grafting in ancient China, as a way of producing predictable varieties. It was so early in history!

Tutor: But it's the natural development of the original wild apple into new species that people wanted more about. Which says a lot for your presentation. You enthused your audience! So, now we need to discuss the form your follow-up work will take. Are you going to produce a paper? Or are you thinking of putting it all up on the department website?

Anita: Um, I felt we could do both. And we could do a poster of some of the data. But Lee wasn't sure.

Lee: No, **(25)** I think it would be enough to use the website. We can offer a link to our email for queries. That would save time and trees!

Tutor: I think Lee's right. A poster would be nice, but it'd take too much time.

Anita: OK.

Before you hear the rest of the conversation, you have some time to look at questions 26 to 30.

[Pause the recording for 30 seconds.]

....

Now listen and answer questions 26 to 30.

Tutor: Now I just want to give you a few pointers about the techniques of your presentation. Mostly it was good, but there are a few things you need to bear in mind next time you do one. **(26)** You both managed the hardware, I mean the projector and things, very well indeed, which is always a great help.

Anita: Good.

Lee: Thanks.

Tutor: You'd obviously checked it out carefully.

Lee: Yes. But **(27)** unfortunately we hadn't finished our maps when we did the practice on my computer at home, that's why there were some the wrong way up.

Anita: We didn't realise the software on the laptop was a bit different from the one I have.

Tutor: But you sorted out the problem very quickly and didn't let it fluster you, so it wasn't a big problem. We could all read the map when we needed to.

Anita: So it was OK, but we could have done better, we realise.

Tutor: Mm. There was a bit at the end where I felt something didn't go as you'd planned – am I right?

Lee: We had a few maps which we ended up leaving out, because we needed to get on to our conclusions.

Anita: Yes, **(28)** it took longer to explain the technical aspects of grafting than we'd expected.

Lee: So sticking to the time limit for each part of our presentation is something we didn't manage at all. Which means we've definitely got to improve before we do another one.

Anita: Yes.

Tutor: Apart from that, well, **(29)** the handout was perfectly adequate for a seminar like this, it gave all the key information, and of course, now I realise the sources are listed at the back. But you need to do those references in the correct format, as footnotes in future.

Anita: OK.

Lee: Yes, sorry, we will.

Tutor: And finally, other students will be presenting projects later in the course. I shall be reminding them **(30)** how well you both spoke and that no one had any problem hearing or understanding either of you. In that respect your talk was a model that the others can follow.

Lee: Oh, thank you.

Anita: Yes, thanks very much. This feedback has been very helpful.

Tutor: Well done, both of you. See you in a fortnight.

Anita and Lee: Bye. Thanks.

That is the end of section 3. You now have half a minute to check your answers.

[Pause the recording for 30 seconds.]

Now turn to section 4.

You will hear a lecturer describing some investigations into the sense of taste. First you have some time to look at questions 31 to 40.

[Pause the recording for one minute.]

Now listen carefully and answer questions 31 to 40.

Lecturer: This morning I'm going to describe for you a few of the kinds of experiments that have been used to investigate the sense of taste, which is now recognised as being a far more complex and important area of neurological science than was previously believed by most people. The results of some of these experiments can be quite fun and I shall suggest that you may want to choose one or two to try out in groups before having a go at designing a new experimental procedure of your own and trying to pinpoint the cause of your findings.

The first one concerns a marketing exercise by a soft drinks company. **(31)** The green colour of some cans was altered by the addition of yellow, so they were a brighter green. Then test subjects were asked what they thought about the flavour of the drink in the new-style cans, and **(32)** they stated that there was more lime in the drink if it was in the ones with the new colour. This was because the brain picks up cues from the way the product is presented, as well as the product itself, which trigger taste sensations. Before food was packaged, humans used colour to gauge the ripeness of fruit, for example.

Next there's the old problem with chewing gum. Everyone knows that after a few minutes' chewing it loses its minty flavour. However, **(33)** if you ask people to chew up to the point where it becomes tasteless, and then ask them to eat a little sugar and continue chewing, to most people's surprise, what happens is that **(34)** the original mintiness actually returns because it is the sweetness which is needed to make the mintiness perceptible. So combinations of flavours can be significant, as the brain needs one of them in order to recognise the other.

Another experiment demonstrates something we've all done. Drink half a fizzy drink straight from the fridge and then leave it at room temperature for a while. Take a sip and you may well decide you don't like it. **(35)** The warm drink is too sweet to be refreshing. So put the rest back in the fridge until it's chilled again. Now try it. Much better. Of course the sweetness doesn't change, it is our perception, because how sweet it tastes depends on the temperature. The extent to which the drink is sweetened is less evident if the drink has been cooled.

Another interesting result has been derived from experiments with sound. **(36)** One of these involved eating crisps. Subjects were put into soundproof rooms and given batches of crisps to eat. As they ate, the sound of crunching which they made as they ate the crisps was played back to them. This was adjusted so that they sometimes heard the crunching as louder, or, at other times, more high-frequency sounds were audible in the sound feedback that accompanied their eating. **(37)** Fascinatingly, if the sound level was louder or higher frequency they reported that the crisps were actually fresher. Of course, the crisps were in fact the same every time! So, it was clear that the level and quality of what they were hearing was influencing their taste perceptions.

So, we've looked briefly at colour, at complementary flavours, at temperature and sound. It seems that all the senses are working together here, but what about the sense of touch? A number of experiments have been done in this area. If you take, for instance, cheese sauce and prepare different versions, some thicker and some thinner, but without any alteration in the strength of flavour, what do you think the subjects perceive? Yup, if the sauce is thicker, they'll say the cheesy flavour is less strong. It was clear that the thing **(38)** that was influencing the subjects' judgement about the flavour of the sauces was the texture of each one. Now, this result is important for dietitians as well as marketing executives.

Lastly, another variation on the two flavours theme. This concerns the capacity of the brain for bridging a sensory gap. **(39)** The subjects in this experiment stuck out their tongues so that the testers could drip two liquids onto them simultaneously, one strawberry flavoured and one sugar flavoured. The testers then took away each flavour in turn. When the sweetness was taken away, the subjects reported they could hardly taste anything, **(40)** but they continued to think they could taste strawberry even after it was taken away! So that taste gap was filled.

Well, that's just a quick look at some of the examples in the current literature. The references will be in the handout you'll get at the end of the session. Now let's see about trying a few of them for ourselves.

That is the end of section 4. You now have half a minute to check your answers.

[Pause the recording for 30 seconds.]

That is the end of the listening test. In the IELTS test you would now have 10 minutes to transfer your answers to the Listening Answer sheet.

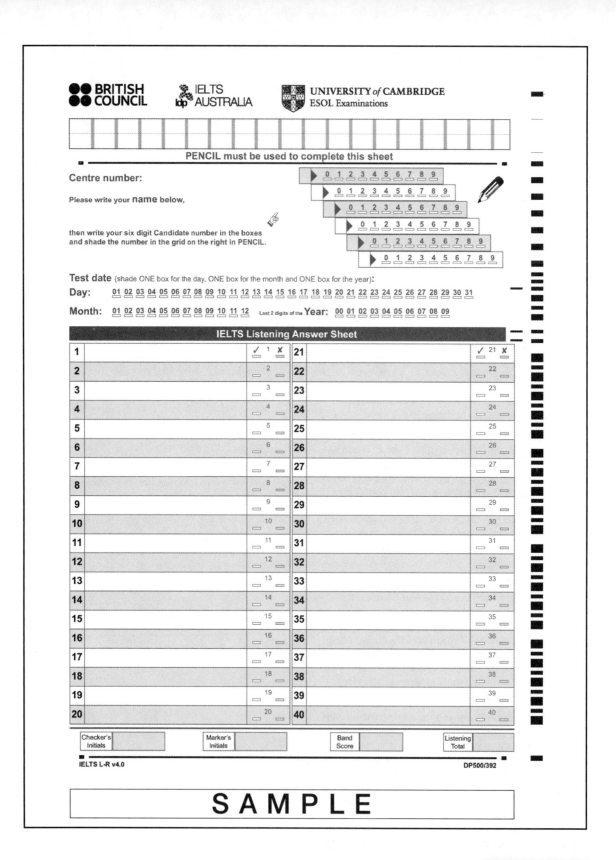

REPRODUCED WITH THE PERMISSION OF CAMBRIDGE ESOL

Photocopiable

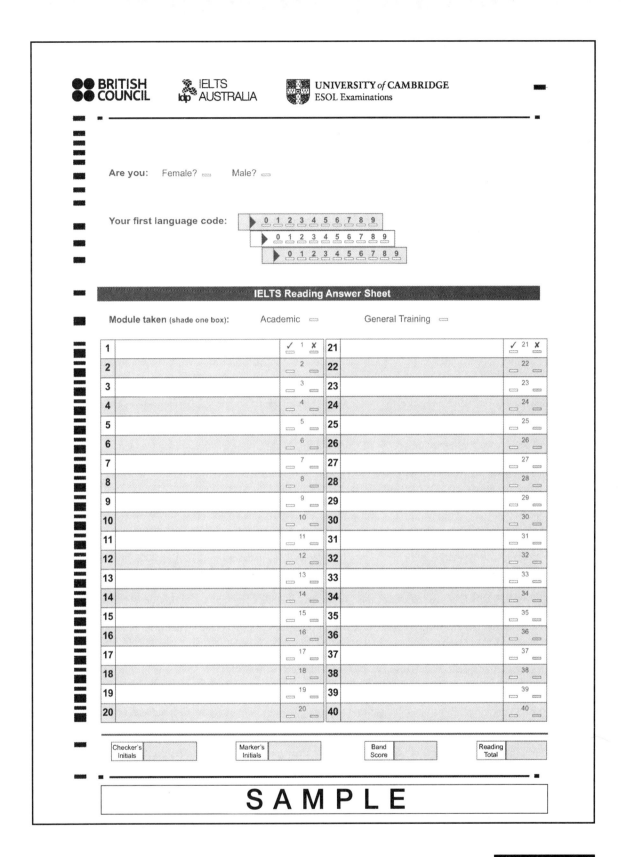

BRITISH COUNCIL   **IELTS AUSTRALIA**   **UNIVERSITY of CAMBRIDGE** ESOL Examinations

Are you: Female? ⊂⊃   Male? ⊂⊃

Your first language code: ▶ 0 1 2 3 4 5 6 7 8 9
▶ 0 1 2 3 4 5 6 7 8 9
▶ 0 1 2 3 4 5 6 7 8 9

IELTS Reading Answer Sheet

Module taken (shade one box):   Academic ⊂⊃   General Training ⊂⊃

	✓ X			✓ X
1	1	21		21
2	2	22		22
3	3	23		23
4	4	24		24
5	5	25		25
6	6	26		26
7	7	27		27
8	8	28		28
9	9	29		29
10	10	30		30
11	11	31		31
12	12	32		32
13	13	33		33
14	14	34		34
15	15	35		35
16	16	36		36
17	17	37		37
18	18	38		38
19	19	39		39
20	20	40		40

Checker's Initials	Marker's Initials	Band Score	Reading Total

S A M P L E

REPRODUCED WITH THE PERMISSION OF CAMBRIDGE ESOL   Photocopiable

Acknowledgements

The authors would like to thank Jane Coates for her efficient and patient editing, and Lynn Townsend, Annabel Marriott and Una Yeung at Cambridge University Press for all their encouragement and support. They would also like to thank Rowland Thomas, Christina Wylie and Ann Grubb for help with research. Many thanks also to Azadeh Hashemi for her help with the writing tasks and to Abbas Hashemi for patiently interpreting rough sketches. The authors and publishers are grateful to the staff and students of the Bell School, Cambridge, for their contributions to the writing exercises. They would also like to express their gratitude to the following for reviewing the material: Anelise Chicherio, Pauline Cullen, Sarah Emsden-Bonfanti, Jessica Errington, Merryn Grimley, Brendan Ó Sé.

Development of this publication has made use of the Cambridge International Corpus (CIC). The CIC is a computerised database of contemporary spoken and written English which currently stands at over one billion words. It includes British English, American English and other varieties of English. It also includes the Cambridge Learner Corpus, developed in collaboration with the University of Cambridge ESOL Examinations. Cambridge University Press has built up the CIC to provide evidence about language use that helps to produce better language teaching materials.

The authors and publishers acknowledge the following sources of copyright material and are grateful for the permissions granted. While every effort has been made, it has not always been possible to identify the sources of all the material used, or to trace all copyright holders. If any omissions are brought to our notice, we will be happy to include the appropriate acknowledgements on reprinting.

Natural Environment Research Council for the text on p. 24 'Walking with Dinosaurs' by Peter Falkingham. *Planet Earth*, Spring 2009. Reproduced with permission; Penguin Books Ltd and Random House (US) for the text on pp. 29–30 'The robots are coming – or are they?' from *Physics of the Impossible: A Scientific Exploration into the World of Phasers, Force Fields, Teleportation and Time Travel* by Michio Kaku. (Allen Lane 2008). Copyright © Michio Kaku 2008. Reproduced by permission of Penguin Books Ltd and Doubleday, a division of Random House, Inc.; Peter Monaghan for the text on pp. 35–36 'Endangered languages' from 'Never mind the whales, save the languages', *The Australian*, 24.6.09. Reproduced with permission; Population Reference Bureau for adapted bar charts on p. 40 and p. 47 from *Population Bulletin*, Vol 62, no 3, 2007 and Vol 63, no 3, 2008. Reproduced with permission; National Geographic for the text on pp. 69–70 'Our Vanishing Night' by Verlyn Klinkenborg. *National Geographic*, November 2008. Reproduced with permission; The British Psychological Society for the text on pp. 74–75 'Is there a psychologist in the building?' written by Christian Jarrett, *The Psychologist*, October 2006. www.thepsychologist.org.uk. With permission from the British Psychological Society; New Scientist for the text on pp. 78–79 'Have teenagers always existed?' from 'Teenagers Special: The original rebels' written by Lynn Dicks, *New Scientist*, 5 March 2005, and for the text on pp. 122–123 'Can animals count?' from 'Animals that count' written by Ewen Callaway, *New Scientist*, 20 June 2009. Copyright © New Scientist Magazine; The University of Bristol for the adapted chart on p. 87 'The Young Ones, 100 years of Bristol's Students'. *Nonesuch* Summer 2009. Copyright © The University of Bristol; The Financial Times for the text on pp. 103–104 'Seed vault guards resources for the future' from 'In case of emergency, break ice' by Fiona Harvey, *The Financial Times*, 26 April 2008, and for the text on pp. 127–128 'Is it time to halt the rising tide of plastic packaging?' from 'Plastic: the elephant in the room' by Sam Knight, *The Financial Times*, 25 April 2008. Copyright © Financial Times Ltd; The Economist for the text on pp. 106–107 'What cookbooks really teach us' from 'Pluck a Flamingo', *The Economist*, 18 December 2008. Copyright © The Economist Newspaper Limited, London, 2008; Prospect Magazine for the text on pp. 110–111 'Is there more to video games than people realise?' from 'Rage against the machines' by Tom Chatfield, *Prospect Magazine*, 29 June 2008. Reproduced with permission; National Tax Journal for the table on p. 133 'How much do drivers spend on petrol?' from *The National Tax Journal*, June 1997, 50 (2), 233–259. Reproduced with permission; Princeton University Press for the text on pp. 140–141 'Nature on display in American Zoos' from *Animal Attractions*, written by Elizabeth Hanson. Copyright © Princeton University Press, 2002 and for the text on pp. 166–167 'The Deep Sea' from *The Eternal Darkness* written by Robert Ballard. Copyright © Princeton University Press and Robert Ballard, 2000. Reprinted by permission of Princeton University Press; Geographical magazine for the text on pp. 143–144 'Can we prevent the poles from melting?' from 'Can space mirrors save the planet?' written by Mark Rowe, *Geographical Magazine*, November 2009. Reproduced with permission; Current Publishing for the text on pp. 147–148 'America's oldest art?' written by George Nash, *Current Archaeology*, Issue 37. Reproduced with permission; Control Publications for part text on pp. 159–160 'Communicating in colour' written by Devi-Stuart Fox, *Australasian Science Magazine*, June 2008. Reproduced with permission; The Guardian for part text on pp. 159–160 'Communicating in colour' from 'Snake spits out new species of Chameleon at scientist's feet', by Esther Addley, *The Guardian*, 23 November 2009. Copyright © Guardian News & Media Ltd, 2009; Psychology Today for the text on pp. 162–163 'The Pursuit of Happiness' from *Psychology Today*, 15 December 2008; Rough Guides Ltd for the weather charts for Brasilia and Recife on p. 170 taken from *Rough Guide to Weather* by Robert Henson (Rough Guides 2002, 2007). Copyright © Robert Henson, 2002, 2007. Reproduced with permission of Rough Guides Ltd.

For permission to reproduce photographs:
Alamy/© Arcticphoto p. 103, /© Peter Alvey p. 127; Corbis/© Wayne Lynch/All Canada Photos p. 159; Photolibraryuk/© BildagenturShuster p. 69, /© Fabio Colombini Medeiros p. 147, /© Jeffrey L. Rotman p. 166
Illustrations: Abbas Hashemi pp. 20, 64, 138, 151; Janos Jantner pp. 26, 29, 105, 118

Audio recordings by John Green TEFL Audio. Engineer: Adam Helal; Editor: Tim Woolf; Producer: John Green. Recorded at ID Audio Studios, London.

Designed and typeset by eMC Design Ltd

Notes

Notes